What Did We Do Right?

Global Perspectives on Ireland's 'Miracle'

Edited by

MICHAEL J. O'SULLIVAN AND RORY MILLER

BLACKHALL
Publishing

Published by Blackhall Publishing
Lonsdale House
Avoca Avenue
Blackrock
Co. Dublin
Ireland

e-mail: info@blackhallpublishing.com
www.blackhallpublishing.com

ISBN: 978-1-84218-192-8

A catalogue record for this book is available from the British Library.

Printed and bound in Great Britain by CPI Antony Rowe, Chippenham, Wiltshire.

Preface

What did we do right?

It's not a question that many people in Ireland are asking themselves at the moment. And why would they? The economy is in tatters. Debt is piling up while the Government attempts to make amends for years of runaway spending, an absence of regulation and long-term planning, and a culture of cronyism, greed and complacency.

Not surprisingly, at the time of writing in early 2010, the mood in Ireland is one of confusion, anger and growing bitterness at the financial follies of the last few decades and the economic burdens they have brought for generations to come. In a sad reminder of times past, thousands are now emigrating to look for a better life in the UK, Canada, Australia or the US.

Moreover, while most other developed economies are in recovery, the Irish economy is still very much in rescue mode. Growth is negative, and the National Asset Management Agency (NAMA) recapitalisation plan is seen by some as being barely operational.

Thus, it is hardly surprising that the current debate in Ireland on the way forward is coloured by emotion and, at times, as in the case of the debate on NAMA, has become sharply polarised.

For Irish people, and those in other countries who wish to learn from Ireland's experience, an honest and unsentimental assessment of the situation demands acknowledgment of all this.

Gone are the days when we could ignore the warnings of the Organisation for Economic Co-operation and Development (OECD) and the International Monetary Fund (IMF) in the false belief that our property bubble would never burst and that our banking sector could regulate itself in a prudent manner.

On top of this, the new global realities demand that we now take a much more global view than we took in the past. On one level, this is happening. In the face of the decimation of our economy by builders, bankers and policy-makers, we have become hypersensitive to what people in other countries think of us.

In the last weeks of 2009, for example, there was much talk over a high profile piece in the *Washington Post* published on 22 December. The article, entitled 'In Ireland's deep budget cuts, an omen for a heavily indebted United States?', related how the Government's 'drastic steps' to turn the economy around now placed the once formidable Celtic Tiger on the 'front lines of the global battle against runaway government spending' and 'exploding budget deficits'.

But this book is not simply intended to feed the curiosity that Irish people have for what the outside world thinks of us. It has a far more serious goal. Those same policy-makers and politicians who, with very few exceptions, led us from boom to bust have responded to the economic crisis by becoming more inward-looking in terms of practical steps and remedies. One of the things we wanted to do in putting together this collection was to counter this 'head in the sand' attitude by highlighting the need to pay more attention to the new trends and rules of the world post-credit crisis.

After almost two decades during which we took much pride and confidence from the fact that wise men and women from across the globe made a pilgrimage year in and year out to learn the mysteries of the Celtic Tiger and the secrets of the Peace Process, it is now essential to shine a light on the lessons that we can learn from other countries as we set out on the massive task of returning to socio-economic stability and growth.

But, at the same time, from the moment the idea for this book was conceived, our primary aim has been to draw attention to the, now all too oft forgotten, positive lessons of the Irish experience over the last two decades. We believe that it is just as important to salvage the worthwhile policies, regulations and programmes of the boom years as it is to discard to the dustbin of economic and financial history those which ultimately had a disastrous impact on the Irish economy and society.

In doing this, we didn't want to provide a platform for the familiar home-grown commentators, but instead have brought together a dozen high-profile non-Irish experts from the worlds of politics, economics and academia. We asked them to provide a 'second opinion' not only on the all-too-apparent failings of the roller-coaster ride from boom to bust, but also to disentangle the good policy moves from the bad, the beneficial strategies from the costly and the brave economic decisions from the crass ones. And they have.

Many of our contributors write from the point of view of countries that, like Ireland, have enjoyed great prosperity but have also suffered crashes and crises. Combined with their objectivity, this provides their analyses with a sense of perspective for the debate on Ireland.

In addition, our contributors take a longer-term view of the changes that have occurred in Ireland, in contrast to the shorter memory of some contemporary home-grown commentators. For example, at the moment there is a widespread tendency to dismiss as, at best, insensitive and, at worst, insulting anyone who raises the fact that during the 1980s there was a wide-ranging consensus around the assumption that Ireland was destined to face long-term, perhaps even permanent, economic underperformance. Yet, within a very short time things had changed beyond recognition as a young, educated, English-speaking workforce coupled with a number of progressive economic policies transformed society.

Our contributors from across the globe place great import on this and the many other positive achievements that are currently unfashionable to draw attention to at home. This helps us to understand what we did right at a time when almost everybody only wants to recall what we did wrong.

As Scotland's First Minister Alex Salmond underlines in his chapter in this book, other countries, perhaps now more than ever, can still learn from such Irish experiences. In making this point, Salmond and his co-contributors have provided an original, illuminating and informative second opinion on Ireland's move from boom to bust.

The contributors also provide us with a constructive starting point in the debate on the way forward for Ireland. And that is a debate that we all need to have right now. In this way, we hope our readership is comprised of Irish people who care about the future of their country, and those in other countries who are eager to learn the lessons of the great transformation in Ireland's economic and political fortunes over the past twenty-five years.

Michael J. O'Sullivan and Rory Miller
London, January 2010

Contents

Contents

List of Abbreviations

ABP	Area-Based Partnership
BPO	Business Process Outsourcing
CAP	Common Agricultural Policy
CIA	Central Intelligence Agency
CIT	Corporation Income Tax
DUP	Democratic Unionist Party
EEA	European Economic Association
EEC	European Economic Community
EFTA	European Free Trade Association
EI	Enterprise Ireland
EMS	European Monetary System
EMU	European Monetary Union
ERM	Exchange Rate Mechanism
ESC	Economic and Social Council
ESRI	Economic and Social Research Institute
ETDZ	Economic and Technology Development Zone
EU	European Union
FBI	Federal Bureau of Investigation
FDI	Foreign Direct Investment
FE	Foreign Enterprise
FIE	Foreign Investment Enterprise
FII	Foreign Institutional Investor
GEM	Global Entrepreneurship Monitor
GDP	Gross Domestic Product
GNP	Gross National Product
HPSU	High Potential Start-Up
ICT	Information and Communication Technology
ICTU	Irish Congress of Trade Unions
IDA	Industrial Development Agency
IFSC	International Financial Services Centre

IMF	International Monetary Fund
IPSI	Industrial Policy and Strategy Institute
IRA	Irish Republican Army
IZ	Investment Zones
MNC	Multinational Corporation
MNE	Multinational Enterprise
NAFTA	North American Free Trade Agreement
NAMA	National Asset Management Agency
NBER	National Bureau of Economic Research
NESC	National Economic and Social Council
NGO	Non-Governmental Organisation
OECD	Organisation for Economic Co-operation and Development
PCPI	Per Capita Personal Income
PNR	Programme for National Recovery
PRC	People's Republic of China
R&D	Research and Development
SDLP	Social Democratic and Labour Party
SME	Small to Medium Sized Enterprise
SNP	Scottish National Party
UNCTAD	United Nations Conference on Trade and Development
VAT	Value Added Tax
WEF	World Economic Forum
WTO	World Trade Organisation

We would like to dedicate this book to the memory of
Georgina Long (1910–2007) and Leslie Silverstone (1920–2007).

About the Editors

Michael J. O'Sullivan is the author of *Ireland and the Global Question* (Cork University Press, 2006). He was educated at University College Cork (UCC) and Balliol College, Oxford, from where he obtained M.Phil and D.Phil degrees as a Rhodes Scholar. He has taught finance at Princeton University and Oxford University, and has worked in the City of London for the past twelve years.

Rory Miller was educated at Trinity College Dublin (TCD) and the University of London. He is currently professor of Middle Eastern Studies at King's College London, where he is also a College Innovation Fellow. He is the author or editor of seven books.

About the Contributors

Alex Salmond is First Minister of Scotland and leader of the Scottish National Party (SNP). He is MP for Banff and Buchan, and the MSP for Gordon.

Joseph Morrison Skelly is associate professor of history at the College of Mount Saint Vincent in New York City. He is the author of *Irish Diplomacy at the United Nations, 1945–65: National Interests and the International Order* (Irish Academic Press, 1998) and co-editor of the books *Irish Foreign Policy, 1919–66: From Independence to Internationalism* (Four Courts Press, 2000) and *Ideas Matter: Essays in Honour of Conor Cruise O'Brien* (University Press of America, 2000).

Jonathan Powell was chief of staff to Prime Minister Tony Blair, 1995–2007 and chief British negotiator in the Peace Process in Northern Ireland from 1997–2007.

Christophe Gillissen is a lecturer at the University of Paris, Sorbonne, specialising in British and Irish studies. He has written several articles on Irish foreign policy, in addition to a book on Anglo-Irish relations.

Pedro Lains is research professor at the Institute of Social Sciences at the University of Lisbon.

Andreas Antoniades is a lecturer in Global Political Economy at the University of Sussex.

Amalia Fugaru is an economist and adviser at the Romanian Central Bank.

Dana Denis-Smith is the managing director of Marker Global, the London-based emerging markets risk advisory firm.

Ashraf Mishrif is a senior lecturer in International Business and Finance at Ashcroft International Business School, Anglia Ruskin University, Cambridge. He is visiting senior research fellow at the Middle East and Mediterranean Studies Department at King's College London.

Yanky Fachler is co-founder and chief learning officer of Bookbuzz Ltd, an international learning company based in Dublin. His books include *Fire in the Belly: An Exploration of the Entrepreneurial Spirit* (Oak Tree Press, 2001) and *Chutzpah: Unlocking the Maverick Mindset for Success* (Oak Tree Press, 2006).

Liming Wang is the director of the Irish Institute for Chinese Studies at University College Dubin (UCD).

Chang Liu is a lecturer in International Business at Nottingham Business School China, University of Nottingham Ningbo, China (UNNC).

Francis Kane is a lecturer at the Irish Institute for Chinese Studies, University College Dublin (UCD).

Khuong Minh Vu is assistant professor at the Lee Kuan Yew School of Public Policy, National University of Singapore.

P.S. Raghavan is Indian ambassador to Ireland.

What Did We Do Right?

Over the last hundred years Ireland has evolved from a poor but defiant nation on the margins of Europe into – until recently – a political and economic success story at the centre of the global economy. Ireland was arguably the most transformed developed nation in the world over the past twenty years and, by the turn of this century, was widely regarded as being the 'poster child' for globalisation and as having an economic model that other countries could copy. This book is about how this great transformation of Ireland into a 'brand state', as Peter van Ham writing in *Foreign Affairs* has termed it,[1] has inspired other countries and how, in turn, we in Ireland must learn from others in order to sow the seeds of our economic recovery.

The rapid onset of the financial crisis in 2008 and the ensuing sharp contraction in the Irish economy has sown deep doubts about the quality of the Irish economic miracle. This is a critical point in Irish history, perhaps the most important period since the foundation of the state in the early 1920s. At the time of writing, most other nations are now in recovery and are studying necessary post-credit crisis reforms. Ireland – once an economic leader – is still in rescue mode, and the sense that we are now lagging behind is very hard to escape.

There is still little serious debate in Ireland on what our long-term recovery may look like, or indeed what its place might be in a post-financial crisis world. This book aims to contribute to the debate on how Ireland can recover by seeking the views of outsiders to help underline what we, the Irish, did right in the first place, and to uncover what we did wrong. We have become too used to other countries sending their wise men and women to admire our economy; it is time we invited them to take a more critical approach and, very importantly, that we also learn from other countries.

What Is the Book about?

What Did We Do Right? aims to identify the factors that drove Ireland's economic and political catch-up in the first place, to disentangle 'bubble' from 'miracle' and, importantly, it focuses on what other nations across the globe can still learn from the Irish case at a time of global credit crisis and recession. In this way, we try to highlight four things: what Ireland did right; how other countries can learn from Ireland; how Ireland can learn from what we did right in the past; how Ireland can learn from other countries.

If anything, the damage being wrought in the world economy at present makes it more important than ever that the driving factors behind the Irish transformation in recent decades is understood. After all, the implementation of wrong policies or the adoption of unsuitable economic models could be costlier now than at any time in living memory.

This book is unique in that all the contributors (save the editors) are policy-advisers, senior politicians and leading academics from outside Ireland. Their chapters are ordered in this book largely on the basis of geography. We start with chapters from Scotland, England, the US and France, which make up the set of Atlantic countries that have played key roles in Irish history. This is followed by views from Portugal, Greece – two of Ireland's former economic peers – and Romania, and then opinions from the Middle East, specifically Egypt and Israel. We end with three views from the Far East – from China, Vietnam and India.

All of the contributors have spent the last number of years thinking deeply about the implications of the Irish experience for their own countries and wider regions. None are Irish. This avoids the pitfalls of parochialism and allows for the extrapolation of the wider lessons of the Irish experience, both positive and negative. This detached and objective approach not only provides an illuminating 'second opinion' on the 'Irish model' that will make an invaluable contribution to the current debate on the economy in Ireland, but allows for the distillation of the key factors and trends that lie behind Ireland's successes and failures. No less importantly, it allows for the identification of the political and economic measures employed by Ireland in the past twenty years that can be applied or 'exported' with relative ease to other nations.

There is a growing literature on the great changes that have taken place in Ireland over the last thirty years. This book seeks to move beyond this literature in a number of important ways.

First, it seeks to set out the lessons that other countries can learn from Ireland's economic transformation from the 1990s to the late part of the last decade, in addition to the lessons that can be learnt from Ireland's struggle for independence. There are few, if any, books that seek to map out how Ireland's experience can be used to the benefit of other, mostly developing, nations. In this way, the focus of the book opens it up to a broad global audience. Indeed, within the literature on development, there are relatively few books that discuss how individual case studies or success stories can be used to the benefit of a wide range of emerging states.

Second, as mentioned, the authors are exclusively 'non-Irish'. This helps to give the book an international scope, lending it a unique angle on the analysis of Ireland's political economy. During the boom years, we as a nation were always curious as to what those in other countries thought of our success. We should be no less curious about their views of us now that the financial crisis has taken its toll.

This book provides an answer to the 'What do they think of us?' question, in addition to sowing the seeds for the necessary debate on Ireland's economic future. In this respect, at a time of great uncertainty over Ireland's economic future, this book serves to remind policy-makers of what worked and perhaps, with the benefit of outside perspectives, to illuminate a path forward. The strong conclusion of the authors is that commentators in most other countries are cognizant of Ireland's classic asset price bubble that developed in recent years, and they focus much more keenly on Ireland's 'catch-up' years (effectively 1990–2001) as representing something for other countries, including their own, to learn from. In this respect, the authors highlight the value of what we refer to as 'intangible infrastructure'(see below) as a very important driver of growth.

What Makes the Irish Case Interesting?

The decade of the 1990s, which began with the collapse of the Soviet Union and ended with the collapse of the Twin Towers, was a period of uncertainty, hope, realignment and, ultimately, disappointment and tragedy in world affairs. Equally, at the start of the 1990s, writers like Francis Fukuyama were prematurely and triumphantly proclaiming the 'end of history' in the sense that liberal democracy and, by extension, the Anglo-Saxon socio-political model had won the day. Yet, at the beginning of 2010, this economic model and the certainty that many invested in it have been left ravaged by the credit crisis. It now faces credible alternatives in the shape of some European models and the Asian 'do it my own way' approach.

In many respects Ireland was the exemplar of the 'Anglo-Saxon' model and, in keeping with the zeitgeist, the 1990s and beyond was a period when Ireland and the Irish came of age at home and abroad. In so doing, we left behind decades, if not centuries, of economic underachievement as summed up by Joe Lee in 1989: 'How has Ireland achieved and sustained this level of relative retardation?'[2]

Ireland's meteoric transformation from one of Europe's poorest and least developed economies into the 'Celtic Tiger' increased its global profile and prestige. Politicians, economists and business people from California to China tried hard to work out the best way to emulate the Irish model.

During the 1990s, Ireland's newly gained status as an economic powerhouse was matched by a more substantial role in the cultural sphere and, notably, by our growing reputation as skilled practitioners of conflict resolution and soft power following our key role, along with the UK, in facilitating the 1998 Good Friday peace agreement in Northern Ireland. In his chapter, Jonathan Powell sketches how difficult Ireland's relations with Britain and the British were up to the mid 1990s; he also provides a testimony of how Ireland, the 'Troubles' and the relationship between Britain and Ireland changed before his eyes. His role in helping to engineer and bring about these changes has been vital.

All of these developments, topped off by Ireland's election to a temporary two-year stint on the United Nations (UN) Security Council beginning in 2000, and of course Ireland's presidency of the EU in 2004, had fundamentally altered the world's view of Ireland's international relevance and opened the way for a decade during which all things Irish flourished in the international arena.

There is no doubt that the hard-won achievements of recent years are now being thoroughly stress-tested by the global financial crisis, which may well uncover social, political and foreign policy fault lines as the Irish approach comes of age. But this in no way reduces the value to policymakers and scholars from across the world of examining the key aspects of the Irish story for their own countries. Khuong Minh Vu, a leading expert on Asian economies and a contributor to this collection, reminds us of the 'method' behind Ireland's early success:

> the lessons learned from the success of the Irish are relevant for all countries. This is especially true for developing countries for the following two reasons: Ireland's success did not come from a good 'design' but from a vigorous process of reviews and reforms. In fact, Ireland's take-off was enabled by a thoughtful review and decisive reform initiatives sparked at the depth of a severe economic crisis [in 1986] ... Ireland's success did not rely on a unique political model....The success came from the society's shared determination to reform and a strategic partnership among key social partners.

Indeed, the unprecedented challenges that both the developing and developed worlds face currently makes an examination of the lessons of Ireland's journey by experts from around the world more relevant than ever. For instance, countries in Ireland's old economic peer group, as the chapters in this volume on Greece and Portugal show clearly, face profoundly difficult economic and financial challenges ahead. Other countries, such as Vietnam and India, have arguably brighter economic futures, but even they are concerned that they have strayed off the path to growth and have much to learn as they move to the next level of economic development.

In all these cases, the changes in Irish policy-making from the late 1980s onwards suggest a number of strands for policy-makers. It is possible to divide our economic 'miracle' over recent decades into two independent, though overlapping, phases. Both of these phases provide many lessons, positive and negative, for countries across the world looking to build and consolidate sustainable economic growth and political stability at a time of global turmoil.

The first, 'catch-up' phase was based primarily on investment in Ireland by foreign multinationals and an increasingly stable investment climate. Foreign Direct Investment (FDI) inflows increased from US$2.6 billion in 1996 to approximately US$26.9 billion in 2003, and explained the extraordinary fact that US investment in Ireland in 2003 was more than two and half times greater than US investment in China, for example.

It is hardly surprising then that inward investment to Ireland over the last two decades led to the creation of an export-oriented and high-skilled Irish industrial sector that is based on high technology manufacturing such as electronics, health care and pharmaceuticals. By the early 2000s, according to Enterprise Ireland (EI), thirteen of the top fifteen world pharmaceutical companies had substantial operations in Ireland, and six out of ten of the world's top-selling drugs were produced there. Ireland also played host to seven of the world's top ten information and communication technology (ICT) companies such as IBM, Intel, Hewlett Packard, Dell, Oracle, Lotus and Microsoft, with annual exports exceeding €21 billion and direct employment of around forty-five thousand people.

Buoyed by the boom in jobs, money and optimism achieved through attracting such investment, the second phase saw the domestic economy, especially the property and construction sectors, come to the fore, aided and abetted by low real interest rates and easy credit. Since the latter half of 2008, this has followed the patterns of asset price bubbles through international economic history back to the Mississippi Scheme of 1721[3] and, as such, serves primarily as a warning to other nations tempted to base economic growth on an unsustainable property boom and cheap, unaccountable credit.

The first phase is both more difficult and arguably more important to understand, and most of the contributors here focus on this period as still representing something that they can learn from. Although most expert opinion concurs that Ireland's economic success emerged due to a number of factors including the Irish education system, an English-speaking workforce, credit growth, the state's role in supporting inward investment, membership of the European Union (EU) and a flexible labour market, there is significant divergence of opinion when it comes to pinpointing the relative weight of each of these individual factors in igniting Ireland's economy after so many years of slumber. This is even more relevant given that many of these factors – from an English-speaking workforce to government underwriting of foreign investment – were in place during the darkest, most stagnant years for the Irish economy.

The contributors to this volume, in addressing this and other issues relating to the Irish experience in terms of the specific circumstances faced by their own home countries, have drawn numerous relevant lessons. While they differ in some areas, it seems that there are certain opinions on which contributors, whether they are from Vietnam or Egypt, Scotland or the US, are unanimous.

For example, all agree that the Irish case highlights the need for countries to marry positive domestic factors (such as those evident in Ireland) with external factors such as the falling cost of international capital, the opening up of international markets and the advent of new technologies – in other words, the ingredients that we now view as key to economic globalisation. They also agree that the Irish case highlights the increasingly significant role of intangible infrastructure in economic success and social development.

Intangible Infrastructure: The Secret of Ireland's Success?

Little else is requisite to carry a state to the highest degree of opulence from the lowest barbarism but peace, easy taxes, and a tolerable administration of justice: all the rest being brought about by the natural course of things.

Adam Smith, 1755[4]

From the writings of Adam Smith through to the most contemporary literature on economics, there is increasing consensus that intangible factors like human capital or institutional quality are determinants of economic performance, especially where structural change is concerned. We use the following definition of intangible infrastructure: 'the set of factors that develop human capability and permit the easy and efficient growth of business activity.'[5]

These factors can be essentially political, legal or socio-economic in nature, such as the rule of law, a strong institutional framework or intellectual property. However, in terms of hard dollar spend, they relate mostly to companies in the education, health care, technology and innovation, and financial and business services sectors.

The strands of intangible infrastructure are closely interrelated and interdependent. It is unlikely, though not impossible, that a country with a high degree of technology penetration would not also have a fairly comprehensive education system. In the same way, financial systems would struggle in the absence of a legal framework and advances in technology might falter without property rights to support cutting-edge research and development (R&D). Importantly, the role of intangible factors in driving economic growth is supported by economic theory, by a growing store of empirical evidence and by numerous surveys (such as the AT Kearney/ Foreign Policy Globalization Index) that link intangible factors to a country's growth and ability to globalise.

Finance is a good case in point, as the power of intangible factors such as legislation, regulations and standards (notably, international accounting standards) influence how financial systems evolve. Moreover, they are decisive in determining why some countries and cities have strong financial sectors and others have weak ones. Also, important issues such as investor protection, transparency, political stability and regulation are by nature intangible, but are nonetheless vital in determining the strength of banking systems and flows of capital into countries. At a time when the world's financial markets and regulators are facing unprecedented scrutiny, the Irish experience provides a very valuable case study of what went right and what went wrong in the unprecedented boom years since the mid-1990s.

Thus, our successful economic transformation over the past decade, and especially our success in attracting FDI, which remains a priority for all nations even in the current economic situation, was due to a willingness to harness an educated, English-speaking workforce to a number of progressive economic policies that are at the core of the intangible infrastructure model – most notably, low tax rates, flexible business practices and a strategic goal to 'promote a competitive enterprise environment which will foster enterprise development and meet the emerging challenges and opportunities of an increasingly knowledge-based economy', as explained in the Department of Enterprise, Trade and Employment's 2001 annual report. A key message of this book is that Ireland, which is today struggling in terms of competitiveness, has seen a range of institutions perform poorly and appears to have lost its way in terms of policy-making, and very much needs to learn the lessons of its own earlier success. If we fail to do this and are reluctant to embark on a programme of renewal of Ireland's intangible infrastructure, we will likely see economic growth fall to a lower trend rate.

Plugging into Globalisation

The notion of intangible infrastructure is a rapidly evolving subject of research in the fields of economics, finance and development studies. What is particularly important about the Irish case is that it is now widely accepted that it was the existence of strong intangible infrastructure that helped Ireland to overcome its small size, its location on the margins of Europe and lack of natural resources, and become a success.

As the contributors to this volume acknowledge, Ireland's approach to intangible infrastructure is filtering through to the policy-makers and politicians in their home countries. In these terms, one lesson of the Irish experience is that a low and simplified taxation system (such as the one Ireland has championed for many years) is not enough in itself to attract FDI. As a number of Eastern European countries are now finding, low taxes need to be complemented by a variety of other factors including political stability, the rule of law and transparency. While intangible infrastructure will be a key to economic success going forward, it will also need to be adapted to meet new global economic challenges at a time when the credit crisis demands that both leverage and deregulation give way to lower leverage and more regulation.

At a very broad level, the rising relevance of intangible infrastructure is driven by globalisation. If we define this as the growing interdependence and integration of markets, economies and societies, then, by nature, much of globalisation rests on the spread of intangible factors like international institutions, the diffusion and patenting of ideas, financial innovation and the diffusion of cultural trends. Amongst other things, globalisation breaks down barriers to the flow of services and information, and helps to relegate geography as a driving factor in economic development.

Globalisation means that many economic and cultural activities are increasingly played out in the world as a single place, rather than within national borders. While the nation-state is still very much a viable entity, power is increasingly placed in the hands of unelected policy-makers and this is reflected in a number of quarters, such as the standardisation of accounting and financial rules and indicators.

Increasingly, institutionalisation seems to be replacing the role played by the gold standard, Pax Britannica and the mercantile ideological consensus that prevailed in the nineteenth century. It is manifest in bodies like the EU or International Monetary Fund (IMF), and has, broadly speaking, been beneficial in preventing and resolving crises, as evidenced by the remarkable role of institutions like the US Federal Reserve in the current credit crisis.

Irish society has embraced the globalisation of the world economy to a greater extent than many of its EU partners. For example, a comprehensive EU-sponsored poll of 2003 on attitudes to globalisation inside the European Community showed that the Irish were second most in favour of globalisation inside the community after The Netherlands, and led the way in the EU in terms of their positive attitude to the impact of globalisation on themselves and their families in the future. Eurobarometer statistics show that, even in the aftermath of the first rejection of the Lisbon Treaty, Irish people still had a much more positive attitude to the EU than many of their European neighbours. Specifically, the Eurobarometer survey of Autumn 2008 showed that 67 per cent of Irish people thought of the EU as a positive, versus an EU average of 53 per cent.

Contributors to this book from countries of varying size and development, from India and Portugal to Vietnam, Scotland and Greece, have all drawn different conclusions from Ireland's encounter with globalisation. For example, the impact of globalisation on small countries is likely to be greater than on large ones and the chapters on Portugal, Scotland, Romania and Greece look at the Irish experience very much from the 'small nation' perspective. On the other hand, as the chapters on Vietnam and India show clearly, Ireland's experience of globalisation can be mapped onto some larger developing countries, who take heart from the fact that the Irish experience shows that poor physical infrastructure, a lack of competitive advantage and an unsuitable geographic location now matter less as determinants of wealth in the globalised world. Equally, we in Ireland need to now recognise that a country cannot go without factors like competitive advantage and quality infrastructure if it has ambitions for a sustainable level of high quality growth.

More generally, all contributors to the book agree that the Irish embrace of globalisation – attracting foreign multinationals, engaging successfully with transnational institutions, and capitalising on the education and skills of its domestic workforce – has clear and important lessons for their own countries.

The Folly of Imitation

With its stable political climate, business friendly economy, and general respect for intangibles like the rule of law and education, Ireland has fitted well into a globalising world, and there is no doubt that the dramatic phoenix-like turnaround in its economic and political fortunes, combined with its title as 'most globalised', makes it an interesting test case of the process of globalisation.

In the past, policy-advisers, academics, business schools, journalists and institutions like the IMF have all made reputations from preaching that one country should adopt the policies of another more successful one. There is also significant academic literature devoted to mapping the experience of one country onto that of another. One has only to think of the dissection of the Japanese manufacturing sector 'miracle' of the 1980s, which sought to apply Japanese management techniques to US companies, as well as the more recent attempts to show European governments and companies the need to adopt a more 'Anglo-Saxon' financial approach.

However, blindly imitating another country's success can prove foolish because, despite the growing integration of national economies, deep structural economic, cultural and legal differences exist between states. For example, one of the main complaints of opponents of global institutions like the World Bank is that such institutions readily apply a policy formula to developing countries that has had success in some developed countries, and, in so doing, take little account of local factors and complex structural differences between nations.

Even within the EU, which more than any other regional integration project has stripped away social and economic barriers, measures that would be acceptable in, say, Ireland would be found unworkable in France. This is the main reason why the EU's Lisbon Agenda for economic reform has so far proved anything but a success.

Being aware of these pitfalls, all the contributors to this book directly address the question of exactly how much of what has worked for Ireland can be applied in their own countries. Ireland, for example, is perhaps the leading nation in terms of emigrant ties to other English-speaking countries. One should not underestimate the practical significance of such ties in explaining Ireland's successful embrace of globalisation.

The contributors to this volume rightly acknowledge that the benefits of these relationships with English-speaking nations based on profound emigrant links cannot be replicated in the case of their own countries. However, such considerations aside, the fact is that many policy measures, such as structurally low tax rates, can and are being copied. It is also the case that the Irish model is not singularly explained by the customs, culture and legal structure of the country, certainly when compared with, for example, the Danish flexible labour market model which dates back to 1899 (*September-forliget*) or the Swedish concept of 'the people's home' (or *Folkhemmet*) that arose during the early twentieth century. In addition, the Irish model doesn't have any of the cross-holding structures[6] found in the Korean, Japanese and German corporate sectors, structures which would be both difficult and costly to replicate.

One example of a 'catch-up' policy was the way in which the extent of Ireland's economic problems in the 1980s led its political class to jettison political ideology (i.e. nationalism) in favour of a much more pragmatic attitude to policy-making and a sharp focus on the need to create jobs. In turn, this approach bolstered the consensus-led social partnership agreements. Indeed, it is fair to say that this pragmatism was the glue that bound together many of the other intangible factors that were the key to Irish success. What is appealing about the Irish approach here is that this pragmatic attitude is relatively easily copied (though it often requires very poor economic circumstances as a catalyst), and does not rely on a cultural or legally embedded approach.

This is the point made by the contributors to this volume from the Mediterranean and Middle Eastern nations of Israel, Greece and Egypt, which attach significant importance to willingness to adopt the pragmatic and broad consensus-based approach to policy-making exhibited by Ireland in recent times (both in the economic sphere and in working for peace in Northern Ireland) for the development of their own economies.

Conclusion

The great transformation of Ireland in the past twenty years is one of the most interesting case studies in the area of political economy. This has been highlighted by the seemingly endless dispatch of emissaries to Ireland from all corners of the globe to study its economic turnaround, political processes and social changes.

Take Israel as an example. Between July 1999 and December 2008, nineteen high-level delegations from Israel visited Ireland, commencing with a visit by the head of the Israeli Dairy Board, followed by the Israeli trade minister, as well as the chief scientists of the Israeli ministries of Agriculture and Industry, and Trade and Labour. Subsequent visits included those by representatives of the world-renowned Technion Institute of Management and the head of the Federation of Israeli Chambers of Commerce. In 2005, Amir Peretz, then head of the Israeli Trade Union Congress, the *Histadrut*, and later leader of the Israeli Labour Party, travelled to Ireland to examine the social partnership model. *Histadrut* leaders, accompanied by members of the Federation of Israeli Economic Organisations, returned two years later in 2007. The year 2007 also saw visits from the Ireland–Israel Chamber of Commerce, the Israel Mobile Association, senior civil servants from the Ministry of Transport and, most importantly, the director generals of all Israeli government ministries, who spent a number of days shadowing their Irish counterparts in the relevant departments. The next year, 2008, saw a visit from Israel's Accountant General and senior members of the Israeli ministries of Agriculture and Finance as well as a visit by the Chairman of the Israel Centre for R&D.

This book takes a unique perspective on the Irish changes in that it offers a wide range of independent opinions from experts who for years have studied what the Irish example has to offer their own countries. Importantly, one attraction of the Irish 'model' that is stressed by almost all of the contributors is that it is exportable – in other words, new policies pursued by the Irish can be copied and applied with relative ease and some success in other nation-states.

The different perspective provided by our authors comes at a crucial moment in global economic history. Governments everywhere are concerned as to how they can rejoin the path to prosperity and, in Ireland itself, policy-makers and above all the Irish people are eager to rediscover the policies that first propelled Ireland's economy forward. In this respect, the model of Ireland's 'catch-up' period (between 1990 to 2001) stands out, and is now even more relevant because of the credit crisis. On the other hand, the overheating of the Irish economy from 2003 onwards also serves as a powerful counter example of what is likely to go down in the annals of finance as an asset price bubble, with all its attendant ugliness, chaos and misery.

In summary, the diverse contributions to this book show that, no matter what part of the world you come from or whether your nation is rich or poor, large or small, there is much to be learnt from the things that Ireland did right. The common factors that the contributors highlight here are a focus on intangible infrastructure as the bedrock for a modern society and a developed economy; pragmatism in policy-making; harnessing your country to the forces of globalisation while constructing buffers to limit the side-effects of this; an acute wariness of asset price bubbles; and the adoption of innovative fiscal policies to counteract larger, 'inappropriate' macro effects.

Above all, the one country that now needs to take heed of these lessons is Ireland, as we search for a path to economic recovery and very necessary institutional rebuilding. Having been admired by so many other countries, Ireland now needs to look at how other countries are changing, adapting and developing, and learn from their example. We very much hope that *What Did We Do Right?* provides a constructive starting point for this journey.

CHAPTER 1

Scotland and Ireland: Towards a Common 'Celtic Model'

Alex Salmond

Back in May 1997, *The Economist* magazine published a special edition on the Irish economic boom.[1] After a rundown on how the Irish economy was reaching maturity following years of relative underperformance, the correspondent concluded with the crisp observation that 'If Ireland has another decade as successful as the last one, it will be a miracle economy indeed.' The credit crisis may have temporarily dented confidence in countries around the world, but when it has run its course we should have a much clearer idea of the factors that drove the turnaround in the Irish economy, in particular from the late 1980s onwards. These factors are still of great interest to Scotland and to the wider world in the post-credit crisis period.

The credit crisis must not blur the many positives that have been achieved. I feel that adopting a 'what did Ireland do right?' attitude is a good starting point in trying to build recovery. One lasting benefit to Ireland from its economic success of the past twenty years is the changed way in which it is now regarded by other countries. Our position in Scotland, as neighbours and perhaps 'cousins' of the Irish, means that we have sufficient perspective to gauge what Scotland can take from Ireland's economic experience of the past twenty-five years.

Though there are, of course, a number of differences in our national experiences, there are also a number of lessons that Scotland can learn from her Irish neighbours, and take to heart in considering her own future. The overarching theme here is that Ireland has based her long-term success on human capital and institutions – two areas where Scotland has also

15

traditionally been strong and in which we as a government are continuing to invest.

More specifically, the first and perhaps the most important lesson is that, just as no man can set bounds on the march of a nation, there are no limits to the success of a nation that is united by a common purpose. While the reforms initiated by Seán Lemass and T.K. Whitaker in the 1960s can be seen as marking the beginning of Ireland's economic catch-up, it still took the lean period of the early 1980s and the resulting 1987 economic plan to truly turbocharge Ireland's subsequent growth.

In Scotland, through our Government's Economic Strategy, our new partnership with local government and through the National Economic Forum, we are seeking to build the same strong and lasting cohesion among our institutions. By doing so, we can lay the foundations for the same economic success that was achieved in Ireland over the past twenty years.

The second point is that, while independence is vital if Scotland is to achieve its full economic potential – by offering Scotland a great many more policy options than she enjoys currently as part of the UK – it is what you do with that independence which really matters. With the right policies, and when engaged fully with the recovering global economy, the economic rewards for Europe's smaller independent countries can be great indeed.

Third, with particular reference to the histories of Scotland and Ireland, we should never forget the counterfactual. While Ireland has the recent experience of independence which Scotland lacks, the history of both countries appears to show that nothing about membership of the UK guarantees economic success.

Today's UK economy is heavily centralised, with policies and resources being focused on its major pole of growth – London. The credit crisis does not seem to have shifted the UK Government's priorities away from the South and toward the English regions, Scotland, Wales and Northern Ireland – and I would argue that this underlines that the UK's political system is simply not able to respond quickly or accurately to the needs of Scotland's economy. That is why my Government believes that the Scottish Parliament is best placed to take all the major economic decisions affecting the people of Scotland.

Fourth, it is now widely accepted in policy circles that investment in human capital – the education, skills and potential of our people – is a basic determinant of economic success. One of the foundations of Ireland's current success was the education and training reforms of the 1960s. While these enabled Ireland to play catch-up with her European neighbours, it also paved the way for today's Irish strength in high-tech sectors such as IT and pharmaceuticals. Scotland has always placed great emphasis on education. At its heart is the idea of the 'democratic intellect' – that education should be open to all who are capable of benefiting from it, regardless of their means or background. It's an ideal grounded in the recognition that education should be valued for its own sake. It is not just for the betterment of the individual, but also for the betterment of the economy and the broader society which have helped shape the individual and have given him or her the opportunity to study in the first instance.

In many ways, free education was a Scottish invention. It is a principle which has become dearly held elsewhere. It is precisely because we can appreciate the societal, cultural and economic benefits of free education that it was reintroduced in Scotland with the Government's abolition of tuition fees. I have no doubt that removing the burden of tuition fees will prove to be a cornerstone of Scottish economic revival.

The fifth lesson to draw is one relating to the interdependence of our economy with that of our neighbours and the wider world. It is a statement of the obvious, but one which bears repetition nonetheless: the countries of the EU are, and will remain, the source of our most significant economic relationships.

As recently as 1960, three quarters of Ireland's exports were to the UK. Today, while the UK remains Ireland's single largest national market, it accounts for a much more manageable 18 per cent of exports.[2] In the context of wider access to European markets, this diversification of the export base and spreading of risk has been a generally healthy and positive experience.

It is only fair to recognise that there are significant sectoral differences within that figure. For example, some 42 per cent of Irish food and drink exports are to the UK. While the UK remains an important market for Ireland – with the intertwined history of the two countries, the UK's proximity to Ireland and its large market of 14 per cent share of EU gross domestic product (GDP), it could scarcely be anything else – the remainder of the EU-27 economy is six times larger, and is unquestionably where the greatest opportunities lie for the Irish – and Scottish – economy in the future. If anything, the impact of the credit crisis makes this lesson all the more clear.

The sixth lesson is that, in Ireland, just as is the case in Denmark, Finland, Norway and Sweden, prosperity is dependent upon the openness of the economy and the development of comparative advantage. Again, the impact of the credit crisis is a lesson here. One notable trend is that exports from Ireland have not fallen by quite as much as in other small countries, and by nothing like other sectors of the Irish economy. This shows the benefits of trade globalisation (as opposed to financial globalisation). And when it comes to securing and maintaining a comparative advantage, Scotland can only look on enviously when it comes to the ability the Irish have to set corporation tax rates.

The seventh lesson – a vital one and an expensive one to ignore – is that an economic windfall must be used wisely. The weak state of government balance sheets across the developed world is a testament to this. In this regard, many emerging and energy-rich economies stand out because they have used prosperity to build up financial reserves. Norway stands out here, as a model to both Ireland and Scotland. Less prosperous than Scotland at the time oil was discovered, Norway now sits at the top of the United Nations (UN) Development Report Index as one of the wealthiest countries on earth. The Norwegian Government created its oil fund in the 1990s, which today is worth over £200 billion. Their oil fund is one which will safeguard the future prosperity of Norway, ensuring that the oil windfall continues to cascade down through the generations long after the last wells have run dry.

This is an important lesson for Scotland because we have benefited, and continue to do so, from a similar economic windfall in the form of revenues from North Sea oil and gas. Since the late 1970s, these revenues have provided us with a great economic opportunity, albeit one which has been largely squandered over the past thirty years. However, for the Government in Westminster labouring under the mounting economic crises of the 1970s, it was an economic lifeline. While successive Westminster governments took the opportunity to use the revenues to ameliorate the balance of payments, a toxic combination of high interest rates, high exchange rates and high inflation wrought devastation throughout Scottish manufacturing industry.

There are estimated to be 25 billion barrels of oil remaining in the North Sea and, given global trends in oil prices, there is likely more value left to be extracted than has already taken place in the past 40 years. By establishing an oil fund, the Scottish Government is determined to secure the same legacy for Scotland as the Norwegian Government has already done for its own people. Future generations will judge us on how we use the hydrocarbon resources which remain. Scotland is also fortunate enough to have some of the most exciting renewable energy potential anywhere in Europe. That is an opportunity we cannot afford to squander in the same way that successive UK Governments have wasted our oil and gas reserves, and is why the Scottish Government is putting such an emphasis on development of renewables.

The eighth point is one which we would do well to remember, not only in pursuit of our own ambitions in Scotland, but also in evaluating where Ireland's 20-year boom has taken her – that economic growth creates its own challenges. It is important to recognise that economic growth is not of itself a panacea; it does, though, create the potential to solve those self-same challenges and, in the process, raise everyone's standard of living. The credit crisis brings this home all the more powerfully and helps to support the argument for a more balanced view of the relationship between society and economy.

The Scottish Government is seeking to match the enviable longer-term growth record of Ireland. Although, as already mentioned, we as yet lack the powers in Edinburgh to alter levels of corporation tax, we have been able to reduce the local taxes levied on small businesses – the lifeblood of town and village centres and, indeed, the whole economy. We are also pre-pared to work as hard in Scotland to maintain social justice and to continue to renew the foundations of economic success.

Scotland has a lot of advantages when it comes to being a place to do business: a well-developed market in legal and professional services; excel-lent infrastructure, particularly in telecoms; a good environment; a well-educated workforce; and good links to key markets in Europe and the US. Scotland is also part of the EU, shares, like Ireland, an intimate famil-iarity with anglophone culture and also enjoys hydrocarbon security along with a wealth of clean, renewable energy sources.

We see raising our competitiveness and growth levels as being the key to securing the resources to help overcome social problems and delivering the public services to which we aspire.[3] It is also a key component in attract-ing the skilled migrants and returning expatriates we need to bring additional skills to our country and help to tackle the demographic trends we face. It is through so doing that we can emulate many of the key drivers which have made possible Ireland's turnaround of the past two decades.

The ninth lesson to draw is not really about economics at all. Rather, it concerns the position of smaller countries in the world and the influence they can exercise internationally. In the past, it was assumed that influence in the world was synonymous with being able to muster military might on land, sea and air; with having a permanent seat on the UN Security Coun-cil; with having nuclear weapons. However, there is a clear lesson for Scotland from Ireland and our neighbours in the Nordic countries – that small, peaceful countries can exercise major global influence.

Today, we strive to extend this positive influence, especially by taking the initiative on climate change, an area in which Scotland has recently passed world-leading legislation, and we also have a key role to play in green energy. Boosted by the recognition of the international community, through the award of the 2014 Commonwealth Games to Glasgow, I am confident that our sights will be raised to go on to even greater achievements in the future.

Much has been made of Ireland cornering the market in anglophone pro-Europeanism in the 1980s and 1990s. Where Ireland has succeeded before us, Scotland can succeed in the future.

Scotland, like Ireland, is part of the English-speaking world. Nearly nine out of ten schoolchildren in the EU learn English, with at least two billion people around the world having either full or at least some understanding of the language. Our universities help teach the world, both by bringing students to live in Scotland and through distance learning. People around the globe are as curious about us as we are about them, which gives us a huge potential audience for our cultural output.

Notwithstanding the challenges of the credit crunch, I feel that looking at what Ireland has 'done right' over the past twenty or so years could provide a compelling example to the rest of the world. Scotland, just like Ireland, with our history, experiences of empire building and retrenchment, centuries-long exposure to globalisation, history of immigration and emigration, outlook, culture, and philosophical and religious traditions, has a truly unique voice and perspective we can bring to bear. Fundamentally, both Scotland and Ireland have great stories to tell, and a world audience queuing up to hear them.

Finally, the tenth lesson concerns the process of becoming a successful nation-state. That is, for all the parallels it may be possible to draw, there is no blueprint for a transition to full independence which Scotland can draw from Ireland.

While the steps towards Irish independence were inexorable, the pace of change in the face of Westminster intransigence most certainly was not. Although Scotland had to wait much longer for home rule than Ireland, it still took Westminster three attempts to pass the Irish Home Rule Bill before it finally succeeded in 1914. The foundation of the Irish State followed within a decade. Yet, still, for more than twenty-five years after gaining independence, Ireland remained a dominion of the Empire.

Voluntarily, if for some perhaps a little grudgingly, Westminster has yielded power to devolved administrations in Edinburgh, Belfast and Cardiff. This has forever changed the political makeup of the British Isles.

From the Labour hegemony which seemed guaranteed by Tony Blair's landslide victory in 1997, there is now a Scottish National Party (SNP)

Government in Edinburgh, a Labour–Plaid Cymru administration in Cardiff and a Democratic Unioninst Party (DUP)–Sinn Féin power-sharing executive in Belfast. This accession to government of parties uncommitted to the maintenance of the British State would have seemed unthinkable just a few short years ago.

Furthermore, there has been a sea change in the attitudes of the Scottish political parties to constitutional change since May 2007. From a position of insisting that further constitutional change was neither necessary nor desirable, opposition parties established the Calman Commission to examine where they think devolution ought to go from here. It is impossible to separate this development from the accession to office of a government committed to independence for Scotland.

The hardest question for parties committed to the British Union was never going to be whether 'more powers' should be devolved to Scotland. Rather, the question that would always pose the greatest difficulty would be 'which powers?' For example, parties may agree that Holyrood[4] should have greater fiscal freedoms, but how should that be reflected in practice? Would powers over broadcasting regulation be devolved? On these, and many other matters, there is no unanimity amongst Calman participants. Other parties may be united in agreement that they do not want independence, but getting to a point where something can be produced on which all agree and which also meets the rising aspirations of Scottish voters seems some way off.

Nevertheless, a direction of travel has clearly been established and expectations set accordingly. The Scottish Government's 'National Conversation' on the constitution continues apace. Crucially, all parties to the Scottish constitutional debate accept the right of Scottish voters to choose independence. The Scottish Government is determined to give the people of Scotland a free and fair choice on their country's constitutional future and that is why we will introduce legislation to Holyrood[4] to enable an independence referendum to be held. If full self-government is endorsed by the people in such a referendum, Scotland would then become an independent state, taking her place alongside Ireland in the EU and UN, while remaining within the Commonwealth.

While participation and pooling of sovereignty have enhanced the role of smaller nations in Europe, the proximity of government to the people in smaller countries lends weight to the view that Scotland and Ireland would find themselves strong partners in the post-Lisbon EU.

In the context of the credit crisis, it should also be noted that, at the time of writing, both Ireland and Norway are tipped by the International

Monetary Fund (IMF) to continue to outstrip the UK in terms of GDP per head into the future. It would seem that, even in the toughest of times, the benefits of independence for smaller European nations remain abundantly clear.

Both Scotland and Ireland have a unique contribution to make, and much to learn from each other in so doing.

CHAPTER 2

Celtic Tiger, American Eagle: Irish Lessons for a Regional Economy in the US

Joseph Morrison Skelly

Over the past two hundred years, the relationship between Ireland and the US has worked out as mutually beneficial. The contribution of Irish emigrants to the growth of the US in the nineteenth and twentieth centuries is well known. So, too, is the role of American investment in the strength of the Celtic Tiger, which flexed its muscles in Ireland for fifteen years before fatigue set in with the onset of the current recession in 2008. What is less often discussed is whether the next step in this transatlantic relationship will take place. That is, will lessons gleaned from Ireland's era of economic expansion travel westward to the US? More specifically, this chapter examines whether some of the things that Ireland did right for nearly a decade and a half are transferable to an economically depressed region of the US – like Upstate New York – during a time of global financial uncertainty. In stormy weather, can the Celtic Tiger teach the American Eagle to fly?

The answer to this question is a qualified yes: certain Irish lessons are applicable to slow-growth areas like Upstate New York, but to a limited extent. Not all variables of Ireland's economic calculus are relevant, but some of the more profitable strategies Ireland employed have real value, namely the ability to attract foreign direct investment (FDI); the development of high-tech, export-oriented industries; the low corporate tax rate; the commitment to free trade; and the well-educated, flexible labour force. This is the case even at the tail end of a harsh global recession in 2010. Now is not the time to recoil from innovative thinking. As the international financial situation stabilises, Upstate New York and other economically challenged regions can better position themselves for future growth by reflecting on what went right with the Irish model.

The American Eagle in Upstate New York

The overall narrative of the Irish economic revival that began in the early 1990s and lasted until 2008 is well known. Its sheen has dimmed, however, as the recession has taken its toll. A vigorous debate that began several years ago has now accelerated regarding the facade of the Celtic Tiger, which concealed the issues of hidden costs such as the long-term economic impact of high public sector salaries, the fate of elements of the population who did not benefit from the boom period, and the blindness of policy-makers to an asset bubble in the housing market – conditions made all the more immediate due to rising unemployment and the collapse of house prices.[1] Still, the nation's progress remains a notable achievement overall, especially in the context of lacklustre economic performance elsewhere during the same years.

Contrast Ireland with Upstate New York during the same decade and a half from the early 1990s, for example. This region, defined as the 52 counties outside of New York City, Long Island, and the suburban Westchester, Putnam and Rockland counties, includes a population of close to seven million people.[2] Its primary urban centres are Albany (the state capital), Syracuse, Rochester, Buffalo and Binghamton. Previously an engine of growth, this swath of New York has been stalled in neutral since the late 1980s. Its economy is anaemic. 'Is Upstate New York going the way of Appalachia?' a report by the Public Policy Institute of New York asked in 2007.[3] It continued to note that

> as recently as the 1970s, the question would have seemed absurd. Since Erie Canal days, Upstate New York had led the nation's economic development. It entered the second half of the 20th Century with a huge and highly advanced industrial base, a world-beating workforce, vital cities and excellent infrastructure. But high costs and stiffening competition from other states and countries gradually took their toll. Job growth declined, businesses moved out, people followed – and by the late 1990s there was growing concern that Upstate's economy was dead in the water.

A study by the Brookings Institution a few years earlier sounded the same tragic note: 'In the 1960s, few people would have expected that this region, with its strong manufacturing base, outstanding infrastructure system, and diverse network of metropolitan areas, would by the 1990s be among the slowest-growing areas in the country.'[4]

Statistics tell this sad tale, which clearly emerged in the final decade of the twentieth century. 'The economy of Upstate New York, by nearly all major measures, worsened in the 1990s, lagging both the nation and its own performance in the 1980s,' report Pendall, Drennan and Christopherson.[5] The region's employment gains during the 1990s, for instance, trailed well behind the national average. The numbers then dropped significantly between 2000 and 2003, 'paralleling the nationwide decline in employment that began in mid-2001 and accelerated with the full onset of the recession and the effects of September 11, 2001'.[6] While other 'Rust Belt' states – those states in the area stretching from the North East, across the Mid-Atlantic States and along portions of the Upper Midwest, which used to be the industrial heart of North America – have recovered faster. For example, while Ohio recovered from this post-9/11 slump, Upstate New York's performance has been consistently weak.[7] In 2008, the state's unemployment rate increased from 5.2 per cent in May to 6.1 per cent in November, while, according to Peter A. Neenan, director of the New York Department of Labour's Division of Research and Statistics, 'The rate of over-the-year private sector job growth has decelerated – from 1.5 per cent in the first half of 2007 to 0.7 per cent in the first half of 2008.'[8]

The Brookings Institution has uncovered chronic wage and income stagnation, noting that '[i]n 1969, per capita personal income (PCPI) in Upstate exceeded that of the US, but by 2000 it trailed the national average by 11 per cent.'[9] Indeed, the only 'broad economic measure' in which Upstate New York leads the way is in the receipt of transfer payments, a measure of dependence on Government.[10] More worrisome, income erosion has slowed population growth as the best educated and highly skilled move to other parts of the country. Upstate New York's population 'grew by a mere 1.1 per cent in the 1990s, slower than the growth rate of every state but West Virginia and North Dakota.'[11] Between 1995 and 2005, only three Upstate counties experienced population growth greater than the national average,[12] and the young, especially those in the crucial 20 to 34 age group, are leaving the region.[13]

Lessons from Ireland

In Upstate New York the Eagle's wings are clipped. What can be done to restore it to flight? It can learn from the Celtic Tiger. As mentioned, there are limits to this exercise, to be sure. Not all Irish economic lessons are transatlantic in nature. There are fundamental differences between the two economies. Upstate New York, like the Rust Belt states of Pennsylvania,

Ohio and Michigan, has a substantial, albeit declining, heavy industrial and manufacturing base, which post-industrial Ireland does not possess to a significant degree. It is necessary to exercise caution when utilising a comparative framework, since some scholars believe that there is not a clearly defined Irish economic model.[14]

Still other factors militate against employing the Celtic Tiger as a growth template. Ireland is now experiencing a severe economic slowdown, led by turbulence in vital sectors like housing, construction, banking, software development and computer manufacturing. It officially entered a recession in 2008 and its gross national product (GNP) contracted sharply in 2009.[15] Hidden social problems persisted in Ireland at the height of the economic boom, such as an uneven distribution of wealth and a steeply rising cost of living.[16] These challenges are re-emerging with the current downturn. For over a decade, economists have noted pockets of weakness in the indigenous Irish manufacturing sector (often in contrast to the Asian 'Tigers', notably Singapore, South Korea and Taiwan), which is not an example for New Yorkers to emulate.[17] There is also the international context to consider, which has deteriorated compared to the 1990s, when, according to Michael J. O'Sullivan, domestic Irish growth variables 'were triggered by outside factors, principally by the falling cost of capital, the trend towards the opening up of international markets and trade, diminished geopolitical risk and the advent of new technologies – all of the ingredients of what are now taken to drive economic globalization.'[18] The US economy itself is experiencing stress in several sectors, including housing, mortgage lending and the credit markets, which represents a challenging economic climate that may not be conducive to importing examples from Ireland.

The identification of lessons from the Celtic Tiger are therefore not numerous. Nonetheless, it is legitimate to consider the relevance of recent Irish economic growth within an American regional setting under certain headings.

Foreign Direct Investment

Let us proceed with this exercise by assessing specific policy prescriptions from Ireland, their utility in a global context and their bearing on the challenges that bedevil Upstate New York.

One relevant lesson is Ireland's success in transforming itself into an attractive recipient of FDI, especially in export-oriented, high-tech industries such as pharmaceuticals, information technology and computer software.[19] While there is international consensus regarding the significance of FDI, the question arises: is this aim worth considering for Upstate New York? Yes, according to the data. At the macro level in the US, the impact of FDI has been substantial, especially its ability to generate high-paying jobs. In 2005, according to the *Wall Street Journal*, in-sourcing companies employed nearly 5.1 million Americans, or 4.4 per cent of the private-sector labour force,[20] and compensation per worker at these firms was 31.8 per cent above the average for the rest of the private sector.

Since these economic gains are transferable to the state level, the importance of export-oriented FDI for Northern New York cannot be overstated. In 2004, FDI accounted for over 7 per cent of the New York State economy (or US$66 billion) and was responsible for over 455,000 jobs state-wide. FDI created nearly one in every ten dollars of new economic activity in the state between 2002 and 2004.[21] FDI linked to exports is an even more powerful formula. A Brooking Institution study argues that New York 'state policy should focus relentlessly and strategically on export industries, those activities that directly contribute to the generation of new wealth for Upstate.'[22]

The same report detects a ray of hope amidst the gloom of previous decades, especially in the development of knowledge-based services such as education and health care, two sectors in which innovation is occurring.[23] Another Brookings bulletin observes that capitalising on Upstate's 'rich endowment of educational and health care institutions' would most likely 'increase the demand within Upstate for well educated workers and boost wages at the top' and, at the same time, encourage outside firms to invest 'in their local communities and surrounding regions and to use local small businesses as major suppliers'.[24]

High Technology, Enterprise Zones, Flexible Labour

What about manufacturing in the region? True, there is downward pressure on wages in traditional smokestack industries, which pay 'less for every manufacturing job – about US$46,650 in 2000 – than the average for manufacturing in the US of over US$51,300 per job'.[25] Since high-end manufacturing pays higher wages, the focus should be on developing knowledge-intensive manufacturing activities, such as photonics, environmental engineering and specialised food processing.[26]

New York would do well to follow the Irish model, in other words, to focus on high-tech industries in combination with the state's emerging strengths in education and health care. There are sophisticated production platforms to build upon, especially in the Capital region centred on Albany (which is home to the State University of New York's prestigious College of

Nanoscale Science and Engineering), the mid-Hudson Valley (where IBM has a strong presence in the manufacturing, research and development of advanced semiconductors) and Rochester, a centre of world-class imaging and optics technology, the resiliency of which demonstrates the viability of the Irish paradigm in limited circumstances.[27] It is true that Rochester's three main employers, Xerox, Kodak, and Bausch & Lomb, have outsourced jobs, but the city has continued to retain important advantages in optics and imaging technology. Small and medium-sized firms in these and other industries have also played their part, ensuring that the city has maintained its crucial role as a source of exports over the past decade, with the US Department of Commerce reporting in 2006 that it led the Upstate region overall, shipping US$4.6 billion in manufactured goods to Canada, Mexico, China and beyond.[28] 'This speaks highly of the mid-size Rochester companies', according to local business consultant Deepak Seth, 'which have picked up the slack.... The spirit of innovation and out-of-the-box thinking which drove Rochester in the past can continue to do so in the future.'[29]

New York is combining its commitment to promoting high technology industries with another Irish lesson – the creation of enterprise zones in order to maximise this opportunity. One analysis of these trends mentions that the state government's two primary initiatives 'to stimulate growth in the Upstate economy are the Empire Zones programme, and high-tech efforts'.[30] The former, like their parallel in Ireland, 'offer virtually tax-free treatment for some growing businesses – a total package that economic developers say no other state can match (although it directly impacts only a few businesses)'.

Like Ireland two decades ago, Upstate New York's labour market today is positioned to take advantage of new industries if they can be persuaded to establish a presence in the area. Throughout the 1980s and 1990s, the Irish labour force became better educated and more flexible, which facilitated growth, while in the latter decade a series of social agreements between unions and management across the public and private sectors encouraged wage stability and a 'flexible labour market'.[31] Northern New York has similar advantages. One of them is a university-educated labour pool that has recently outpaced the national standard. In 1980, 'only 15.8 per cent of Upstate adults had college degrees, compared to 16.2 per cent nationwide', but by the year 2000 32.8 per cent were university graduates, a larger percentage than the US overall, at 30.7 per cent.[32] In the face of declining wages, New York needs to hold on to this human capital by embracing innovative policies. A creative approach to financial aid would be helpful, one that would encourage young men and women 'to stay in Upstate by providing scholarships to promising graduates that would convert to repayable loans if the student takes a job outside Upstate' – combined, of course, with a growing demand for college-educated employees.[33] An announcement in July 2008 that the College of Nanoscale Science and Engineering in Albany will partner with IBM's semiconductor facility in the Hudson Valley, the State of New York and private firms as far away as Buffalo to carry out applied research into nanoscale technology, thus creating up to a thousand new high-tech jobs across the region, is a good start.[34]

Corporate Tax Rates

Attracting FDI will keep workers and families in Northern New York. But how can this be achieved? Here, the Irish experience is again compelling. It demonstrates that the correct business policies are essential. At the height of the Celtic Tiger, a Central Bank of Ireland study reported that the reasons that 'foreign investors find Ireland an attractive investment location are consistency of economic policy, economic openness, and a focus on employment and enhancing productivity'.[35] One specific example is the country's low corporate tax rate of 12.5 per cent. Economists have concluded that there is a relationship between lower corporate taxes and increased FDI, which has been observed not only in Ireland, but measured in the US.[36] This linkage also explains why there is widespread international interest in adopting Ireland's policy of minimal corporate taxes in countries as diverse as Northern Ireland, Vietnam, Singapore and Colombia.[37]

What about New York State? Its corporate tax rate stands at 7.5 per cent, which, in combination with the national figure of 35 per cent (or an adjusted rate of 39.9 per cent), does not compare favourably to Ireland's over the past decade. Nor does it compare well to other states across the US, with thirty having lower adjusted rates.[38] Its high corporate rate should be seen as part of an oppressive state-wide tax regime that weighs like an anchor on the New York economy. In 2003, the Public Policy Institute asked, 'How does our overall business tax burden compare to the competition?' The answer – not well. Calculations by economists at the Federal Reserve Bank of Boston, which uses a 'representative tax system', show that New York's state and local taxes on corporate profits were third highest among all the states and 82 per cent higher than the national average.[39]

When translated into real figures, the dollar amounts that New York companies shell out in taxes at the state and local levels are excessive. In 2003, they paid over US$10.5 billion to support the state budget. At the local level, businesses contributed some US$19.9 billion, including US$6.6 billion in school taxes.[40] This total of US$30.4 billion represented 34.1 per cent of total tax revenue. As if these numbers are not high enough, a comparative analysis reveals that, in 2004, Upstate New York's businesses and taxpayers paid state and local taxes that were 'about US$5 billion to US$6 billion a year higher than they would be if they were living in, say, Ohio'.[41] This burden represents 'a significant drag on the region's economy [and] one reason Upstate's job growth has lagged behind competing states for so long'.

Economic Freedom

It is imperative to lower corporate taxes and reduce the tax burden overall, which will help to attract FDI into Upstate New York. These steps will improve the business environment in the region. So, too, will a more restrained spending policy. Making the case for limits on taxation and government expenditure is Benjamin Powell, a lecturer in Economics at Suffolk University, who links these policies to the principle of 'economic freedom', which, he believes, accounts for much of the economic growth that Ireland experienced from the early 1990s. This concept may also hold out a lesson for Upstate New York. According to Powell's research, 'no one particular policy is responsible for Ireland's dramatic economic growth. Rather, a general tendency of many policies to increase economic freedom has caused Ireland's economy to grow rapidly.'[42] He defines 'economic freedom' as low taxes, restricted spending, reduced levels of government debt, the deregulation of the economy, free trade, the practice of limited government and a commitment to the rule of law.

In terms of restrained expenditure, New York can learn from Ireland's actions two decades ago. In order to avert a major debt crisis in 1987, the Irish Government engaged in serious belt-tightening across the board. 'Through early retirement and other incentives', Powell notes, 'public sector employment was voluntarily cut by nearly 10,000 jobs.'[43] That was just the start. 'A budget was set for 1988, which had the biggest spending cuts Ireland had seen in 30 years.' Current spending was reduced by 3 per cent and capital spending was cut by 16 per cent, thus rescuing Ireland from its fiscal crisis.

What was the result of this cost-cutting? It reduced the level of debt, limited the size of the Government's role in the economy and improved the domestic business climate. Powell argues that, as 'Ireland increased economic freedom, per capita GDP rose',[44] but his main thesis is that the 'rapid growth of the Celtic Tiger only occurred once all aspects of economic freedom were largely respected at the same time.'[45] According to the Fraser Institute's index of economic freedom, which he cites, Ireland in 1995 'was the world's fifth freest economy, and in 2000 it was the seventh freest economy, achieving scores of 8.2 and 8.1 respectively. From 1985 to 2000, Ireland improved its score on all five of the freedom index's broad categories.'[46]

In Northern New York, many business leaders, policy-makers and lawmakers concur with Benjamin Powell's analysis: they believe that greater 'economic freedom' will enhance economic performance, as it did in Ireland. According to the Public Policy Institute, for 'Upstate to compete on an even footing with places like Ohio, let alone Virginia, may require that Albany give the region the freedom it needs to get its costs down.'[47] Spending, for example, needs to be pared. In particular, there needs to be a reduction in the number of local government employees (the region has a 25 per cent higher rate of local government workers to the population than the national average[48]) and a decrease in the budget of New York's Medicaid programme (health care for the poor), which costs Upstate taxpayers about US$1 billion more a year in state and local taxes than it would if it matched the national average per recipient.

Upstate New York, after all, is vying for jobs with 'places like Ohio, and Virginia. In that competition, costs *do* matter. If a corporation is trying to decide whether to locate a new plant in Elmira, New York, or Roanoke, Virginia ... [w]hat is relevant is if property taxes and energy and workers' compensation and health insurance cost more in Elmira than in Virginia. That's the competitive game Upstate is in. If it isn't allowed to change, it can't compete, and it won't win.'[49]

Economic freedom has a proven track record in the region. From 1995 to 2000, New York's growth rate reached 80 per cent of the national average and nearly equalled it towards the end of this cycle.[50] These years did include a bull market on Wall Street, but they also encompassed Governor George Pataki's success in creating a more favourable business climate. He spearheaded a series of reforms – tax reductions, new workers' compensation laws, administrative improvements, regulatory changes and the introduction of competition into the electric utility business – that were directly linked to the state's strong economic performance in the late 1990s.[51] Economic freedom, in other words, can lead to economic progress in New York.

Limits and Lessons

Several caveats are in order. Factors exist in the US that may limit the efficacy of Irish economic lessons for New York. At the federal level, does Congress possess the will to lower the national corporate tax rate? The answer in the current economic climate, alas, is no. The recession has cooled enthusiasm for free trade. The Obama administration may follow through on its campaign pledge to renegotiate the North American Free Trade Agreement (NAFTA), while Congress has refused to approve trade pacts with several countries, including Colombia. Limiting free trade will neutralise the use of a lower corporate tax rate to attract FDI into New York by diluting the state's potential as a platform for exporting goods and services. The Upstate region is also suffering from a long-term structural change underway in the national economy, namely the shift in population, wealth and resources to the Sun Belt – those areas of the south and southwest of the US which have exploded in size in recent decades – away from New York and the northeast.[52]

At the state level, New York's Legislature and Governor need to push through much needed economic reforms, such as reducing the tax burden and limiting public spending. But will they do so? The record is mixed. In May 2007 the State Senate approved a comprehensive piece of legislation entitled 'Upstate *Now*', an ambitious ten-point economic development programme that Ireland's Industrial Development Agency (IDA) would admire. Yet the State Assembly and Governor have failed to fund it sufficiently or to implement all of its components.[53] Perhaps this is because the Downstate region, which consists of New York City and its suburban counties, is a stumbling block to Upstate aspirations in terms of attracting investment and blocking any developments at the expense of the urban areas.[54]

There are signs that attitudes may be changing, but the current recession may put reform efforts on ice for the time being. In June 2008 Governor David Patterson, who is from New York City, announced that he would introduce legislation to cap local school property taxes at 4 per cent or 1.2 times the rate of inflation, whichever is less. 'The growth rate of property taxes in this state is unsustainable, especially for the elderly, working families and small businesses just starting out,' he said.[55] Echoing some of the pro-growth arguments articulated above, his statement added, 'New York is a premier destination for individuals, families and entrepreneurs, but the state's rising tax burden has impacted its ability to retain young families, seniors and businesses – especially in the face of a national economic downturn.' The Empire Centre for New York State Policy registered its approval, having earlier argued in a white paper that '[h]eavy property tax burdens strain household budgets and drive up the cost of doing business throughout Long Island, the Hudson Valley and Upstate New York.... In less affluent Upstate communities, high tax rates undermine property values and feed a vicious cycle of disinvestment in urban real estate'.[56] The sooner the property tax cap and other reforms are turned into law the better, but it is more likely that the record multibillion dollar deficit New York State is facing in 2010 due to the economic slowdown, combined with the income tax hikes proposed to shrink it, will delay their passage, at least in the short term.

Another factor complicating the efficacy of the Irish model for Northern New York is that there may be limits to wage performance in some of the strategic industries identified above. Health care is 'the fastest growing sector in Upstate and now employs a larger share of Upstate residents than the sector's average in the nation; however, average wage growth in the sector lags the nation.'[57] In the Rochester region, the home of optics technology, modest increases in employment have been accompanied by wage slippage in recent years, with Kodak experiencing acute challenges.[58] Salaries in the information sector (education, financial services, office support) are soft, and jobs in information industries pay less than those in the high-tech and manufacturing sectors.[59]

Some Irish lessons, upon closer inspection, may not be relevant to the US. The social partnership model, which limited upward pressure on wages in the early years of the Celtic Tiger, may lack appeal in New York due to differences in business cultures.[60] The international economy, the expansion of which was pivotal to Ireland's performance in the 1990s, will not be favourable to Northern New York for the next several years. (A weak dollar, however, may spur FDI into the US.) There are other growth models, namely the 'Asian Tiger' models, that may be more germane to the complex conditions found across the state. It may therefore be best to apply lessons from Ireland and other countries, a combined approach that could ultimately yield a greater growth curve.

Still, there are limited Irish lessons for Upstate New York. These include the development of a viable strategy to attract FDI, particularly in high-tech industries; a pro-business climate; a low tax burden; restrained government spending; an educated workforce; and a commitment to economic freedom. Truth be told, these lessons apply not only to New York, but also to other regions in the US. This is so even in the challenging economic environment of 2010. Eventually, the business forecast will improve, while in the meantime New York and other states can prepare for future growth by considering the more effective elements of the Irish economic experience. To a limited extent, the Celtic Tiger can teach the American Eagle how to, if not soar, at least to fly.

CHAPTER 3

The New Anglo-Irish Relationship

Jonathan Powell

Anglo-Irish relations have been difficult since at least the time of Strongbow[1] and probably before. Perhaps relations between small countries and their big neighbours are always filled with resentment, like the relationship between Portugal and Spain, even though the Portuguese war of independence was in the fourteenth century rather than the twentieth century.

When you add to this disparity of size the history of colonial rule from London, the rebellions bloodily put down, the discrimination against Catholics, Ireland's economic dependence on Britain and the relationship of mutual incomprehension between the countries, perhaps the resentment on the Irish side is not so surprising.

My mother was a scion of the Anglo-Irish Ascendancy and her view of Ireland was formed by the series of books *The Irish RM*,[2] which depicted the Anglo-Irish squires enjoying their balls and foxhunting and patronising the comic 'bog Irish'. However, the comic aspect waned and became bitterness following the foundation of the Irish State in 1922 and the estrangement between the Protestant and Catholic communities across Ireland. From a British point of view, Ireland's neutrality during World War II and then the beginning of the Troubles[3] made things more difficult. Specific events like the murder of Earl Louis Mountbatten[4] by the Irish Republican Army (IRA) and the IRA attempt to blow up the British Cabinet in the Grand Hotel in Brighton in 1984 turned the mood in Britain to fully-fledged rage.

It appeared to the British that the Irish had a chip on their collective shoulder. And of course there were good reasons for the chip, from the British establishment's handling of the Great Famine[5] to opposition to

Home Rule for Ireland (until the bill was enacted in 1914), surrender to the 'Orange card'[6] in the North and ability to turn a blind eye to the way the Catholics in the North were treated by the majority community. Monumental injustices like the imprisonment of the Guilford Four[7] and the Birmingham Six,[8] and suspicions of collusion between Northern Ireland's security forces and loyalist paramilitaries turned the chip into a huge block. For most of the twentieth century, each side was given good cause to hate the other.

Even when I joined the Foreign Office in 1979, relations between Irish and British diplomats were marked by deep suspicions. Irish colleagues thought the British were patronising and perfidious. The British diplomats called the Irish diplomats 'green' and thought they were part of a pan-nationalist front with the nationalist parties of Northern Ireland, the Social Democratic Labour Party (SDLP) and Sinn Féin, and wanted to force their nationalist agenda on a reluctant unionist people. Irish officials kept telling the British that it was their job to deliver the unionists to the negotiating table when the British thought they had trouble enough just keeping Northern Ireland quiet and avoiding a repeat of the loyalist Workers' Strike of 1974 that had brought the whole place to a halt. For their part, the British could not understand why the Irish would not take effective steps to cooperate on security and allow hot pursuit after terrorists across the border into the South. The negotiations on the Sunningdale Agreement,[9] the Anglo-Irish Agreement[10] and those after, although always polite, were often characterised by this mutual suspicion and recrimination.

I saw this competition firsthand in Washington from 1991 to 1994. The Irish Embassy was far more effective at cultivating Congress, playing on the heritage of many Irish-American congressmen and senators, while we in the British Embassy concentrated on the administration. The battle came to a head in January 1994 over the issue of a visa for Gerry Adams. We marshalled the Washington establishment on our side – the State Department, the Department of Justice, the Attorney General, the FBI and the CIA. All agreed with us that it would be wrong to grant Adams a visa before the IRA declared a ceasefire. We were certain we had won the debate with such a powerful coalition, but we had not reckoned on the Irish Embassy's ability to influence the Clinton administration through Senator Ted Kennedy and their network in Congress. We lost and didn't even realise we had done so until we read about it in the news. The decision led to a major breakdown in the special relationship, until Bill Clinton remedied it by inviting Prime Minister John Major for a sleepover in the White House a few months later.

And yet, by the time Taoiseach[11] Bertie Ahern addressed a joint session of the British Houses of Parliament on 15 May 2007, all that had changed. It was not just that the problem of Northern Ireland had been resolved, but that relations between Ireland and the UK had been put on a completely new footing. The ghosts of the past had been exorcised, and finally the UK and Ireland were looking to the future together rather than arguing about who had done what to whom and when. Prime Minister Tony Blair said on that occasion: 'These islands have at last escaped their history.' How had the relationship changed so completely in less than a decade and a half?

First, Ireland had changed beyond recognition. This book chronicles the remarkable birth of the Celtic Tiger, built on a favourable tax regime, a liberal economic consensus and, most importantly, massive investment in a world-class education system. What had been an unending wave of emigration of the best and the brightest became a wave of immigration, with the return of young, qualified Irish men and women and then Eastern European migrants keen to find better-paid work. The unionists in Northern Ireland did not wake up to this transformation quickly. As late as 1998, deputy leader of the Ulster Unionist Party John Taylor was still talking about the priest-ridden, backward, impoverished country to the south. But that caricature was by then hopelessly out of date. And the economic growth meant that the Irish people gained a new self-confidence.

Interwoven with this economic success in a globalised economy, Ireland found a new role in Europe which allowed it to escape its obsession with its big neighbour. It was now a partner with the UK in something much bigger than either country. Ireland was able to play a leading part in the European institutions and amplify its influence in the world without having to pass through London. Europe was able to help Ireland's growth, contributing particularly to the spectacular transformation of its infrastructure with unprecedented financial assistance. When, later, we in the UK Government were negotiating the 2006 budget deal with Poland and the Baltic Republics, we pointed out to them the experience of Ireland in maximising its benefit from membership of the European Union (EU). The process of joining the EU had similarly helped to remove any enmity between Spain and Portugal, and finally allowed the integration of their economies that had previously been prevented by the corporatism of their respective leaders, Franco and Salazar.

Second, the UK had changed too. Its economy was humbled in the 1970s and 1980s. It looked on enviously at the rate of growth in Ireland. A country previously associated only with Kerrygold butter was now seen as the seat of hi-tech and software industry. The UK could no longer afford to be so patronising about its small neighbour. Under Tony Blair the UK began, finally, to apologise for the Great Famine, for the Guildford Four and for the events of Bloody Sunday.[11]

Third, huge steps had been taken towards resolving the issue of Northern Ireland. Northern Ireland had been a bone of contention between the two Governments from the creation of the civil rights movement there in the 1960s. Irish Minister for Finance Charlie Haughey's association with gunrunning (Haughey later became taoiseach) and Taoiseach Jack Lynch's statement that Ireland could not 'stand by'[12] were seen by the British as direct threats. The British Embassy in Dublin was burned down; the British Ambassador to Dublin was killed on his way to work. But in the end it was the ability of the British and Irish Governments to work together as a team with a common strategic objective that brought the Troubles to an end.

According to the official record, when Tony Blair and Bertie Ahern first met each other in early summer 1997, Tony said that Bertie 'came to the issues with no ideological or historical baggage. He regarded the present situation as irrational and stupid and he simply wanted to stop people killing each other.' In response, Bertie Ahern said that Tony 'too came to Northern Ireland with no historical baggage.' They were from a new generation of political leaders who did not carry with them the burden of history and were able to work together pragmatically and seamlessly for over a decade in power. They were very different men. Bertie did not have the soaring rhetoric of Tony or his messianic zeal, which was crucial in driving the peace process forward, but he had the calm good sense of a seasoned negotiator – a skill honed on the social partners in Ireland and in Europe – without which we would not have been able to close the deal. Bertie Ahern also had the cardinal virtue of politics – bravery. Sometimes he had to take a political risk by overruling the orthodoxy of Irish officialdom to get to an agreement, and when he had to do so he did not hesitate.

Tony Blair and Bertie Ahern managed not just to achieve the breakthrough of the Good Friday Agreement[13] through their teamwork, but to stick together in the nine years of hard grind that followed, before we got devolved government established on a lasting basis in Northern Ireland. Over the ten years from 1997 to 2007, we in the British and Irish Governments had our disagreements, particularly over suspension in 2000,[14] but we always managed to contain them and never allowed a gap to appear that could be exploited by the parties. The Irish Government took on the difficult task of reaching out privately to the loyalists and was patient in dealing with the leader of the Democratic Unionist Party Ian Paisley, who refused even to shake the Taoiseach's hand until the St Andrews Agreement[15] at the end of 2006. When eventually we faced the extraordinary sight of Ian Paisley and Sinn Féin's Martin McGuinness taking the oath together to serve as first and deputy first minister of Northern Ireland in May 2007, the partnership between the UK and Ireland was cemented by the success.

It was not just the outcome of negotiations but the process itself that helped put relations between the two countries on a new footing and build trust. The often twice-weekly meetings or video conferences between the two sides established a partnership that spilled over into other areas, such as Europe. In Downing Street we got to know our remarkably talented Irish colleagues better than colleagues from any other European country and that paid off in working together at a series of difficult European Councils. The UK and Ireland became close allies, and we often turned to the Irish Government first when we faced a new challenge.

None of this is to say that relations between Ireland and the UK will always be harmonious in the future. We will continue to disagree about Common Agricultural Policy (CAP) reform and about the speed of integration in Europe, on nuclear power stations and on certain aspects of foreign policy. There are new issues that could provoke disputes between us from the tax flight of major British companies to Ireland to the development of European defence. And there is the danger that, now the intensity of working together on Northern Ireland is passed and there is a new generation of leaders in charge in both countries, we could find ourselves drifting apart with less to say to each other.

But my personal hope and belief is that we will instead come together in the face of new common challenges like the issues of immigration, economic reform in the EU, and the global financial crisis that is challenging Ireland's economy and the strength of the City of London. I hope and believe that the UK and Ireland have finally established a relationship of equals and a new habit of talking to each other that will permanently replace the barbed relationship of the past.

CHAPTER 4

From Phoenix to Tiger: French Views of Ireland

Christophe Gillissen

A moving ceremony was held in Dublin Castle on 19 June 1969. The main staircase was adorned with replicas of the flags of the Irish brigades that had fought in the French Army in 1745 at Fontenoy, in order to welcome General de Gaulle, who had just spent several weeks in Ireland following his resignation from the French presidency. Government ministers, leaders of the main political parties and senior officials attended a lunch organised in his honour. Taoiseach Jack Lynch made a speech in which he detailed Ireland's historical debt to France. He mentioned his people's Gallic ancestors who had crossed the seas, bringing the language and the culture that were the basis of the Irish nation; he also evoked the leader of the Irish 1798 Rebellion, Wolfe Tone, who had found both inspiration and support in France for his dream of an independent Irish republic. De Gaulle's response stressed France's debt to Ireland, in particular the important contribution of the many Irish saints, scholars and soldiers who had lived in France. In his conclusion, he outlined the coming together of two ancient friends:

> There has been, it seems, for some generations past a kind of screen between Ireland and France, but it appears that that time has passed and that it is now possible for both of us to get through it, to find one another and to be together again in spirit and action. The impression I have gained in my brief stay amongst you and the wish I would like to express [...] before I leave your country is that henceforth Ireland and France may get to know each other better every day, that they may meet and remain together in thought and action.[1]

Indeed, during most of the twentieth century, relations between France and Ireland were much more distant than one would have expected given their close historical links. They had been on the same side in most European conflicts and divisions and had assisted each other in times of difficulty until the late nineteenth century, but from the 1880s onwards their bonds gradually loosened, both for domestic and international reasons. On the domestic front, the Third Republic was deeply anticlerical, sometimes anti-Catholic, and its perception of Irish nationalists was distorted by its hostility towards French Catholic nationalists.[2] The main international reason for the change in French policy – the 'screen' mentioned by de Gaulle – was the Franco-British Alliance. As late as the Boer War, the French Army had been preparing plans for an invasion of Ireland in order to destabilise the UK, but these were hastily abandoned with the signing of the *Entente Cordiale* in 1904, a series of agreements signed between Great Britain and France. It created a divide between France and Ireland, as Paris could not afford to vex its new ally over the increasingly sensitive Irish Question.[3]

France and Irish Nationalism

In 1916, the French and the British were fighting a desperate war against Germany. French reactions to the Easter Rising[4] were therefore extremely negative: with the exception of the socialist *L'Humanité*, the French press unanimously condemned the rising as a *coup de force* perpetrated by a small group of German-backed radicals against the wishes of the majority of the population.[5] The overriding concern of the French Government was to prevent any crisis that would hinder the war effort of its British ally and it organised a campaign in Ireland to discredit Sinn Féin, but with very limited success. The French High Command, which was anxious to obtain a further 200,000–300,000 Irish soldiers to relieve its exhausted troops, pleaded for a rapid resolution of the Irish Question. French authorities participated in an attempt to boost recruitment in Ireland through the intervention of the Primate of France Mgr Amette, who approached Cardinal Logue, a prominent opponent of conscription, in order to persuade him to encourage Irishmen to join the French Army.[6] Alfred Blanche, who was appointed French minister in Dublin in 1917, was more aware of the situation on the ground, but he found it hard to convince his authorities in Paris to take any risk in relation to Great Britain. When he stated in April 1918 that France did not approve of British policy in Ireland, he was disowned by his Government.[7]

Despite the works of some dedicated writers like Yann Goblet, a French academic who worked closely with Irish diplomats in Paris, French public opinion became indifferent to Ireland after World War I. Between November 1918 and June 1919, the French press only devoted two articles to Ireland. This changed with the Versailles Peace Conference held in Paris, where Irish authorities tried to mobilise international opinion for their cause. French journalists were sent to Ireland to investigate the situation and twelve books on the Irish Question were published between 1919 and 1921, most of them supportive of nationalist positions. In Paris, one of the main tasks of Sinn Féin's representative George Gavan Duffy was to counter the negative impression left by the 1916 Rising. He published a selection of French-language press articles on Ireland, one of them calling for a renewal of the old Franco-Irish alliance:

> In the middle of the last century, and until the fall of the second empire, the French felt a platonic but endless pity for the misfortunes of those two victims, Poland and Ireland. We had memories of friendship, of brotherhood, of common ordeals with each of them, memories that stretched over several centuries. Our poets celebrated them in verse; our politicians addressed them in lyrical or revolutionary prose. And then, silence! Ireland disappeared. Because of the English alliance, no more Ireland! [...] The French must reflect on the value of this passionate people's friendship. [...] What about becoming once again the friends of the oppressed?[8]

Yet this point of view held little sway in official circles: the right-wing National Bloc Government, elected in 1919 with an overwhelming majority in parliament, was fiercely anti-German and thus opposed to Sinn Féin.[9] It declined six times between September 1919 and March 1921 to recognise the Irish Republic, and Gavan Duffy was expelled from Paris in 1920 because of his propaganda activities. The French Government refused a request to organise the Congress of the Irish Race in Paris in September 1921 but, after consulting the British Foreign Office, it agreed on condition that Dáil Éireann ratify the Anglo-Irish Treaty.

There was no notable change in Franco-Irish relations in the following years, though they improved enough to establish full diplomatic relations in October 1929.[10] Yet contacts remained limited as both countries dealt with their own priorities. In 1930 the newly appointed French Minister to Ireland Charles Alphand, while recognising the 'intellectual sympathy' that existed between both countries, noted that 'for the time being at least, France has little to ask Ireland politically speaking, and Ireland has little to expect from us.' Thus, during the 1930s, Ireland was, from the French point of view, like one of those 'old friends whom one constantly promises to write to or to visit, but who must satisfy themselves with vague desires of the sort and fond memories'.[11]

Brittany

There was one region in France where interest in Ireland was much less vague, however, and where Irish history held ominous relevance for the present: Brittany. This can be explained by several similarities between the two Celtic nations of Ireland and France that were referred to in an article published in the *Télégramme* on 21 August 1919:

> Why try to conceal it? We French have much sympathy for Ireland. She's the sister of our Brittany. Beyond the fogs of the Atlantic Ocean, a few miles from our coasts, we feel that we have brothers in this green island, people of the same breed. Their lofty, generous souls have always stirred in unison with the national soul of France. History and tradition have sealed a deep friendship between them and us.

Several Breton nationalists were inspired by the Irish experience and they had strong sympathy for Sinn Féin. Louis Napoléon Le Roux, who founded the Parti Nationaliste Breton (PNB) in 1911, spent some time in Ireland during World War I, where he befriended nationalist leaders. He wrote the first biography of 1916 rebel Patrick Pearse and obtained Irish citizenship. In the 1930s, the PNB published a pamphlet on Irish history, seeing it as a model for their own struggle for independence and emphasising the practical lessons that could be drawn.[12] In 1932 a paramilitary organisation was created on the model of the early IRA and in 1936 it commemorated the 1916 Rising with several bombings. In 1939, a gunrunning operation – Operation Casement – was organised with German support.[13]

During World War II, some Breton separatists sought to promote the Breton language and culture, while others took action to achieve independence. There were cases of collaboration with the Germans. At the end of the war, about 30 Bretons fled to Ireland, which had no extradition agreement with France. Taoiseach Eamon de Valera, who had met some of them at the 1925 Congress of the Gaelic League, granted them asylum.[14] This contributed to negative perceptions of Irish neutrality in France, where the provisional government established in 1944 initially refused to recognise the Irish Taoiseach on account of his accreditation of the Vichy regime.[15] It took General de Gaulle's personal intervention to end the diplomatic crisis.[16]

European Partners

In the same way, de Gaulle's visit to Ireland in 1969 helped to improve Franco-Irish relations prior to Ireland's accession to the European Economic Community (EEC) in 1973, and since then both countries have often worked together within the organisation.[17] This *entente* is based on several elements: both countries have common interests, in particular concerning the Common Agricultural Policy (CAP). In 1984 they adopted a common position during the difficult reform of milk quotas.[18] The personal diplomacy of François Mitterrand (president of France 1981–1995) and Garret FitzGerald (taoiseach of Ireland 1981–1982 and 1982–1987), who held each other in high esteem, also contributed to the Franco-Irish *rapprochement*. In 1988, Mitterrand made the first official visit to Ireland by a French president. After his meeting with President Mary Robinson in 1992, an Irish cultural year, *L'imaginaire irlandais*, was held in 1996, the first event of its kind in France.

This reflected strong French interest in Ireland, evidenced by the development of Irish studies in French universities.[19] This was partly due to the conflict in Northern Ireland, with events like the 1981 hunger strikes arousing much sympathy for the nationalist cause: some 20 streets were named after Bobby Sands in French towns like Nantes, Nîmes, Chambéry, St Etienne, Brest and Amiens, though the boulevard Bobby Sands in Le Mans was renamed after the 1987 Enniskillen bombing.

Yet, by the late 1990s, Ireland's capital of sympathy among its European partners was in decline.[20] The French Finance Minister expressed his annoyance at the fact that Ireland was using European Union (EU) funds to finance corporate tax cuts.[21] The reprimand of the European Commission (EC) against Ireland's generous 2001 budget and the results of the first referendum on the Nice Treaty[22] in June 2001 also led to critical comments; the French Prime Minister blamed Ireland for refusing the applicant countries the benefits it had itself enjoyed and which had helped it achieve economic prosperity.[23] Ireland seemed to be moving from its close links with the European continent towards the Anglo-American sphere of influence.[24]

The Celtic Tiger

France and Ireland may indeed be considered to some extent as representative of two different models of capitalism, the European social market one and the American free market one. This was the gist of Tánaiste Mary Harney's remark in 2000, when she claimed that Ireland was 'spiritually a lot closer to Boston than to Berlin', emphasising the attractiveness of her country's political and social environment from the point of view of corporate America: 'When Americans come here they find a country that believes in the incentive power of low taxation. They find a country that believes in economic liberalisation. They find a country that believes in essential regulation but not over-regulation.'[25]

Between the mid-1990s and the financial crisis of 2007–8, Ireland's exceptional economic boom was often seen as a vindication of neo-liberal politics, whereas the difficulties experienced by France were attributed to its excessive regulation, high wage costs and lack of fiscal incentives. In 2001, Ireland had one of the lowest rates of tax pressure among the fifteen EU members, while France was in tenth position. The Irish corporation tax rate, at 12.5 per cent, was the lowest in the EU prior to the 2004 enlargement, and thus very attractive for foreign companies wishing to set up in Europe in order to have access to the single market. With over a third of US investments in Europe going to Ireland, the success of this rate was regularly mentioned in the French press, which often compared it favourably to the 34.3 per cent rate in France, but sometimes criticised it as a form of fiscal dumping.[26] One news magazine reported that, in 1998, an American company had been thinking of setting up in France, its second largest foreign market, but that in the end it opted for Ballinasloe in County Galway, where wage costs, social contributions and building costs were lower. France was competitive only in relation to transport costs.[27]

The French press also noted the low levels of income tax in Ireland, the small number of civil servants, 'the reduction of public spending, the flexibility of the labour market, as well as the privatisations and deregulation that followed the neo-liberal watershed of 1987'.[28] Some observers, after comparing the growth and unemployment rates of both countries, advocated a more neo-liberal approach in France, in order to reduce the persistently high unemployment that has had a corrosive effect on its social fabric.[29] The neo-liberal reforms of Reagan in the US and Thatcher in the UK, and the collapse of state-managed economies in Eastern Europe had already led to similar demands, but Michel Albert, a French economist, emphasised the advantages of the Rhineland or continental model.[30] Its long-term approach in the field of investments, the search for social agreements, the predominance of companies over shareholders and its active state were compared favourably to the short-termism of the Anglo-Saxon model, which is dominated by finance and individual profits, and where the limited role of the state encourages individual initiatives but also the development of inequality.

In addition, the trade-off between economic growth and equality is not as simple as that, as the examples of Sweden and Denmark suggest. This led to more detailed analyses of economic models and, for instance, Robert Boyer, another French economist, identified four major European models.[31] He accepted the distinction between the Rhineland and free market systems, but considered that the social democratic economies of Sweden and Austria constitute a distinct model, just like the statist capitalist systems of France and Italy. From his point of view, each country should try to develop solutions in conformity with its own traditions, rather than accept the dominant ideology of globalisation. This is a point that has also been made by the economist Joseph Stiglitz, who has argued cogently in favour of autonomous solutions, developed by national authorities according to local conditions, instead of the 'one size fits all' policies advocated by the proponents of the Washington consensus.[32]

'Ireland: A Miracle, Not a Model'

It is debatable, furthermore, whether the Celtic Tiger could have been exported to France through the implementation of neo-liberal reforms. Many other factors contributed to the transformation of the Irish economy since the mid-1990s, such as state intervention, European integration, social partnership and demographic changes.[33] French newspapers have often emphasised the important contribution of European structural funds to the Irish economy.[34] If one adds to those funds the payments made through the CAP, Ireland received a total of €45 billion from Brussels between 1973 and 2001, a very significant amount in relation both to the size of the population and to gross domestic product (GDP) per capita before the 1990s.[35]

As to multinational companies, they have undoubtedly been attracted to Ireland by its business-friendly environment, but some elements of Ireland's attractiveness are of another order. In particular, state investments in the education system have been quite effective in forming a large skilled workforce, which has the advantage of being English-speaking. The emotional bond between Irish-American businessmen and Ireland, though difficult to quantify, is also an undeniable asset.[36]

From a demographic point of view, the diminishing number of dependants per worker increased purchasing power. At the same time, the demand for labour was partly met by the high numbers of young people and women entering the labour market and of emigrants returning to their home country – an elastic labour force that was an essential ingredient of the Celtic Tiger but that cannot be easily transposed either.[37]

Another difference between the two countries was highlighted by Professor Paul Brennan of the University of the Sorbonne Nouvelle, who noted that 'in Ireland, with its rural tradition, there was no real working class as there was in France and Britain, which explains the absence of a communist party and of powerful trade unions defending wage claims.'[38] The social partnership and the ensuing wage restraint that were fundamental to the Irish economic recovery would indeed be much more difficult to achieve in France.

Social Protection and Inequality

In the same way, the low level of Irish public spending on health would certainly face protest in France where the notion of quality public services is highly valued, both in terms of social protection and of redistribution of wealth. Despite recent fiscal reforms, the French tax system remains more progressive than the Irish one, and social transfers play a more effective role in the reduction of poverty than in Ireland. Both countries have broadly similar rates of people at risk of poverty before pensions and social transfers: 44 per cent in France and 39 per cent in Ireland, the EU average being 41 per cent. But their respective rates *after* pensions and social transfers – 14 per cent and 21 per cent – show the impact of state intervention in France.

French observers have underlined the 'dark side' of the Celtic Tiger, such as a deficient infrastructure, high levels of inequality and of relative poverty.[39] The fact that Ireland had one of the highest growth rates in 2005 but also one of the highest rates of poverty in the EU was noted with some surprise.[40] Even though this can be partly explained by the poverty of specific groups like farmers and pensioners, there was the perception that the Irish State had not played the role of reducer of inequalities expected of its French counterpart.[41]

The 1999 International Social Survey Programme showed that there is no correlation between actual levels of income inequality and perceived levels. France, for instance, was characterised by a fairly low level of inequality, yet a high proportion of respondents still considered that it was too high.[42] Such expectations contribute to shape government policy, notably in relation to social protection.

In 2005, André Sapir identified four main social models in Europe according to two criteria (see Table 4.1): the equity of their society (levels of inequality) and their efficiency (levels of unemployment).[43] He considered the two efficient models to be adapted to globalisation: the

Table 4.1: The Four European Social Models

	High Equity	Low Equity
High Efficiency	Nordic group: Denmark, Finland, Sweden and the Netherlands.	Anglo-Saxon group: Ireland, and the United Kingdom.
Low Efficiency	Continental group: France, Belgium, Germany, Austria and Luxembourg.	Mediterranean group: Italy, Portugal, Greece and Spain.

Source: André Sapir, 'Globalisation and the Reform of European Social Models', Bruegel Policy Brief, vol. 1, November 2005, p. 5, available at:<http://www.bruegel.org>.

Anglo-Saxon group, composed of the UK and Ireland, and the Nordic group, which both managed to create high numbers of jobs. But the first group ranks low in terms of equity, while within the second group are the most egalitarian societies in the world. As to the inefficient models – the Mediterranean and the Continental one – they were deemed unsustainable in a globalised economy because of their persistently high unemployment. But whereas Mediterranean countries like Italy also have high levels of inequality, Continental countries like France manage to maintain a fairly high degree of equity.

Given France's cultural attachment to equality, the model that seems most compatible with its tradition is the Nordic one, not the Anglo-Saxon one.[44] This is consistent with the ambitions both of the Lisbon Strategy, launched in 2000, which aims to promote economic growth and social cohesion in Europe, and of the EU in general, which aims to preserve political control over globalisation.[45]

French and Irish Perceptions of Globalisation

From the late 1980s until recently, it seemed that Ireland had successfully seized the opportunities created by globalisation on the whole, while France was still trying to adjust to the new context. This was apparent in the results of a poll on the perceptions of globalisation conducted in the EU in October 2003.[46] It revealed some notable divergences between the Irish and the French. Thus, 34 per cent of French people believed that EU trade policy was too liberal – the highest proportion among the fifteen member states – compared to only 18 per cent in Ireland (EU average: 26 per cent).

The Irish came second in their support for globalisation, with 71 per cent of responses being favourable. Over two-thirds believed that the intensification of globalisation would be advantageous to them and their families, compared to only 43 per cent in France (EU average: 56 per cent).

Logically enough, 72 per cent of the Irish believed that globalisation had a positive effect on economic growth in their country – the highest rate of positive answers among the fifteen countries – while only 45 per cent of the French agreed with that statement. The divergence was most marked on the issue of employment, the Irish being the most convinced (63 per cent) of the positive effect of globalisation on job creation in their country, while the French were in last place, with only 27 per cent agreeing. The French were the most convinced that the US had excessive influence over globalisation, at 83 per cent, while the Irish, at 75 per cent, reflected the European average.

Yet, the survey also revealed some interesting similarities between French and Irish perceptions. In both countries a fairly high proportion believed that globalisation could be effectively controlled and that more regulation was in fact necessary. In the case of both France and Ireland, there was considerable trust in the EU as an agent of regulation – 70 per cent and 76 per cent respectively compared to a European average of 61 per cent – even though almost one Frenchman out of two (49 per cent) considered that the EU did not have enough influence, an opinion shared by one Irishman out of three (32 per cent). In both countries, there was strong agreement with the statement that anti-globalisation movements raised relevant issues, with France coming in first position with 88 per cent agreement and Ireland second with 84 per cent. In other words, it would seem that both peoples, despite their divergent experiences of globalisation, do agree on the need to establish more effective forms of international economic regulation. Given the current economic recession, that agreement becomes all the more relevant.

An Anglo-American State or a European Republic?

Even though Ireland was not among the countries surveyed in 1999, one may consider that it has a cultural bias towards equality, given the deep influence of Catholicism and of Irish nationalism, both of which are conducive to egalitarianism.[47] This tendency is reinforced by the anthropological nature of Irish society, according to Emmanuel Todd, a French demographer and historian who has studied the long-term influences of traditional family structures on contemporary societies. He has concluded that the nuclear or stem-family structure – prevalent in Germany, Japan, Sweden and Ireland – tends to contain the rise of inequalities generated by globalisation, contrary to the 'absolute nuclear family' typical of English and American societies.[48]

This may seem difficult to reconcile with the increase of inequality observed in Ireland in recent years, yet several points should be noted. First of all, globalisation has generated greater inequality in many countries, notably in the UK and the US. Ireland's geographical position and its close relations with those countries subject it to strong Anglo-American influences that compete with its native cultural substratum. One must also take into account the gravity of the economic situation in 1987: the trade unions did make significant concessions in terms of wage restraint, but there was very little choice at the time.

In addition, the growth of inequality in Ireland must be qualified. Various Organisation for Economic Co-operation and Development (OECD) studies on income distribution tend to show that Ireland's evolution in recent years has been closer to that of France than that of the UK. One study concludes that Ireland now belongs to an intermediate group of European countries – along with France, Germany and Belgium – and not to the most unequal group of countries, which includes the UK and Portugal.[49] Another study emphasises that Ireland is one of the few countries – with France, Spain and Greece – where inequality has actually diminished in the last decade.[50]

From this point of view, one may consider that the social partnership agreements did produce a valid 'alternative to the option of aggressively liberal Thatcherite economics'.[51] Irish trade unions looked to the continent for models that would enable Ireland 'to achieve social convergence with the rest of Europe', that is to say to combine economic growth and social cohesion. And in recent years they have insisted on the need to address issues of social justice and to defend the European social market model of capitalism against the effects of globalisation.

This pressure has led to an increase in the level of public spending on social protection in Ireland. Even though it remains significantly lower than the EU average, it has risen more quickly than in other member states. On a per capita basis, it rose by an average of 7.8 per cent a year between 2000 and 2004, compared to 2.1 per cent in the EU as a whole and 2.8 in France. Since 2002, the proportion of national wealth going to wages has increased faster than the proportion going to profits.[52]

The electoral setbacks of the Irish Government in 2005 and of the Progressive Democrats[53] in 2007 may be seen as a sign that the electorate is supportive of this shift. While increased inequality was initially associated with increased economic opportunities, Irish voters may have become disenchanted to some extent with the unfairness of income distribution.[54]

One may conclude from all this that there is a tension between two conceptions of Irish society, a rivalry between two different narratives of Irish identity – to use the terminology proposed by Ben Tonra: that of a European republic and that of an Anglo-American state.[55] If the latter understandably prospered during the boom of the last two decades, it may be that the former will reassert itself as hard times challenge widespread assumptions about social and economic policy.

Conclusion

The two main efforts of the Irish nation in the last century – to obtain its own sovereign state and to 'consolidate the economic foundations of [its] independence'[56] – were misunderstood in France despite the ancient links between both countries. In 1916, the German connection with the Easter Rising prevented France from supporting the Irish struggle for independence. Though the two countries did come together again within the framework of the EU, the neo-liberal dimension of the Celtic Tiger led to mixed reactions in France.

Yet, the two republics have common cultural positions on issues like equality, both within and among the states of the world, and the French and Irish peoples seem to share a desire to exert more democratic control over global capitalism. If the EU seems a natural political space in which to achieve this, there are real doubts about the direction it is taking. One could argue that, among the many different reasons the French voted against the European Constitutional Treaty in 2005[57] and the Irish against the Lisbon Treaty in 2008, one important issue at stake in both cases was the perceived threat to national labour markets.[58] Former French Prime Minister Michel Rocard thus claimed that the French 'No' was not a rejection of Europe but 'the rejection of a deregulated labour market'.[59] Similarly, David Begg, the secretary general of the Irish Congress of Trade Unions (ICTU), stated that 'the management of the labour market post enlargement in 2004 was a factor' in the rejection of the Lisbon Treaty by Irish voters.[60] In other words, many French and Irish voters pronounced themselves against a blueprint for Europe which they perceived as conducive to greater precariousness in the labour market and to weakened public services.

Whatever one might think of that interpretation of the treaties, support for Europe will only be forthcoming when a majority of people believe that it stands for a model of society corresponding to their wishes and values. As the economic crisis reveals the shortcomings of corporate US-driven globalisation, there is increasing necessity to propose a vision for Europe that is endorsed by its peoples. Were France and Ireland to come together to work for the establishment of a European model of development based on high social and environmental standards, they could help to shape an alternative that would both enjoy considerable international support and constitute an objective worthy of the old Franco-Irish alliance.

Chapter 5

The Portuguese Economy in the Irish Mirror, 1960–2004

Pedro Lains

Introduction

Ireland and Portugal spent much of the second half of the twentieth century in the same economic category – that of largely backward European periphery economies. However, from the late 1980s onwards they diverged, with Ireland developing into the stronger economy. This chapter assesses the relative slowing down of gross domestic product (GDP) and total factor productivity in Portugal relative to Ireland and, by extension, examines where Ireland managed to get it right. Although lately Ireland is going through a much worse recession than Portugal, it may be argued that her economy is better positioned to recover more quickly, due to the extent of its structural transformations since the late 1980s. During the period 1960–73, Portugal caught up at an unprecedented speed to the levels of income per capita of the more developed European countries. Yet, the catch-up lost momentum since the 1973 oil crisis and there have been periods of divergence from the European average since then. Rapid growth in the years to 1973 was accompanied by structural change, marked by the decline of agriculture in GDP and total employment and the increase in the shares of the industrial and service sectors. Within manufacturing and services, there was also considerable structural change. Such change was common to all European economies but it was felt more intensely in Portugal, as well as in the rest of the poor periphery, simply because of lower levels of industrialisation there.

Ireland, initially also a poorer country on the European periphery, tells a different story. In fact, the Irish economy *diverged* during the period from

1960–73 and caught up thereafter. Ireland is also different because of her earlier commitment to higher levels of economic and monetary integration within the EU, having joined the Common Market in 1973, the Economic and the Monetary Union (EMU) in 1979, and, with Portugal, the single European market in 1992 and the Euro in 1999.[1] In this respect, the study of Ireland may help to identify alternative paths of growth for the periphery during recent years.[2] Was Irish growth after 1973 and particularly in the 1990s accompanied by significant changes in the structure of her economy? Or was it due to increases in productivity in existing or more traditional sectors? We shall see in this chapter that the answers to such questions have relevant policy implications, especially relating to the very different labour market regulations in the two countries.[3]

In this context, the impact on national economic structures of changes in international trade and capital flows can be either positive or negative.[4] The deepening of European integration during the 1990s led to an increase in international trade and capital flows, which led to a higher level of geographical specialisation and higher productivity growth in the core European countries and Ireland.[5] Recent Irish growth has been associated with the growth of those sectors which use or produce goods with a high content of information and communication technologies (ICT) and with the role of foreign direct investment (FDI) and exports, as well as special tax regimes.[6] Why didn't Portugal benefit from the increase in economic and monetary integration during the 1990s? This chapter shows that labour productivity slowdown in Portugal was determined by adverse structural change – or a 'structural cost' – that is, by the increase of employment shares in sectors with low productivity or low productivity growth, contrary to what happened in Ireland.[7]

The role of structural change in explaining economic performance is neglected by growth models based on aggregate production functions.[8] These models are thus less useful for countries at earlier stages of development, where it is expected that structural change has an important role.[9] Moreover, the impact of structural change on growth can be of greater relevance if factor returns[10] across sectors are not in steady-state[11] growth equilibrium due, for example, to institutional bottlenecks or barriers to trade. Again, this is presumably more significant for less developed economies.

The assessment of the role of structural change has led to fruitful explanations of long-term international differences in factor productivity growth.[12] For example, the overtaking of the UK economy by that of Germany since the 1890s and by the US after World War II was, to a large extent, due to productivity gains obtained from shifting resources out of agriculture, as well as due to sectoral productivity growth in the service sector. It has also been argued that differences in sectoral productivity growth has been one of the most important factors explaining economic catching-up within the Organisation for Economic Co-operation and Development (OECD) economies and during the period 1950–1985, together with the spillover of technological progress across borders and changes in preferences and thus in the structure of demand.[13]

Differences in economic performance and pace of structural change relate to other factors such as technological progress, changes in corporate organisation, investment in physical capital, and the quality of the country's institutional setting. For example, Portugal faced a competitiveness problem in the international markets as real wages increased faster than labour productivity in the 1990s, due in part to rigid labour markets.[14] The measurement of the impact of such factors on the performance of labour productivity provides a complementary analysis to the one discussed in this chapter.[15]

Trends in Economic Growth

Decennial growth rates for Portugal's GDP per capita since 1960, as well as for the other three countries in the cohesion group,[16] namely Spain, Greece and Ireland, and for the EU (EU-14) and the US are shown in Table 5.1. One relevant conclusion to be drawn from that data is that there is no common pattern for growth cycles across the periphery countries. In fact, Portugal and the two other southern European countries had very high growth rates of income per capita in the period 1960–73, between 6.6 per cent and 7 per

Table 5.1: Growth of Real GDP per Capita in the Cohesion Countries, Europe and the USA, 1960–2004 (annual growth rates, %)

	1960–1973	1973–1980	1980–1990	1990–2004
Portugal	6.64	2.24	3.13	1.83
Greece	6.75	2.58	1.23	2.43
Ireland	3.70	3.19	3.07	5.83
Spain	6.96	2.62	2.74	2.58
EU-14*	4.18	2.19	2.02	2.03
USA	2.88	1.95	2.09	1.96

* EU-14 – Luxembourg excluded.
Source: Computed from Groningen Growth and Development Centre, Total Economy Database, March 2006, available at: <http://www.ggdc.net>.

cent per year, whereas Irish growth during the same period was considerably slower, at 3.7 per cent, and below the average of the EU-14 countries. From 1973 to 1980, economic growth in all four peripheral countries slowed down, although in Ireland the fall was relatively smaller. During the decade 1980–90, economic growth in Portugal gained some speed, whereas in Spain and Ireland growth rates remained at similar levels. Greek economic growth slowed down considerably in the 1990s to 1.2 per cent. During the period between 1990 and 2004, Portuguese growth slowed down to 1.8 per cent per year, which is below the rate of growth of the EU-14 group. At the same time, Irish growth accelerated to 5.8 per cent per year. In terms of relative income per capita levels, Ireland started from a higher income position in 1960, compared to the average of the EU-14 members, and it was relatively unchanged until 1980, increasing rapidly after 1990. The Spanish relative position increased rapidly between 1960 and 1973 and again after 1980. Portugal and Greece were the two poorest of this group. From 1960, they leaped forward in the decade to 1973, but their relative positions changed little afterwards.

The evolution of GDP per capita levels as a percentage of the average for the EU-14 is shown in Figure 5.1.[17]

Table 5.2 shows the decomposition of output growth in Portugal and Ireland in terms of growth of labour productivity and labour participation rates since 1979. The labour participation rate evolved differently in the two countries, as before 1986 it declined in Ireland whereas in Portugal it increased at 1.04 per cent per year. After 1986, the labour participation rate increased rapidly in Ireland and stalled in Portugal. Changes in Irish employment were due to the decline in emigration and a net flow of immigrants which led to an increase in labour supply and average labour participation rates.[18] Labour productivity growth in Ireland increased much faster, particularly in the period 1994–2002 (see Table 5.2).

Two Paths into the Economic and Monetary Union

Today, Portugal and Ireland are virtually fully open economies in the context of the European Union (EU), with few barriers to international trade and capital flows, participation in the common currency, and decreasing levels of regulation and state intervention. The Irish economy is probably more deregulated than the Portuguese, particularly where the labour market is concerned. Ireland is also more open to the extent that she is presently a large receiver of capital imports, including FDI.

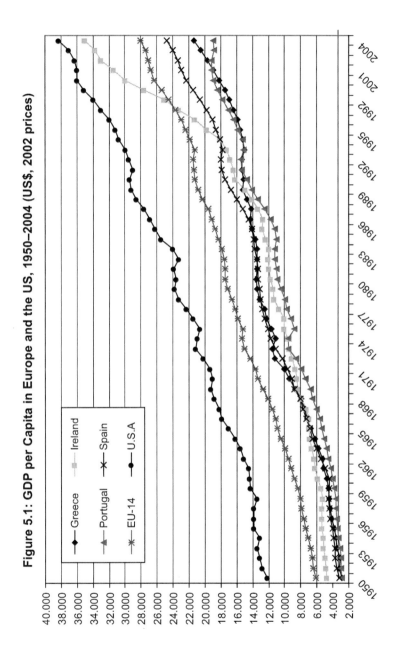

Figure 5.1: GDP per Capita in Europe and the US, 1950–2004 (US$, 2002 prices)

Table 5.2: GDP, Labour Productivity and Participation, 1979–2002
(annual growth rates, %)

	Portugal			Ireland		
	1979–1986	1986–1994	1994–2002	1979–1986	1986–1994	1994–2002
1. GDP per capita	1.77	3.41	2.66	1.68	4.48	7.50
2. L productivity	0.73	3.61	2.46	3.20	3.60	5.80
3. L participation (2-1)	1.04	0.20	0.20	-1.52	0.88	1.70

Note: GDP/Pop = GDP/L x L/Pop
Sources: Table 5.1 and computed from Groningen Growth and Development Centre, Total Economy Database and 60-Industry Database, March 2006, available at: <http://www.ggdc.net>.

In the 1950s and early 1960s, the two countries were in a different situation, with high barriers to trade and capital imports, and high levels of state intervention and market regulation. The move away from autarky and state interventionism started at about the same time in both countries, namely in the early 1960s. The first steps to opening up borders were almost contemporaneous, but the two countries followed different institutional arrangements because of their historical, political and geographical idiosyncrasies. At its earlier stage, the gradual reduction of trade barriers was accompanied in both Ireland and Portugal by the increase of state intervention in the economy.[19]

Ireland's most important step towards trade liberalisation was the signing, in 1965, of the free trade agreement with the UK, her main trading partner.[20] The treaty was signed when the Industrial Development Agency (IDA) was already in place in Ireland, which provided grants to promote domestic and foreign investment. This was the start of an 'industrialisation-by-invitation strategy'.[21] During the 1960s, the Irish Government's role in terms of spending and taxes as a percentage of GDP increased significantly, although this was largely the consequence of the increase in transfer payments, including social security, welfare, health and education. The share of the state in total investment remained small, around 5 per cent of total gross capital formation[22] throughout the decade.[23]

Yet, the Irish economy changed little following the demise of autarky. In 1973, when Ireland joined the European Economic Community (EEC), its economy was still highly protected and unable to explore markets abroad. But joining the Common Market was a definitive blow to longstanding Irish protectionist policies. In fact, four years later, Ireland abolished all its tariffs with the other member states. Ireland also joined the European Monetary

System (EMS) in 1979. The immediate implications of openness were considerable. Because of tariff removals, according to one account, 44 per cent of firms closed, including 88 per cent of those in the textile sector and 50 per cent in chemicals and metal products. In 1986, employment in 'traditional' sectors fell 76 per cent from its 1980 level (72.6 per cent in 1992).[24] Since the early 1990s, capital imports also increased substantially and, together with the existence of comparative advantages in industries with high levels of factor productivity and expanding international demand, accounted for the rapid rise of the Irish manufacturing sector. The data on Irish FDI is in fact impressive. In 1973, foreign firms, of which 7.3 per cent were from the US and 14.6 per cent were from the UK, employed 32.3 per cent of the total labour force. In 1994, foreign firms, of which 23.2 per cent were from the US and just 5.8 per cent were from the UK, employed 44 per cent of the labour force. Ireland's European integration led to the growth of her Atlantic links. But such changes in the structure of firm ownership occurred before the big spurt in Irish growth that essentially took place after 1994.[25]

Portugal joined the free trade club through its accession to the European Free Trade Association (EFTA) in 1959. But, again, the process of opening up was slow and too intertwined with state intervention. EFTA led to a substantial change in the structure of Portuguese exports, which followed the slow change that had been occurring in the manufacturing sector. But, during these early stages, industrial change was led by a 'traditional' sector, namely textiles. Moreover, the Portuguese Government received special treatment from its more industrialised EFTA partners (the UK, Denmark, Norway, Sweden, Switzerland and Austria) and could therefore continue to protect its industrial sector. Economic policy – under French-type six-year government 'plans' – was marked by strong state intervention through public investment in infrastructure, namely communications and energy, as well as in industrial branches considered by the Government as essential, namely chemicals, cement, and metallurgy and metal work.

In 1972, in preparation for the first enlargement of the EEC, Portugal signed a trade agreement with the EEC which led to a substantial reduction in her trade barriers.[26] After the first oil shock of 1973 and the political revolution that followed during 1974–75, the trend towards increasing openness was reversed. A decade of political instability, high inflation, increasing unemployment, distressed public finances and external imbalances ensued. Moreover, the expansion of the foreign sector, which had jumped from 20 per cent to 35 per cent of GDP during the decade that followed the EFTA accession, stalled and the economy became increasingly protected by tariffs and other forms of state intervention. After a long process of negotiation, Portugal joined the European Community (EC) in 1986, and in 1992 signed the Maastricht Treaty. Portugal joined the European single currency in 1999. Portugal was also a large recipient of EU cohesion funds, which contributed considerably to total investment in social overhead capital[27] and education.

When Portugal joined the EEC in 1986, its manufacturing sector was already markedly different from the situation in 1973, but the process of 'creative destruction'[28] was not as intensive as in Ireland.[29] In the years following accession, the Portuguese economy achieved high rates of growth due to the expansion of exports, as well as the effect of investment in infrastructure which, like Ireland, was partially financed by EU structural funds. At the same time, the economy underwent a structural transformation with a sharp decline in employment in the primary sector, once again made possible by European sources of finance through the Common Agriculture Policy (CAP). In these early years investment in education and thus in human capital increased more rapidly than before and, for the first time, human capital made a higher contribution than physical capital in the aggregate production function. Unlike in Ireland in the 1990s, the resumption of growth was not led by the manufacturing sector, as the service sector also expanded rapidly.[30]

In 1992, Portugal entered the Exchange Rate Mechanism (ERM) in preparation for joining the Euro. Joining the ERM led to a sharp drop in interest rates and expectations of faster growth, which ultimately led to a decline in private savings and an increase in investment. Yet, productivity and export growth remained slow and Portugal entered a period of large current account deficits from the late 1990s onwards. Competitiveness in the export markets was further aggravated because low unemployment levels led to the rapid rise of nominal wages and unit labour costs.

The Impact of Structural Change, 1979–2002

Labour productivity growth can be related to changes in the structure of labour employment and domestic output. We now turn to the quantification of the impact of changes in the structure of labour employment in the context of total labour productivity in Portugal and Ireland. In the context of what Ireland did right, the question we need to address here is whether the changes that occurred in the two countries were conducive to higher levels of aggregate labour productivity or not. In other words, we will be looking for the existence of a 'structural bonus', that is, gains in productivity obtained by shifts of resources from industries with lower labour productivity levels or with lower rates of growth of productivity to industries where productivity levels and growth rates are higher. This is a crucial step for the identification of the sources of labour productivity growth differentials, which will be discussed in the next section.

To estimate the contribution of structural change to productivity growth, we use a shift-share analysis[31] that breaks down the growth of aggregate productivity into the following components: intra-industry effect, static effect and dynamic effect (we present the results in Table 5.3). The intra-industry effect refers to changes of productivity within each sector. The static component refers to circumstances in which resources shift towards sectors with productivity *levels* above the average. The dynamic component refers to circumstances in which resources shift to sectors with productivity *growth rates* above the average. This is known as the Verdoorn effect or the 'structural bonus', which associates increases in labour productivity and output through the effects of increasing specialisation.[32]

Table 5.3: Shift-Share Analysis of Labour Productivity Growth, 1979–2002 (%)

	Portugal			Ireland		
	1979–1986	1986–1994	1994–2002	1979–1986	1986–1994	1994–2002
Intra-industry effect	65.2	65.1	139.3	71.2	98.5	71.1
Static effect	36.3	88.4	-0.3	37.2	7.8	2.0
Dynamic effect	-1.6	-53.5	-39.1	-8.5	-6.3	26.9

Sources: See text. Computed from Groningen Growth and Development Centre, 60-Industry Database, March 2006, available at: <http://www.ggdc.net>.

By far, the major factor behind labour productivity growth in Ireland since 1979 is the effect of productivity changes within each industry. In the period 1979–86, the intra-industry effect accounted for 71.2 per cent of that change. It increased to 98.5 per cent in 1986–94 and then declined to 71.1 per cent in 1994–2002. The static effect, which measures the change in the share of industries with above-average labour productivity *levels*, accounted for 37.2 per cent of the change in 1979–86, and that effect declined significantly in the two subsequent periods. Instead, the dynamic effect, that is, the growth of the share of industries with productivity *growth* above average, started as negative and increased substantially to account for 26.9 per cent of total labour productivity growth in the last period in Table 5.3, from 1994 to 2002. Portugal's performance was markedly different, as the dynamic effect was negative in 1986–94 and 1994–2002 and negatively impacted labour productivity growth, which was -53.5 per cent in the first period and -39.1 per cent in the second period. In other words, in Portugal, labour was leaving both manufacturing and service industries with above average productivity growth, in contrast to what was happening contemporarily in Ireland.

Explaining Portugal's Low Structural Bonus

In order to explain why Ireland managed to benefit from the structural bonus whereas Portugal did not, we need to look at structural change in more detail. The literature points to two different types of conclusion which have quite different implications in terms of our perception of the reasons behind the Irish catch-up of the last fifteen years. According to Cassidy, the 'Irish pick-up in growth [in the 1990s] was primarily driven by the performance of a small number of foreign dominated high-technology sectors; productivity growth in the more traditional manufacturing sector and the services sector was more modest.'[33]

Contrarily, Barros argues that 'traditional industries have been at least as important as ICT-producing industries for the convergence process within the European Union.'[34] By the same token, we need to understand what drove structural change in Portugal, namely whether there was a shift towards new sectors or not.[35]

Figure 5.2 provides a comparison of the distribution of employment in the two economies in the years 1979 and 2002. We can see that, in 1979, both Portugal and Ireland had a large share of labour employed in the primary sector, and that that share strongly declined in the years to 2002, although more quickly in the Irish case. In fact, Portugal's primary sector declined by half throughout 1979–2002, from 23 per cent to 10.8 per cent, whereas in Ireland the decline was by about two-thirds, from 18.1 per cent to 6.8 per cent. Figure 5.2 also shows a decline in the employment share of the 'Food, drink and tobacco' sector, which had similar weight in the two countries at the end of the period considered. We can also observe a decline in the share of 'Textiles, leather, footwear and clothing' in both countries, but Portugal's employment remained more concentrated in these industries than Ireland's, where the sector all but disappeared. There are thus strong similarities in the change of the structure of employment in the two economies in what can be considered traditional sectors, although the process was more intense in Ireland than in Portugal. As we move towards the right-

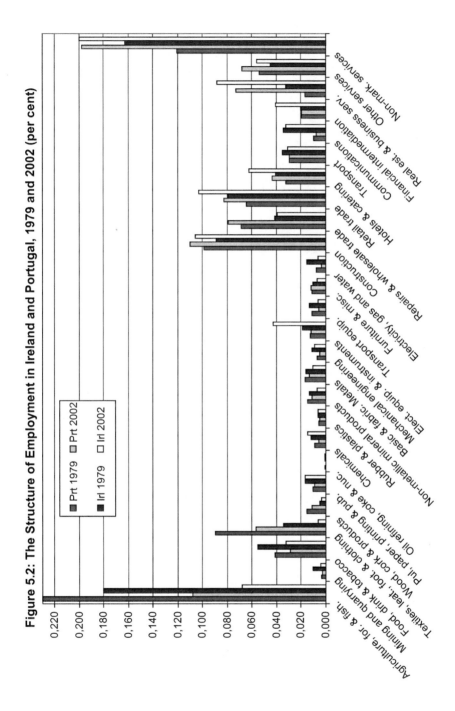

Figure 5.2: The Structure of Employment in Ireland and Portugal, 1979 and 2002 (per cent)

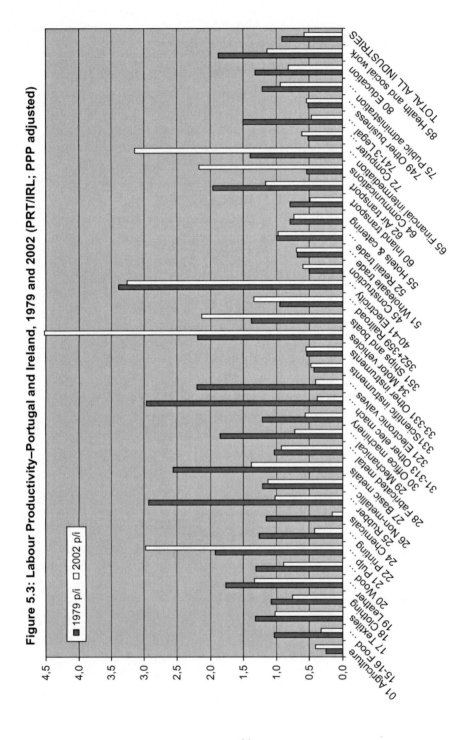

Figure 5.3: Labour Productivity–Portugal and Ireland, 1979 and 2002 (PRT/IRL; PPP adjusted)

hand side of Figure 5.2, we may notice that there are more similarities than differences between the two countries. The share of the 'Non-market services' sector, which includes education, health and public administration, is similar in the two countries, although 'Public administration' was higher in Portugal in 2002, whereas 'Education' was relatively similar in the two countries and 'Health' was higher in Ireland.

Figure 5.3 depicts the evolution of relative levels of labour productivity, also in 1979 and 2002, measured in purchasing power parity (PPP) exchange rates. In 1979, Portugal's total labour productivity was 91.3 per cent that of Ireland and in 2002 that ratio had declined to 57.9 per cent.[36] The most important conclusion we can draw from the relative labour productivity data is that differences are not clustered in specific types of sectors. For example, Portugal had lower labour productivity in 'Agriculture', as well as in 'Scientific instruments' and 'Construction'. On the other hand, Portugal had higher levels of labour productivity in industries such as 'Motor vehicles', 'Electricity', 'Communications' and 'Financial intermediation'. Productivity differentials are thus not clustered in industries that could be classified as more modern or in those using ICT more intensively.

Figure 5.4 provides the distribution of labour force according to the ICT taxonomy given by O'Mahony and van Ark,[37] and here we may see some differences between Ireland and Portugal. In fact, the share of ICT-producing and ICT-using industries in the manufacturing and the service sectors in Ireland totaled 25.4 per cent of the labour force in 1979 and 33.5 per cent in 2002. In Portugal, that share, slightly below Ireland's in 1979, was at 22.1 per cent and remained so in 2002 at 25.4 per cent. Table 5.4 shows the contribution of each sector to total labour productivity growth and we can see that ICT-using and ICT-producing industries accounted for 42.3 per cent of labour productivity growth in Ireland in 1994–2002, whereas in Portugal they accounted for just 25.9 per cent in the same period. Table 5.4 also shows that Ireland outperformed Portugal, particularly in the ICT-producing manufacturing industries where the contribution to labour productivity growth expanded from 9.8 per cent in 1979–86 to 15.8 per cent in 1994–2002, whereas in Portugal that contribution was just 1.4 per cent in the later period.

The data on the composition of the labour force and the contribution to labour productivity growth according to the ICT taxonomy does lead to the conclusion that Ireland's economic performance depended on sectors where ICT is more important. Yet, Portugal did not fare particularly badly in that respect. In fact, we may see that the ICT-using manufacturers contributed in a similar way in the two countries between 1994 and 2002; and

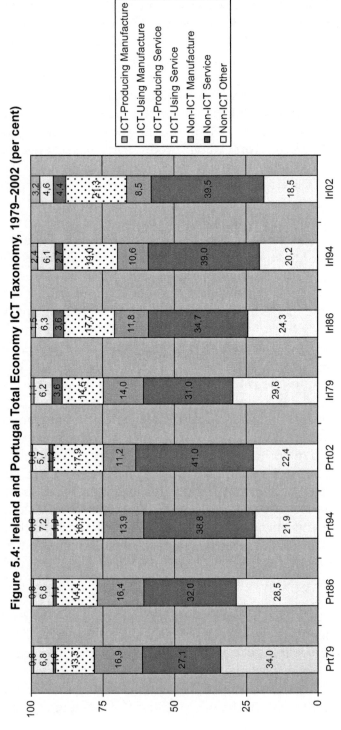

Figure 5.4: Ireland and Portugal Total Economy ICT Taxonomy, 1979–2002 (per cent)

Table 5.4: Contribution to Labour Productivity Growth According to ICT Taxonomy, 1979–2002 (%)

	Portugal			Ireland		
	1979– 1986	1986– 1994	1994– 2002	1979– 1986	1986– 1994	1994– 2002
ICT-Producing Manufacturing	0.6	2.0	1.4	9.8	3.4	15.8
ICT-Using Manufacturing	6.5	6.2	8.5	7.1	6.3	8.4
ICT-Producing Services	1.3	2.3	1.3	2.9	3.6	2.0
ICT-Using Services	11.6	12.2	14.7	10.1	14.3	16.1
Non-ICT Manufacturing	16.4	15.2	16.7	20.1	12.8	11.1
Non-ICT Services	24.3	26.9	35.6	26.4	32.3	30.2
Non-ICT Other	39.3	35.1	21.9	23.5	27.3	16.5
TOTAL	100.0	100.0	100.0	100.0	100.0	100.0

Note: ICT definition according to M. O'Mahony and B. van Ark (eds.), *EU Productivity and Competitiveness: An Industry Perspective. Can Europe Resume the Catching-up Process?*, Luxembourg: Official Publications of the European Communities, 2003, p. 49.
Source: see Table 5.3.

similar contributions can be found in the ICT-using services. Moreover, the data in Table 5.4 also shows that what was happening in the remaining sectors was of paramount importance. In fact, as much as 57.7 per cent of labour productivity growth was due to non-ICT sectors in Ireland, the figure for Portugal being, of course, much higher, at 74.1 per cent.[38]

To sum up, Irish and Portuguese labour productivity differed because of the joint effect of lower levels of productivity in certain industrial sectors and also because of differences in the structure of the two economies. In order to measure the impact of the two different factors, we can compare two counterfactual situations: the structure of the Portuguese economy and the levels of Irish labour productivity compared to the Irish economic structure and Portuguese levels of productivity. Table 5.5 shows actual aggregate labour productivity levels in the two countries and the two counterfactuals. In 2002, Irish total labour productivity was 1.725 times that of Portugal. Counterfactual A measures the situation in which we compare the structure of Portuguese labour employment and the levels of Irish productivity. On the other hand, if we consider a counterfactual where we take Irish employment structure and Portuguese labour productivity levels, the difference is 1.751. This exercise shows that the main cause of the productivity differential of the two countries is the differences in the structure of employment and not differences in labour productivity levels.[39]

Differences in the structure of employment in the two economies can be explained in terms of endowments of physical and human capital.[40] Table

**Table 5.5: Actual and Counterfactual Total Labour Productivity
(2002 US$, PPP adjusted)**

	1979	1986	1994	2002
Portugal actual	19,080	24,002	29,140	31,472
Ireland actual	20,910	26,066	34,596	54,299
Counterfactual A	21,515	24,632	32,329	44,838
Counterfactual B	23,733	30,699	32,887	55,110
Ireland actual/Portugal actual	1.096	1.086	1.187	1.725
Counterfactual A/Portugal actual	1.128	1.026	1.109	1.425
Counterfactual B/Portugal actual	1.244	1.279	1.129	1.751

Notes: Values adjusted according to the implicit PPP deflator of GDP for Portugal and
GNP for Ireland. Counterfactual A: structure of the Portuguese labour employment; levels
of Irish labour productivity. Counterfactual B: structure of Irish labour employment; levels
of Portuguese labour productivity, adjusted by the PPP exchange rate.
Memo (underlying data): (1) Total labour productivity (Portugal/Ireland): 1979 – 0,520;
1986 – 0,509; 1994 – 0,462; 2002 – 0,340; (2) GDP (Portugal/Ireland): 1979 – 0,913;
1986 – 0,921; 1994 – 0,842; 2002 – 0,580; (3) PPP coefficient (2)/(1): 1979 – 1,754; 1986
– 1,810; 1994 – 1,824; 2002 – 1,704.
Source: See Table 5.3.

**Table 5.6: Levels of Capital per Worker in Ireland and Portugal, 1979–2002
(US = 1; and ratios)**

	Physical Capital		Human Capital	
	1980	2000	1980	2000
Ireland	0.83	0.94	0.80	0.85
Portugal	0.37	0.64	0.59	0.68
Ratio Ireland /Portugal	2.24	1.47	1.36	1.25

Source: Migual Lebre Freitas (2005), 'O Capital' in Pedro Lains and Alvaro Ferreira da
Silva (eds), *Historica Economica de Portugal, 1700–2000*, Vol 3, Lisbon, Imprensa de
Cienias Socias, 2005, p. 116.

5.6 shows relative levels of physical and human capital per worker in 1980
and 2000. Three relevant conclusions can be drawn from the figures here.
The first is that the levels of both forms of capital were higher in Ireland.
The second is that the difference in endowments has declined rapidly in
terms of physical capital, from a ratio of 2.24 in 1980 to a ratio of 1.47 in
2000, and less so in terms of human capital, namely from 1.36 to 1.25 in the
same time span. The third relevant conclusion is that the deficit for Portugal in terms of physical capital is *higher* than the one in terms of human
capital.[41]

Conclusion

The structure of the Irish and Portuguese economies changed dramatically in the period from 1960 to 2004, but that change occurred in quite different ways. In both countries, there was a reduction in the share of the labour force employed in traditional sectors, which was compensated for by an increase in the share employed in modern sectors. But that transformation was quicker in Ireland than it was in Portugal. The impact of such structural change on the growth of labour productivity has been quantified in this chapter. As much as 29 per cent of Ireland's labour productivity growth in the 1990s was due to increasing the number of people engaged in industries where productivity was increasing rapidly. By contrast, changes in the structure of the Portuguese economy had a *negative* impact on the growth of the country's labour productivity.

Moreover, the share of ICT-producing and ICT-using industries in manufacturing and service sectors expanded faster in Ireland, increasing from 25.4 to 33.5 per cent between 1979 and 2002, whereas in Portugal that share barely changed, increasing from 22.1 to 25.4 per cent in the same period. ICT-related industries accounted for 42.3 per cent of labour productivity growth in Ireland in 1994–2002 and just 25.9 per cent in Portugal in the same period.

An important question is why did changes in the economic structures of the two economies have such different effects? The answer lies in the structure of the comparative advantages of the two countries. At the start of the period, Portugal had comparative advantages in sectors with lower levels of labour (and thus presumably capital) productivity. The abandonment of tariff protection and the adoption of the Euro implied a higher degree of exposure to international market forces and thus to increases in the output of those lower productivity industries. By contrast, Ireland had comparative advantages in higher labour productivity industries and thus benefited from the higher level of participation in the international economy. The main reason for the better structure found throughout the Irish economy is related to the fact that its endowments in terms of physical and human capital were higher than those of Portugal.

There are some relevant policy implications that we can derive from our conclusions. According to Esteban, if countries (or regions) that lag behind suffer from a 'uniform productivity gap', then one should back 'present EU regional policies based on structural funds essentially geared to improve infrastructures and human capital', and not specific policies geared to promoting ICT-producing industries.[42] Policies directed towards infrastructure and education would help bridge Portugal's lags in physical and human capital endowments, but one shouldn't be too optimistic.

The kind of policies mentioned above were implemented after Portugal's accession to the EEC in 1986, with the financial support of the EU structural funds programme. Importantly, investment in transportation infrastructure had a large impact on growth. Yet the outcome in Portugal was much less impressive than what was observed in Ireland. FDI and export growth are more powerful sources of structural change and productivity growth than governmental transfers within the EU. Financial transfers from the EU could lead to larger benefits if they result in an increase in private capital flows to the country, but that linkage depends on policies that attract foreign investment. Portugal also has a relatively low degree of flexibility in the labour market, which may also hamper higher levels of structural change.

Portugal's adverse conditions for growth in the more recent period can be related to the structure of its economy and to its institutional framework. Those adverse conditions can be changed. The Irish experience from the 1970s to the 1990s shows how this can be achieved, how it can bring gains in the longer term, in terms of increase in labour productivity and welfare, and how lengthy that process of change can be. The changes that happened in Ireland since the late 1980s may havè led to too much dependence on international financial markets and that certainly is one of the reasons why the present recession is so strongly felt in Ireland. Yet, openness also led to the structural change that strengthened the Irish economy and that may help its recovery.

CHAPTER 6

Readings, Misreadings and Politics: The 'Irish Model' in Greece

Andreas Antoniades

This chapter aims to assess how the 'Irish model' was communicated in Greece and how it affected Greek public discourse and policy. The focus is on the period 2001–7, when its influence was arguably most discernable. We can divide this period into two relatively separate chronological phases. The first covers the first four years (2001–4) and is the period in which the left-to-centre party Panhellenic Socialist Movement (PASOK) was in government. It could be said that this period began with an aphorism against the Irish model, by the then Prime Minister Costas Simitis, and ended with its adoption by Simitis's Government as a basis for an effective economic growth strategy (especially with regard to investment incentives). In this manner, the Irish model constituted a significant issue in the national elections that took place in 2004.

The second phase starts with the coming to power of the right-to-centre party New Democracy (ND) in 2004. The conservative leader Kostas Karamanlis was an advocate of the Irish model throughout the seven-year period in question. The beginning of this second phase found the positions of the two major parties converging with regard to the importance of 'learning the lessons' from the Irish model. Towards the end of this period, however, the Irish model became an integral part of an antagonistic binary public discourse that was based on the juxtaposition of the Irish and Swedish economic models. This antagonistic discourse dominated the press and was an integral part of the rhetoric and discourses of Greek political parties during their campaigns for the 2006 local elections (which took place one year before the 2007 parliamentary elections).

Beyond these highly visible effects of the Irish model in Greek public discourse, two less visible but equally important effects should also be stressed. First, notwithstanding the official party positions, Ireland was treated as a source for policy ideas and best practice by several departments of the public administration throughout the period under examination. Second, a critical intervening variable for understanding how the Irish model influenced Greek public policy is the European Union (EU) and its institutions. The European Commission used Ireland as a paragon for successful socio-economic development, and advised several EU member-states on the lessons and policies they could learn and adapt from the 'Irish economic miracle' (despite criticising Ireland for violating the Stability and Growth Pact, an agreement by EU member states, relating to their management of fiscal policy, to facilitate and maintain the programme of Economic and Monetary Union). Thus, along with policy initiatives related to the Irish model that were taking place at the national domestic level, there were also EU-led initiatives and policy suggestions. Although this EU dimension and mechanisms are beyond the scope of this chapter, they remain a defining part of the picture of the influence of the Irish model on Greece.

In what follows, I first present and then analyse the aforementioned two different phases of the influence of the Irish model in Greece, and then offer some general conclusions. As I hope will become clear from the analysis that follows, the dissemination of the Irish model should not be understood as a top-down process of 'translation' of a clear and well-defined text (i.e. a clear set of policies and practices). The signifier 'Irish model' was used by different political and economic actors to serve different and often conflicting purposes. It was used as a rhetorical device to promote or denounce particular understandings and strategies of economic development; it was used as an ideological marker; it was finally used as a compact or substitute for actual policy reforms. It can thus be argued that, through these strategic games and discursive struggles, the Irish model discourse emerged in Greece in a bottom-up manner.

Phase I: From Denunciation to Adoption

A landmark in the communication of the Irish model in Greece was the statement made by Prime Minister Costas Simitis, during a meeting of PASOK's Central Committee in 2001, that 'we will not become Ireland' ('δεν θα γίνουμε Ιρλανδία'). Simitis, in effect, denounced the Irish economic miracle as a neo-liberal creature based on low taxes that deprived the state of its capacity to promote social welfare, help those most in need and invest in infrastructure. Simitis's statement was widely criticised in the Greek press as dogmatic. A good number of journalists and political analysts concluded that Simitis denounced the Irish model without really being aware of what the characteristics of this model were and what had been the achievements of the Irish economic miracle, especially with regard to unemployment and living standards.[1] It was also reported in the press that, after this criticism, Simitis asked the General Accounting Office of the Ministry of Finance for evidence that would substantiate his position. Yet, the evidence that was gathered pointed to the opposite position to that taken by the Prime Minister.[2]

Simitis's statement is an important discursive point for two reasons. First, it can be taken to be the starting point of the 'negotiation' of the Irish model within Greek public discourse. Second, this statement remained an important point of controversy and reference throughout the period under examination. Notwithstanding Simitis's statement, the Greek public policy-making machine did not remain insulated from the Irish economic miracle. As in many other countries in Europe, Ireland turned out to be the first country to which policy-makers would turn to get ideas about successful public policy reforms, almost in every single sector of public policy. Thus, for instance, in January 2002, shortly after Simitis's statement, the Ministry of Development decided to apply the Irish model in the liberalisation of the energy and electricity market in Greece.[3] In most cases, however, these 'technocratic' deliberations and their source of inspiration remained beyond public attention.

The issue that brought the Irish model under the spotlight again in Greek public discourse was a new 'law for economic development' ('αναπτυξιακό νομοσχέδιο') that the PASOK Government put to the vote in the Greek parliament in January 2004, just before the national elections in March of the same year. A significant aim of this law (law 3219/2004)[4] was to increase the attractiveness of Greece as an investment location. To do so, the Minister of Economy and Finance Nikos Christodoulakis adopted key aspects of the Irish model, such as tax stability and low corporate tax rates. For instance, for major investments (above €30 million), the law offered lower tax rates on corporate profits (reduced by up to 10 per cent, from 35 per cent to 25 per cent), tax stability for a ten-year period, as well as improved and simplified inspections by tax authorities (although not 'non-interference' for ten years as had been initially discussed).[5]

During the period in which this new development law was discussed, mostly between the summer of 2003 and the winter of 2004, the Irish model remained prominent in the public agenda. Most commentators read the proposed new law as an attempt by the PASOK Government to adopt the Irish model of economic growth and, consequently, as a change of direction in economic policy towards a more business friendly (or, for some, neo-liberal) approach.[6] Many criticised the Government not for changing direction, but for failing to change direction enough, arguing that any comparison with Ireland on the basis of the development law was unfortunate. The critics' main points were that, unlike the Irish case, the proposed development law was not part of a well-thought-out and well-designed overall economic strategy; it did not address key concerns of the business world; and it was not brave enough (the Irish, for example, gave 20 rather than 10 years of tax stability; 12.5 per cent rather than 25 per cent rates of corporate taxation).[7]

A qualifier is important here. This change of direction in PASOK's economic policy, no matter how small or big, should not be conceived as representing a new consensus within PASOK. It should rather be seen as one more, rather controversial, decision coming from PASOK's 'modernising wing', which at the time was leading both the party and the Government. Thus, the leaning of PASOK towards the Irish model reflected more a consensus among the 'modernisers' than a general new consensus within PASOK.

The Irish model and its reputation in the EU, however, was not only associated with low corporate tax rates. In fact, the distinctiveness of the Irish model, and its key differentiation in relation to the Anglo-Saxon model of political economy, was that the Irish political economy was characterised by a consensual structure of interest representation. It was based on a strong, wide-ranging and well-institutionalised social partnership (which, in fact, is a defining characteristic of the Continental model of political economy). By the mid-1990s it was clear to all commentators in Europe that this social partnership had a key role in the Irish economic miracle, and many countries tried to imitate Ireland's success by attempting to build strong social partnerships.[8] Greece was no exception. Most importantly, in 1994 an Economic and Social Council (ESC) was created by law (2232/1994) in order to provide the institutional framework for the development of a social partnership on the basis of a neo-corporatist model. Furthermore, in the amendment to the Greek Constitution that the country voted in favour of in 2001, there was a provision that described the ESC as an instrument of social dialogue. Through its constitutional recognition, the PASOK

Government aimed to enhance the ESC's institutional role. Yet, neither of these attempts bore any significant fruits.

To conclude, in this first phase, the Irish model seemed to operate at two levels within the Greek politico-economic system. On the one hand, at the policy level, Ireland remained a constant point of reference within the Greek public administration. On the other hand, in the discourse of the ruling party, as this was reflected by its leader, the Irish model was associated with excessive neo-liberalism. Towards the end of this period, however, these two levels converged. The PASOK Government seemed to recognise the success of the Irish model and publically adopted aspects of this model in its economic policy.

Phase II: From an Emerging Consensus to Polarisation

In the 2004 national elections, PASOK was replaced in power by the centre-to-right party New Democracy (ND). The Irish model was on the daily agenda of ND's 'economic team', even before ND's coming to power. Indicatively, in an interview in the newspaper *Kathimerini* in February 2004, Yiannis Papathanassiou MP, a member of ND's 'economic team' (later deputy minister for development, and minister for economy and finance), commented: 'There is a need for additional specific measures to boost the competitiveness of our economy ...Yet there can be no improvement in our competitiveness without adopting the Irish model of development that focuses on entrepreneurship and education.'[9]

Kostas Karamanlis, the new prime minister and leader of ND, was an advocate of the Irish model (since the late 1990s).[10] In one of his first speeches after the elections, Karamanlis compared the economic performance of Greece with that of Ireland and argued that Greece could and should follow the Irish example. He argued that the

[m]ain target of [my] New Economic Policy is the strengthening of competitiveness...Contrary to our country, Ireland...succeeded to increase its per capita GDP from 84.1 per cent of the EC/EU average (in 1994) to 120.6 per cent (in 2003)...In contrast, Greece in the same period moved from 66.5 per cent to 72.9 per cent of the EC/EU average...As a result, Ireland reduced its unemployment from 14.3 per cent (in 1994) to 4.6 per cent (in 2003). In the same period, unemployment in Greece increased from 8.9 per cent to 9.9 per cent...How did this happen? Simply, Ireland adopted and implemented policies that created an environment friendly to entrepreneurship and creativity. At the same time, they invested in new technologies. They

turned their attention to youth – the dynamic ages between 20 and 25 years. They dared and succeeded. We can do the same.[11]

He continued his speech by referring to the economic and tax policies that his Government would follow in order to meet this aim. These included a reduction in corporate tax rates (to 25 per cent for large enterprises and 20 per cent for smaller ventures), a reform of the tax inspection system, a new law for economic development and reduction of the role of the state in the economy.

Thus, with the coming of Karamanlis to power, the Irish model gained a pre-eminent place in Greek media and public discourse as the Government's favourite model for economic development.[12] It would be accurate to say that, in the public discourse, the concept of the Irish model was mostly related to lower corporate taxes and, in general, the creation of a business-friendly and entrepreneurship-conducive environment. Thus, the second central pillar of the Irish model, the existence of a well-institutionalised social partnership, was rather marginalised or ignored in the majority of analyses referring to the Irish model, at least in the press. Of course, the 'economic teams' of both PASOK and ND were aware of this second pillar. For instance, George Alogoskoufis (minister for economy and finance, 2004–9) argued in 2006 that 'key for the Irish model was its consensual base' produced by the institution of the social partnership.[13] Yet the failure of both PASOK and ND to overcome the fragmented, particularistic and party-dominated structure of interest representation in Greece further enhanced the tendency of the press to focus mostly on one of the two pillars of the Irish model.

Taking these developments into consideration and comparing the laws for economic development proposed by the successive governments of PASOK and ND, it could be argued that, by 2004, the Irish model had come to be accepted as the most appropriate model for economic development by the two main Greek parties. Yet, this apparent convergence of the two parties proved rather short-lived. The explicit support of the Irish model by the ND Government, and the constant effort of the latter to present this model as its own economic proposal for Greece's development, led PASOK to diversify its position and counter-propose the 'Swedish/Scandinavian model' as a more appropriate orientation for Greece's economic development.

The new leader of PASOK George Papandreou (who replaced Simitis in 2004) was instrumental in this change, as the development of a discourse about the Swedish model as a counterbalance to the ND's economic proposals was his own initiative. To be accurate, Papandreou, in his public pronouncements, referred to the 'model of the northern countries' or the 'Northern model', in which he also included, with some qualification, Ireland (along with Sweden, Finland and Denmark). His underlying point was that the success of the Northern model was based on the consensual nature and strong social partnerships that exist in the political economies of those countries.[14]

Yet, the juxtaposition of the Irish model proposed by ND and the Swedish model (apparently) considered by PASOK acquired an independent dynamic in Greek public life and came to dominate the Greek public discourse in 2006 (especially before and during the local elections in October). An important moment in this process was the dismissal of George Floridis, PASOK's parliamentary co-ordinator for economics and finance, by George Papandreou on 6 April 2006.[15]

Elaborating on the 'Northern/Scandinavian model' that would be adopted by PASOK when in power, Floridis referred to the flexible nature of the labour market in Scandinavian countries and the right of employers to fire their employees without significant constraints. The other half of his statement referred to the safety net offered by Scandinavian states to those dismissed employees.[16] Yet, this latter half was 'lost in translation', and Papandreou asked and received Floridis's resignation from the post of PASOK's parliamentary co-ordinator.

The damage, however, had already been done. Both Prime Minister Kostas Karamanlis and Minister for the Economy and Finance George Alogoskoufis immediately criticised PASOK for its proposal to apply the Scandinavian/Swedish model in Greece. Karamanlis focused his criticism on the issues of 'free dismissals' and 'high taxes' that characterise the Scandinavian model. In a speech the day after Floridis's dismissal, he claimed that the 'citizens reject those who, on the one hand, say they care about employees and workers and, on the other hand, suggest free dismissals and tax increases.'[17] Along similar lines, George Alogoskoufis pointed out that the Scandinavian model was based on high VAT rates, high tax rates, high public expenditure and flexicurity (where a pro-active market policy directs labour arrangements). It 'is a model effective and useful for [Scandinavian] countries, and at the same time a model compatible with their social and political situation. But it is not a model that has led to very high economic development.' He then contrasted this with the Irish model.

Another model that I deem more appropriate to be studied within the Greek context, is the Irish model, which in many regards is the exact opposite to the Scandinavian model. The Irish model is based on low taxation for corporations and people, low indirect taxation and low public expenditures. This model too, however...is based on political consensus...Of course there can be no implementation of the Irish model point by point, but there are lessons to be learned.[18]

Consequently, Alogoskoufis said that the Greek Government would take advantage of the lessons of the Irish experience, rather than lessons coming from the Scandinavian model. 'The first stage of our tax reform focused on reducing corporate tax rates...The second stage...concerns the reduction of tax rates for people.'[19] Finally, Alogoskoufis closed his speech by acknowledging that a prime problem for any reform in the Greek economy is the lack of social and political consensus (thus acknowledging one of the key differences between the Greek and Irish politico-economic systems).

After Floridis's dismissal, the 'models controversy' reached another climax within Greek public discourse after a parliamentary debate devoted to the status of the Greek economy on 13 April 2006. The debate was presented and analysed by the majority of the press as a 'clash of models' and as one more attempt by the Government to persuade the public that the ND's model (i.e. the Irish) was more appropriate for Greece, in comparison to the Swedish model, proposed by some PASOK members (most notably, Floridis).[20] There were numerous articles in the press on the characteristics of the two models and how the models compare to each other.[21] Most members of ND and PASOK took, or were asked to take, a position on this matter.[22] In addition, Irish politicians and experts who participated in the 'Irish economic miracle' were invited to give speeches and interviews in Greece, including Michael Ahern and Dan Flinter.[23]

This polarised discourse started to gradually lose its intensity after the 2006 local elections. Papandreou's decision to implement a moratorium on statements about economic models within PASOK, and his attempt to change the terms of the debate, and especially the notion that PASOK proposed the adoption of the Swedish model for Greece, helped in moving the spotlight away from the juxtaposition of the two models. Other factors were the dissatisfaction of many members of both parties and part of the press with the abstract terms in which the debate was taking place and the lack of focus on the real problems of the Greek economy.[24]

Alogoskoufis himself seemed to have changed his position by 2007, if only in semantic terms. In his concluding remarks at a conference on European economic models organised by his ministry in April 2007, he concluded that 'it is not feasible to copy a single model per se nor is it recommended due to the various structural differences.... [T]he government today is implementing a policy based on reforms that combine several parts of successful European models. Greece however...does not copy a specific European model and aspires to create its own "Greek" model.'[25]

To conclude, this second phase (2004–7) of the negotiation of the Irish model in the Greek politico-economic system was qualitatively different in comparison to the first. During 2001–4, the Irish model remained mainly an issue for 'the few'. It did emerge as an issue in the public agenda, especially with its initial condemnation by Simitis and its later adoption by the PASOK Government as a model for economic growth, but it was mostly a technocratic issue. Especially after its adoption by the PASOK Government, it did not emerge as an ideological issue and it was not presented in the press as a major political issue. In the second phase of its negotiation (2004–7), however, the Irish model was no longer only discussed within the economic teams of the two main parties and by some economic journalists. Through several means – daily statements by political leaders, ministers and politicians of all ranks in ND and PASOK; frequent newspaper headlines, articles and special sections; the dismissal of Floridis from his role as PASOK's parliamentary co-ordinator for economic issues – the Irish model came to dominate the Greek public agenda and public discourse for a considerable period of time.

After this period away from the spotlight, the subject of the Irish political economy returned to the Greek public discourse with the 2008 economic crisis. The news that Ireland was the first Eurozone member to fall into a recession in 2008 sent shock waves across European countries, including Greece. Within this climate, the emphasis in the Greek press and public discourse was more on the global economic crisis itself (its nature, causes and potential implications) rather than on the Irish model and lessons to be learned. Some commentators, however, related the near 'collapse' of the Irish economy to the failure of the Irish 'neo-liberal' economic model.[26] Within this framework, the Irish recession vindicated all those who had opposed the Irish model, while Simitis's 2004 statement returned to the forefront of the debate. Once more, the 'Irish model' was used in ideological terms as an instrument for political purposes by domestic political actors. Ireland, however, was not to stay alone for long as the 'weak link' of the euro and Eurozone. It was soon joined by Greece, which also faced mounting fiscal deficits and an excessive public debt. This dynamic threw the spotlight back to the Greek politico-economic system and its structural weaknesses. As one commentator put it, 'although we did not follow Ireland in its "miracle", we now leave together the economic "nightmare".[27]

Conclusion

From this analysis of the communication and negotiation of the Irish model in Greece, we can draw four main conclusions. First, in Greek public discourse the Irish model came to signify a model for economic development based on low corporate tax rates and, in general, the existence of a business- and entrepreneurship-friendly economic environment. Other aspects of the Irish model, such as its consensual nature and strong social partnership, were not absent from the public discourse, but they were rather overshadowed by the focus on corporate taxation.

Second, both the main Greek parties adopted aspects of (what *they* defined as) the Irish model (mainly a reduction of corporate tax rates, long-term tax stability for big investors, widening investment incentives) in their economic policies. In particular, PASOK did so with its 2004 development law (3219/2004), and ND did so with its 2004 tax and economic development laws (respectively, laws 3296/2004 and 3299/2004) that were both modified in 2006 (law 3522/2006).[28] It is hard to explain these tax and development laws only in relation to the Irish model. Yet, as I tried to demonstrate above, both the PASOK and ND governments associated their respective economic proposals and initiatives with the Irish model. Especially in the case of ND, both the Prime Minister and the Minister for Economics and Finance declared that their tax and economic reforms were inspired by and based on the Irish model. In terms of real developments on the ground,[29] and especially with regard to the issue of taxation, the corporate tax rate was gradually reduced from 32 per cent in 2004 to 25 per cent in 2007 (and from 25 per cent to 20 per cent for some types of small companies). With regard to personal income tax, tax rates in 2005 were progressive: 15 per cent, 29 per cent, 39 per cent and 40 per cent for professionals; and 29 per cent, 39 per cent and 40 per cent for non-professionals and pensioners (40 per cent in both cases was for income over €75,000). In both cases, the 29 per cent and 39 per cent rates were reduced to 27 per cent and 37 per cent in 2007, and further by 2 per cent to 25 per cent and 35 per cent in 2009. Therefore, there is at least some evidence on the ground that 'confirms' the influence of the Irish model in Greece.

Third, it is clear that the communication and dissemination of the Irish model in Greece was not an outside-in, top-down process. It was not communicated or implemented as a recommendation to Greek governments by external actors, institutions or organisations. Rather, it emerged bottom-up within Greek public discourse. Different political forces used the concept of the Irish model, positively or negatively, to support and enhance their ideas, policies or prejudices. In this regard, the Irish model came to serve the Greek political forces as much as (and possibly much more than) these forces 'served' the Irish model.

Finally, it can be argued that a significant part of the explanation of why the Irish model was communicated in the way it was in Greece lies with the nature of Greek political culture and Greek public discourse. This issue exceeds the purpose of this chapter. Yet it can be said that the way in which the Irish model emerged and was negotiated in Greek public discourse seems to confirm earlier studies about the nature of public discourse in Greece. In particular, it has been argued that debates on public issues in Greece have traditionally been characterised by a high degree of abstraction, a recourse to abstract universalising categories, and a high degree of ideology and polarisation. As one would expect, the analysis of the impact of the Irish model on the Greek politico-economic system tells us more about this system itself than about the Irish model.

CHAPTER 7

The Irish Economic Model in Eastern Europe: The Case of Romania

Amalia Fugaru and Dana Denis-Smith

Introduction

Most, if not all, of the former communist countries in Eastern Europe contemplated the possibility of transforming their uncompetitive economies of the 1990s according to the Irish 'economic miracle'. The 'Tatra Tiger',[1] the 'Czech Lion' and the 'Baltic Tigers' are but a few of the common labels used in political circles to describe the desire of these countries to replicate the Celtic Tiger miracle. 'If the Estonian people have a dream of where they would like to be in ten years' time', said Estonian Foreign Minister Kristiina Ojuland in 2004, 'then they dream of following Ireland's example.'[2]

Romania, which in 1989 emerged from over 40 years of dictatorship, was then one of the poorest former communist countries due to the economic policy introduced by Nicolae Ceauşescu's regime in the 1970s and 1980s. As such, Romania shared Estonia's dream of turning its economy into a 'Dacic Tiger'[3] to catch up with the wealth levels of Western Europe, but it did little in terms of policy to realise this in the post-communist era. The recent global economic crisis has placed Romania at a crossroads. As was Ireland in the 1980s, the country has now been a member of the European Union (EU) for several years and large EU capital inflows have started to arrive. However, like Ireland then, Romania faces significant challenges in order to achieve sustainable economic growth levels and improve living standards in the long term. Romania lacks sound institutions, investment in human capital has been patchy and a strategic partnership among key social players is not in place. Unlike in Ireland, corruption in Romania is widespread, political and economic interests remain closely intertwined, and market fundamentals such as property rights are often infringed as a result.

Eastern Europe and Ireland's Economic Success – the Background

Political thinking in the aftermath of the collapse of the Eastern European communist regimes in 1989 centred on how to ensure a quick fix to a half-century-old problem. Poverty,[4] macroeconomic imbalances, inefficiencies typical of centrally controlled economies and a long period of trade isolation were characteristics inherited – in varying degrees – by all of the post-1989 Eastern European governments. Thus, for most of the early transition to a market economy, these governments were faced with the challenges of the socio-economic breakdown of the communist regimes. Rather than look at specific country models such as Ireland, they were initially urged to choose between more theoretical approaches: 'shock therapy' reform[5] (such as was implemented in Poland and Russia) or a 'gradual' path to reform their economy (as was the case in Hungary and Romania). By the late 1990s, the success of the economic transition was still displaying a mixed picture across the region, and the 1997 rouble collapse resulted in a sharp economic setback for all of Eastern Europe. High unemployment, high inflation, high emigration and, ultimately, a higher degree of political volatility were just a few of the characteristics of Eastern Europe and Romania in the late 1990s.

It was following this sharp economic contraction that Ireland started to be considered more seriously as a possible 'catch-up' economic model to be replicated across Eastern Europe, to the extent that, by the time of the first accession wave in May 2004, most candidate countries were seeking to follow the Irish 'economic model'. In this historical context, Ireland's background as a country on the periphery of an empire, which rose from a long history of poverty to swiftly become a star economic performer, provided a very attractive success recipe for policy-makers in Eastern Europe.

As accession to the EU approached for the CEECs (Central and Eastern European Countries: Estonia, Latvia, Lithuania, Poland, Czech Republic, Slovakia, Hungary, Slovenia, Romania and Bulgaria), the Irish recipe became even more attractive – just as Ireland had joined the EU in 1973 at the bottom of the wealth league table, so would the former communist countries in 2004 and 2007.[6] Policy-makers began to consider how they could borrow and apply elements from the Irish model so that they too could enjoy the same wealth and economic success as Ireland. Ironically –

and as if to continue this parallel between Ireland and the ex-communist East – the first eastern enlargement of the EU took place in 2004 under the Irish presidency, and Brian Cowen, the then Irish foreign minister, emphasised the historical similarities between Ireland and the new entrants.

In Romania, the increased interest in the ingredients of Ireland's success was the result of a number of factors: the country verged on economic collapse in 1997–9[7] at a time when Ireland's economy was booming; as in 1980s Ireland, the 'brain drain' and emigration of labourers intensified as Romanians looked for a more prosperous life elsewhere (Ireland included);[8] Ireland had become by far the most successful EU member state in its use of structural funds and in attracting high levels of foreign direct investment (FDI); and, due to its economic performance, it was very effective in its efforts to lure back Irish emigrants. The similarities between Ireland and Romania do not stop here, however. As they embarked on an economic reform programme, both countries' economies were dominated by a large agricultural sector and heavy industry. Trade was highly dependent on their relations with the empires they now rejected – the British Empire for Ireland, and the former Soviet Bloc for Romania. In the case of Romania, curbing this dependency on exports to a large but highly uncompetitive common market such as the Soviet Union was directly linked to its ability to restructure the country's industrial sector in order to improve productivity and, crucially, produce better products capable of being exported to the West.

Economic Imbalances in Post-Communist Eastern Europe and Romania

Ireland's initial attempt at 'stop-starting' its economy by following the advice of the International Monetary Fund (IMF) in 1981 failed. The IMF had devised a plan for macro-stabilisation intended for all countries affected by high oil prices in the 1970s to bring inflation and current account deficits under control, and to stimulate public investment. The IMF's programme had two key aims: to achieve a low level equilibrium in the real economy through the restructuring of public budget expenditure and to reduce the monetary aggregates by using the exchange rate as an anchor by, if necessary, depreciating the national currency. Ireland adopted the IMF plan in 1981 but the result was a significant drop in private consumption. Ireland then abandoned the plan within the year.

The second attempt in 1987, which aimed to cut public spending and curb inflation, succeeded in achieving macroeconomic stability. The success of the second attempt was widely viewed to be the result of an aggressive liberalisation policy. Taxes were cut to supplement cuts in public spending and monetary mass. Following Ireland's success at achieving macroeconomic stability, the IMF suggested that a similar policy be applied in Eastern Europe in order to address the macroeconomic imbalances inherited from its communist past. Following the Irish example, liberalisation became top of the agenda for economic reform in the immediate aftermath of the Soviet collapse. Romania, however, did not embrace liberalisation from the outset, despite calls from international financial institutions (IFIs) and the EU. Instead, Romania spent a good part of its first decade of economic transition (1990–2000) in a vicious circle of high inflation and high unemployment, with foreign trade hampered by non-tariff barriers as it tried to gradually adjust a socialist economy to a free market model. In the period 1996–1999, Romania recorded unemployment figures similar to those registered in Ireland in 1980, when the Irish unemployment rate was 11 per cent.

In Ireland, the annual consumer price inflation rate peaked in 1981 at 20.43 per cent – a similar rate to Romania's 22.5 per cent in 2002. In the same period, the Irish Government faced a budget deficit of 8 per cent of gross domestic product (GDP), the result of increasing property and consumption taxes to cope with declining economic activity. Similarly, Romanian governments of the 1990s were struggling to control the budget deficit, which continued to rise from 8.4 per cent of GDP in 2004 to 11.8 per cent in 2006,[9] despite starting its transition period on a very low current deficit, at 1.4 per cent of GDP in 1994.[10]

The need to reform Romania's economy had been drummed home by economic experts and IFIs since 1989 and there had been, from the outset, public awareness about the need to modernise the country's production facilities. Romania, however, delayed the privatisation and closure of its large and inefficient socialist plants until the late 1990s. Furthermore, the process of land restitution started in 1991 was so badly executed by the local authorities that it led to a high volume of litigation and a delay in the adoption of modern methods in agricultural production.

The share of industry in Romania's GDP, at 36.2 per cent in 1994, only started to decrease significantly after 2005, when it stood at 24.6 per cent. Similarly, Romania maintained a large share of agriculture as a percentage of its GDP until very recently – the decline from 19.9 per cent of GDP in 1994 to 7.8 per cent of GDP in 2006 was accelerated only from around 2000. It is evident from the above that, unlike Ireland in the 1980s, Romania's economy was in need, not only of a macroeconomic stabilisation programme, but also thorough structural reform. In 1982, Ireland embarked on several exchange-rate-based stabilisation programmes[11] intended to curb inflation and to force an export-led economic recovery. This economic strategy bore fruit as it later resulted in a sharp change in the structure of the economy, which became dominated by the services sector and the manufacture of high value-added products.

The experience of Ireland demonstrated that the country's Central Bank was a key institution in achieving macroeconomic stabilisation. Once the Central Bank was allowed to operate as an independent institution and started to set monetary policy, inflation was brought under control. This link between an independent central bank and inflation was often addressed in the IMF standby agreements and the EBRD (European Bank for Reconstruction and Development)[12] economic monitoring of post-communist economies – throughout the 1990s, the economies with the weakest central banks (especially those of Eastern Europe (South), Romania included, and Central Asia) always had the highest inflation rates.

Before the role of the central banks could be enhanced, all the former communist economies needed to undergo a complete structural reform of their banking sector: the banking sector inherited from the communist regimes was saddled with bad debts which needed to be removed from the balance sheets; the supervision of the banks had to be strengthened; any recapitalisation could only be achieved by attracting foreign capital into the banking sector; and in order to ensure the sector's competitiveness, the banks needed to acquire know-how and expertise from foreign banks. Reforming the banks was a highly complicated process, as it had to effect two major changes.

First, any reform had to lead to an increase in the penetration of the banking sector in the real economy. Second, reform had to strengthen the commercial banks[13] by improving not only their capitalisation but also their competitiveness and effectiveness. The credit problem in the transition economies was severely influenced by hyperinflation. Each country addressed the weakness of its commercial banks through different strategies. Some countries, like Poland, chose to rehabilitate the banks with the consequence that the banks were used to help the real sector to adjust to a market economy. Others, like Hungary, chose to privatise the banks. Romania, by contrast, wavered between rehabilitation and privatisation with the result that a strong, competitive banking sector emerged only once the largest bank, the Romanian Commercial Bank, was sold off to Austria's Erste Bank in December 2005.[14]

Although on the surface Eastern Europe faced a similar challenge to that of Ireland in achieving macroeconomic stability, it also had to deal with the legacy of centralised economies – state ownership of all production facilities and the absence of functioning markets. The IMF's recipe for Ireland therefore could not be transposed to Eastern Europe. For instance, the strategy had to be amended to take into account that the trajectory of inflation could not be forecast accurately in the absence of historical price data, as was the case in Eastern Europe. In order to create a market, the IMF and other IFIs suggested the introduction of a mass privatisation programme aimed at selling off state-owned assets. This, again, was in contrast to the Irish model, as in Ireland the privatisation of state assets occurred before the 1987 macro-stabilisation plan.

As such, there were a number of key distinctions that made the Irish model difficult to apply in Romania in the early transition period, 1990–2000. First, the initial conditions in Ireland compared to Romania were different. The most important element that negatively affected each stage of reform in Romania was the lack of institutional capacity to enable a clear-cut break with the economic practices of the past. For example, it was difficult for government agencies to sever existing relationships between state-owned enterprises and the Government and to replace them with relationships based on the single criterion of marginal cost. Ireland had not encountered such an issue, as markets, private ownership and prices were present before the macro-stabilisation was attempted. A second difference can be found in the way the population related to the macro-stabilisation effort. The entire reform programme was considered and presented by politicians as something imposed from outside, either by the IFIs or by the EU.

Whereas in Ireland the social agreement was an economic trade-off accepted by the political actors, in Romania most reform efforts were presented as a necessary evil to avoid the disapproval of the EU and IMF, as the country's main goal was to meet EU membership criteria. Apart from macro-economic stability, privatisation and liberalisation have often been used as reform tools to solve the issue of financial, physical and human capital deficiencies. Ireland needed fresh capital in order to replenish the resources eroded by inflation and, more generally, to help its economy to grow. Liberalisation allowed new businesses to enter and exit the market without barriers. Romania also needed an injection of capital for two reasons. First, there was an acute lack of capital easily available in the domestic economy – in 1989 Romania had almost no foreign debt but the population had minimal savings. Second, all human capital and physical resources had been misallocated between industries, not least because the markets for which they were producing disappeared. Moreover, the pricing of the physical and human capital had previously been allocated on the basis of a five-year, central economic plan, not on the value dictated by market forces.

Ireland chose to attract new capital in three ways. First, Ireland cut corporation tax as well as social contributions with the intention of attracting FDI and foreign know-how to improve the quality of local management. Second, the Irish Government slashed public spending by reorganising the public administration, public health services and other social services. These cuts resulted in a 15 per cent reduction in public spending in the period 1982 to 1989. Lastly, Ireland, supported by Spain, persuaded the European Commission in the 1980s to agree to the use of the cohesion funds to finance the retraining and development of the workforce. By contrast, Romania introduced flat taxes as late as 2005.

Tax cuts were not viewed as the most important element in attracting new capital. Governments placed a higher premium on sectors that could grow rapidly by having the necessary production capacity that could attract foreign investors. Plans to introduce budget cuts never survived beyond a general election, with the result that only in 2009 was Romania considering a cull of the very large public sector workforce.[15] Romania has a higher number of pensioners than those active in the labour market[16] and pension increases are regular, especially around elections, with the result that all governments to date have found it difficult to bring down public spending on salaries and pensions. As for the use of cohesion funds, which contributed to higher productivity in Ireland, such funds were was not available in an enlarged EU.

The Irish Social Pact

Economic reform often carries a political and social price tag. In Ireland, the first stabilisation programme was abandoned as the Government's loss of popularity led to three rounds of elections in eighteen months. Such political instability did not bode well for any administration which sought to undertake the deep reforms needed. Therefore, Ireland achieved macro-economic stability only once a partnership between the main social stakeholders was signed in 1987. This *Programme for National Recovery* was not a formal arrangement as it was not ratified by Parliament, but it was accepted and respected by the major stakeholders as the only means to improve economic performance.

This partnership was based on a trade-off between wages and taxes such as to allow a gradual but rapid adjustment of the economic imbalance. Such a social pact was absent in Eastern Europe for a number of reasons. At the beginning of the transition period, the attitude of IFIs was inflexible in that they prescribed a plan of action that had to be closely followed. Most of the IMF and EBRD monitoring missions made political as well as economic reform recommendations to the Eastern European governments. This was in contrast with Ireland's case – when Ireland applied the Washington Consensus,[17] the Government did not face any political monitoring when applying hard economic reforms.

For Eastern Europe, the first decade of transition was dominated by 'IFIs in the driving seat'. In the late 1990s, the World Bank changed its approach and coined the phrase 'countries in the driver's seat' as a metaphor for each country's ownership of its policies. Furthermore, Eastern European countries competed directly for EU membership and economic co-operation between them was not fostered. At EU level, the policy of the biggest EU member states favouring individual Eastern European states for accession was also a factor that undermined the formulation of a clear economic strategy, especially in the laggard countries such as Bulgaria and Romania. Uncertainty surrounding Romania's accession to the EU was another factor that was often a political weapon internally, with the result that consensus policies were never formulated. A rare attempt was made to agree a 'National Pact for Education' in March 2008, but it was too little too late, as the Government that initiated the pact was out of power by the end of the year and only a fraction of the political signatories held seats after the parliamentary elections in November 2008.

Education, Migration and Human Capital

There was a contrast in the perception of the quality of education and quality of economy across Eastern Europe, and in Romania, after 1989. Like most of its neighbours, Romania produced a high number of science graduates as the communist system encouraged technology education to support the regime's plans for industrial self-sufficiency. Therefore, in the initial stages of transition, human capital in Romania was very attractive to foreign investors for three reasons: the workforce had a strong science background and linguistic ability; the labour force was cheap compared to workforce costs in Western Europe and Romania; and, finally, the former Soviet Bloc bordered the EU and thus its workforce was accessible.

The skills of the Eastern European workforce were well fitted for the manufacturing sector, in particular the automotive and textile industries. As all these factors were characteristics of the labour force during the economic transition, retraining and new skills were not high on the political agenda.

Table 7.1: Global Competitiveness Rankings

Country	2009–10 Rank	2008–09 Rank	Institutions	Heath and Primary Education	Innovation
Ireland	25	22	19	10	20
Czech Republic	31	33	62	33	26
Hungary	58	62	76	53	61
Romania*	64	68	84	63	75
Bulgaria	76	76	116	58	89
Poland	46	53	66	35	46

*Romania scores 86th in the rankings for basic competitiveness requirements.
Source: World Economic Forum, The Global Competitiveness Report 2009–2010, available at: <http://www.weforum.org>.

It was only as the country sought to expand its services sector that the need for new skills became apparent. Romania remains a highly uncompetitive market and a principal reason for this is the lack of innovation and investment in education. Table 7.1 illustrates Romania's ranking in a random selection of CEECs as well as against Ireland. In 2009, 20 of the 27 EU member states were in the global top 50 for competitiveness out of a total of 133 countries. Romania's rank as sixty-fourth was just above the halfway mark, and in innovation the country ranks towards the bottom of the league.

Similarly, according to the Programme for International Student Assessment (PISA) – the three-yearly appraisal of fifteen-year-olds in the principal industrialised countries, organised by the Organisation for Economic Co-operation and Development (OECD) economic grouping – Romania scores badly (see Table 7.2 below). Romania's overall score is 23 per cent below the OECD average and this illustrates the lack of education reform undertaken in the country in the past 20 years.

Table 7.2: PISA Scores* – 2006

Country	2006 Overall Rank	2006 Score	2006 Overall Rank	2006 Score
Ireland	15	508	5	517
Czech Republic	12	513	22	483
Hungary	19	504	23	482
Romania**	44	418	44	396
Bulgaria	40	434	42	402
Poland	22	498	7	508

*The scores show results on the science scale and reading proficiency (scores based on an OECD average of 500).
**Romania scores 86th in the rankings for basic competitiveness requirements.
Source: OECD, PISA 2006: Science Competencies for Tomorrow's World, available at: <http://www.pisa.oecd.org>.

Table 7.3: Population Changes in Ireland and Romania

Year	Irish Population	Year	Romanian Population
1979	3,368,217	1977	21,559,910
1981	3,443,405	n/a	n/a
1986	3,540,643	n/a	n/a
1991	3,525,719	1992	22,810,035
1996	3,626,087	n/a	n/a
2002	3,917,203	2002	21,698,181
2006	4,239,848	2006	n/a

Source: Data based on Central Statistics Office, 2006 Census and historical data, available at: <http://www.cso.ie/census/documents/PDR%20Tables%201-10.pdf> and from the National Institute of Statistics, Romania, available at: <http://www.insse.ro>.

Due to the drop in the quality of education and the lack of highly skilled jobs in Romania, the adjustment of the workforce was achieved (as in most labour intensive economies such as Poland) through large-scale workforce migration (Table 7.3).

Generally, the CEECs were more severely affected by the migration of their workforce than Ireland (Table 7.4). The rate of migration was linked to economic recovery – the longer it took the economy to return to growth, the higher the number of migrants. Romania registered one of the highest

Table 7.4: Population Migration from Romania 1990–2006

Year	Migrant Numbers
1991	44,160
1992	31,152
1993	18,446
1994	17,146
1995	25,675
1996	21,526
1997	19,945
1998	17,536
1999	12,594
2000	14,753
2001	9,921
2002	8,154
2003	10,673
2004	13,082
2005	10,938
2006	14,597

Source: National Institute of Statistics, Romania, 'Statistical Yearbook: Population', available at: <http://www.insse.ro/cms/files/pdf/ro/cap2.pdf>.

migration levels in Eastern Europe – in the period 1990 to 2002, it was estimated that the population decreased by 10 per cent due to migration.[18]

Despite slight differences between Romania and Ireland, the nature of the migration problem was essentially the same: the economy was not competitive enough to attract as much demand for its output and lacked the production capacity to employ its entire available workforce. Perhaps most important of all was the mismatch between the skills of the workforce and the market demand. When growth started to return around 2001, the Romanian governments started to consider bringing back some of the skilled migrants by introducing some financial incentives. In Romania, the first tentative policy on this issue was initiated by Adrian Nastase's Government in 2002, but without success. Another attempt was made in 2005 by Emil Boc, the current prime minister but then mayor of Cluj-Napoca. In 2005, Boc announced that the Irish Government was helping the Romanian authorities through an institutional mechanism to bring back some of the two million Romanians working abroad. Again, the initiative was abortive and so far no politician has devised a credible plan to incentivise migrant workers to return.

The return of the labour force is an important subject in today's Romania for a number of reasons. First, there is the problem of macroeconomic stability. High economic growth between 2000 and 2008 has brought Romania from high unemployment to a tight labour market, without a transition period to adjust demand of labour to output. This has pushed wages higher than productivity with negative effects on inflation and ultimately on the current account deficit. Second, it encouraged low-skilled immigration to Romania, especially from Asia, in sectors with the lowest wages – textiles and construction – but not in the sectors with the highest growth rate, such as the automotive industry.

In the Irish case, the migratory trend had reversed only after the country reached convergence with the EU average in the mid-1990s and when the population was growing yearly at an average rate of 1 per cent. Based on the Irish experience, it would be fair to conclude that the new EU members such as Romania will continue to face an outward migration of their workforce, even during an economic boom, until living standards in the home country approach the EU average. The need for CEECs to reform their education system to offset this trend therefore remains pressing.

The social cost of transition had been especially high in those economies where there were large industrial sectors, such as the economies of Poland, Slovakia, Bulgaria and Romania. The reason behind this was that the planned communist-era economy computed the necessary set of skills of the labour force as a result of the input–output table of the economy. Thus, talent, innate skills and demand-driven inclinations were not considered. In addition, due to their geographical position, workers in Romania and Bulgaria had less opportunities to have regular access to the labour market in the EU and hence to learn new skills, in contrast with the case of Poles, Czechs, Slovaks and Hungarians.

Unlike CEECs, where education was almost ignored during economic reform, in Ireland there were two reform waves in education – in the 1960s and then again in the early 1990s – which resulted in an educational system that was focused on skills creation. The 1960s reform marked two essential new lines in the way education was considered in society and in the policy mix. Education became the main avenue for investment in human capital.

This new approach towards the workforce, now seen not only as wage earners but also as capital to bring future benefits, was essential in organising the curricula based on what skills would be in demand in the future. Second, investment in human capital became a strategic objective, was part of the national planning process, later to be included in the National Action Plan, and was financed from EU structural funds. In the CEECs, education is still considered just another item of the general consolidated budget, choked by the powerful vested interests of the teachers' trade unions. In Romania, 80 per cent of the total budget of education is allocated to the teachers' wages with the rest directed to material expenditures. This does not allow much room for reform in education, as the most important actor is the teacher and not the result of the education process.

The Irish educational reform was centred on two points: a focus on the education process as the acquisition of skills and on the skills needed by the future workforce. The 1960s reform pressed on the first point, while the 1990s reform was instrumental in delivering a workforce capable of increasing productivity and, ultimately, of delivering the 'Irish miracle'. Education reform, and the Irish experience of it, is the latest subject to be discussed in the CEECs, and also the only reform with the chance of being successful as it will be an entirely domestically designed and implemented project. Presently in Romania there is a continuous debate surrounding a new education law. Furthermore, parents are more and more concerned about the way school curricula are set and what skills their children are going to acquire through education. This bottom-up approach to education reform might lengthen the adjustment period but it is more likely to be successful because it will have the largest possible support.

Structural Funds

The 'Irish miracle' became the subject of the day in the CEECs at the beginning of the 2000s for a number of reasons: accession to the EU became ever closer and therefore catching up with developed Europe was no longer seen as a mere dream; the Irish had been very successful at attracting EU funds and their success was made an example of by the European Commission; the EU itself was interested in the efficient use of pre-accession and structural funds because it underlined its commitment to an enlarged EU. But Ireland invested the nearly £10 billion it received in EU structural funds wisely, with much going towards improving the island's infrastructure. For their part, the ten CEECs wanted to be as successful as Ireland in using EU funds because they represented a free source of capital to be used in order to finish the process of economic restructuring.

This aside, their ability to absorb EU funds was an indication of their institutional capacity as well as their ability to achieve convergence with the EU. Although the CEEC governments were aware that not all of Ireland's economic success was the result of its use of structural funds, they acknowledged that Ireland's ambition for a 'maximum draw' was part of its economic success. This, therefore, became a strategic objective in order to achieve the target of convergence. Ireland took a very pragmatic approach to structural funds and viewed it as a source of capital for a large-scale investment project – the modernisation of the country.

The Irish way of using the structural funds was more effective in allotting finance to a project. Thus, under a specific priority, any investment was certified to use structural funds without going through the usual hoops of the EU administration. Instead, the finance for each project was allocated from the general government budget. The advantages of this approach were twofold: more finance became available for projects that fell within the set of priorities agreed for the country and the procedure of granting finance was much faster, almost replicating the speed of the private sector in approving a transaction.

This unique approach that Ireland applied was not easily replicable in the CEECs for three reasons, which are all linked to the Irish authorities' strategies in using structural funds. First, the central public authorities kept only the role of co-ordinator and paying authority without any other parallel administration for these funds. This was possible because the coordinator had already a specified project to finance and did not have to choose between hundreds of projects in every operational programme, which would have required more expertise and personnel. Moreover, financial control was exactly the same as for government-funded projects. By contrast, the CEECs had to adopt several sector operational programmes under which hundreds of small projects were subscribed. In Romania, this meant that a new management structure was set up to oversee all the ministries which were to use structural funds. Moreover, the Ministry of Finance was part of this new management structure, with the role of deciding on each project as well as that of the paying authority, with the same staff dedicated to both tasks. This increases the risk of conflict of interests.

Second, the Irish model was based on the fact that the entire project was funded from the budget by advancing money to the beneficiaries and then recouping it from the EU. This meant that the Irish budget was able to support the entire invoice of the project. Moreover, the Irish budget was taking the risk of any non-certifiable expenditure in terms of structural funds. The CEECs cannot enjoy this leeway because they simply do not have enough money in the coffers to finance all projects. Furthermore, due to the EU's increased concerns on possible fraud and corruption, the CEEC governments have a higher risk of underwriting projects for which they would not be paid from EU funds.

Third, in Ireland the bulk of the work in designing and implementing each project was carried out at local level. Local authorities were very effective in procuring, drafting and supervising contracts. This was extremely useful for monitoring and evaluation in the constant feedback between the coordinating and implementing authorities. Furthermore, the Irish authorities used structural funds for the reform of the labour market, not least to solve the emigration problem, a problem for Ireland throughout the last century.

In the CEECs, the full focus of the structural funds is at the central level, where the projects are decided. In Romania, it takes two years on average to have a project approved at national level. The CEECs have looked up to the Irish success in using structural funds to achieve convergence, but the drawing rate for these funds is at best around 15 per cent, with forerunners like the Czech Republic with 30 per cent and laggards like Romania with 2 per cent.

Conclusion

The Irish 'catch-up' or economic miracle resulted from a combination of factors, such as achieving macroeconomic stability through a well-designed and well-executed economic programme and the existence in the late 1980s and 1990s of a consensus within society that everyone should benefit from the country's economic turnaround. In Ireland, this consensus was founded with the common goal of catching up with the living standards of the more advanced EU member states. By contrast, Romania was prescribed a macro-stabilisation programme by IFIs and its compliance with that programme was closely monitored by both IFIs and the EU to prepare it for EU accession. As yet, there is little consensus in the Romanian political community on a positive (as opposed to a responsive) objective of economic and financial reform.

Another key lesson that Romania can learn from Ireland is to invest in education, human capital and training and to take long-term strategic decisions. As former Irish Prime Minister Bertie Ahern said in 2005: 'Some people believe that Ireland joined the EU and the following morning they got up and everything was solved. We were 15 years in the EU and many things went from bad to worse. It was when we started taking the difficult decisions ourselves ... that we managed to change things around, obviously with the help of the EU.'[19] For Romania and other countries aspiring to follow Ireland's economic achievement, the Irish example is less a model to be reproduced than an example of the need for initiative.

CHAPTER 8

A Model for Egypt? Foreign Direct Investment in the Irish Economic Boom

Ashraf Mishrif

The Irish economic boom of the 1990s was truly exceptional, and has attracted much attention in developed and developing countries alike. Highly industrialised countries such as Canada have looked for lessons to learn from the Irish economic boom, particularly in areas such as education policy, employment and productivity enhancement.[1] In addition, many developing countries have also praised the Irish experience and sought means to emulate some aspects of Ireland's economic model. This chapter seeks to outline the lessons that Egypt can learn from Ireland's economic 'catch-up' during the 1990s. Indeed, the economic example of Ireland has already registered at the very highest level in Egypt – President Hosni Mubarak, during the first visit by an Egyptian head of state to Ireland in December 2006, expressed much interest in Irish economic success over the previous decade and a half.[2]

The attraction of what Ireland did right is not only that the country transformed itself from being one of Europe's poorest and least developed economies into the 'Celtic Tiger' but also that this experience has practical, potentially transferable lessons for other developing countries. For instance, as discussed elsewhere in this book, the peaceful settlement of the conflict in Northern Ireland in the decade since the signing of the Belfast (Good Friday) Agreement of April 1998 can provide valuable guidance on how to handle longstanding regional disputes such as the Arab–Israeli conflict.

A large body of literature has already examined the Irish experience from various angles, with each aiming to provide an explanation of the causes of the economic boom. To distinguish this chapter from other work, the over-arching focus here is to highlight how foreign direct investment (FDI) contributed to this success. It also stresses that the Irish economic catch-up was not a product of a one-off economic policy package, but was created and sustained by a long-term active economic policy initiative that was aimed at gaining wide access to external markets and making Ireland's domestic economy competitive by exposing it to international competition. I argue here that it was this liberal policy approach that first encouraged exports, by offering tax breaks on profits earned from international sales, and later provided the basis on which efforts were made to attract FDI into the country. In light of this, I will explore the effect of the Irish Government's open attitude towards free trade and investment on the country's economic growth, and how this growth impacted on Irish–Egyptian relations, together with the lessons that Egypt can learn from this experience.

Ireland's Pragmatic Approach to FDI

The liberal and pragmatic approach of the Irish Government towards foreign trade and investment has arguably been the key to the country's economic boom. This policy approach, formed as early as the 1950s, and its effects eventually brought about high levels of economic growth, with Gross Domestic Product (GDP) growth averaging 8 per cent between 1995 and 2000. This growth could not have been made possible without Ireland being a promoter of free trade and investment policies and the significant improvement in its business environment, which turned Ireland into an attractive location for huge FDI flows (in financial services and industry) from the US and also Europe. In realising the positive role of FDI in economic development, the Irish authorities focused on attracting FDI as a means of both overcoming the country's limited natural, physical and financial resources and as a viable solution to unemployment, which reached 17 per cent in 1987. The Irish authorities also showed an impressive ability to utilise the huge FDI inflows, which increased from US$2.6 billion in 1996 to approximately US$26.9 billion in 2003, to develop high-technology-based industries and to turn Dublin into an international financial services cluster.

Successive Irish governments also adopted a very pragmatic perspective in dealing with FDI inflows, an approach that is largely influenced by their perception of FDI as a business process rather than an economic one. The development of this perception helped to foster an entrepreneurial mind-set and business confidence among Irish public and private sector executives, who became eager to exploit business opportunities at home and abroad as evidenced by the rapid growth in Ireland's trade with the rest of the world.

The effect of this liberal and pragmatic policy has been seen in the primarily business-to-business character of Irish FDI inflows, resulting in large transactions and mega projects, while concentrating on capital-intensive industries. It also resulted in the creation of high numbers of new jobs, and had a rapid and visible impact on the country's economic and social development. This enabled Ireland to double its per capita income between 1990 and 2000 and bring the Irish standard of living up to, and indeed to surpass, British and European levels.[3] The impact of this was also notable in the development of collective capability by Irish companies in servicing the needs of foreign investors at home and in investing and trading globally. The pace of this development was seen in key sectors such as financial services, design engineering, biopharmaceuticals and electronics, with significant growth in employment in the latter sector from 92,000 in 1995 to 129,000 in 2004.[4]

One should also stress that Ireland's fostering of free trade and overseas investment was based on its accession to the European Union (EU) in 1973, the European Monetary System (EMS) in 1993 and the European Monetary Union (EMU) in 1999, thus allowing the country to benefit enormously from European financial and regional development programmes. Such external gains have also been notable in Ireland's 'special relationship' with the US, which has contributed the majority of FDI capital flows into the country since the early 1990s.

Relations with the EU and the US

Although Ireland has had 'special relationships' with Europe and the US for over half a century, it was not until the early 1990s that the country was able to capitalise on these ties in its economic development. Ireland's membership of the EU in 1973 brought about dramatic changes in the economic environment as the country had to adapt its regulatory, legal and fiscal policies to those of the EU; nevertheless, this did not lead to a change in the country's economic fortune in the ensuing twenty years.[5] In fact, it was the deepening process of European economic integration in the early 1990s that allowed Irish officials and business leaders to capitalise on their EU membership. This deepening integration process created demand conditions for international firms to exploit and Ireland was among the very first countries to take maximum advantage of this development. Given the favourable conditions in Ireland at that time and the perception of the EU's investment potential among multinational corporations following the creation of the single European market, Ireland was very well placed for international companies to get market access in the new Europe.

Meanwhile, Ireland was blessed by other favourable conditions in the global economy, namely the phenomenal growth of the US economy during the 1990s. The sustained growth of the US economy and the relative appreciation of the US dollar created a dynamic whereby US companies had a real business need and desire to invest internationally. This need was efficiently exploited by the Irish, who were not only successful in selling the comparative advantage of their country as an attractive destination for these companies but were also capable of securing a large share of the huge US capital flows directed into Europe, Asia and the Americas. This is notable in the growth levels of US investment in Ireland, which increased tenfold over the 1991–2000 period from an average of US$100 million FDI inflows between 1986 and 1991. Also, US FDI stock, which accounted for two-thirds of the total Irish FDI stock, increased by US$1 billion in 1995, US$2 billion in 1996 and US$4 billion in 1997, with most investments going into chemical, pharmaceutical, electronics and financial services sectors.

The capacity of Ireland to benefit from these two important developments was apparent in its ability to attract a huge number of US firms to exploit the tremendous business opportunities created by the process of deepening European integration. The increasing business activities of Irish firms with the US and European markets also encouraged and led to the internationalisation of many local Irish firms, some of which acquired international status in key sectors such as building materials, food ingredients, consumer food, paper and software.

This internationalisation process was encouraged by a business-oriented public policy that operated to meet the needs of local firms. The creation of Enterprise Ireland (EI) helped many Irish firms to address the availability of equity finance and support their activities overseas. This public policy approach was successful in establishing the required funds and in attracting venture capital, with over €250 million invested in some 200 early phases, mainly technology-based firms, between 1994 and 2004. It also increased the level of venture capital funds in the Irish economy, enhanced the capability of Irish firms by responding to their financial and technical needs, and supported them in their efforts to gain access to global markets.

The internal–external effect of this public policy approach was best seen in the innovative measures taken by government agencies to identify market opportunities and to establish Irish companies in key international locations such as Silicon Valley, New York and Tokyo, where the provision of office space, to give just one example of support, helped Irish executives to focus on international business development rather than spending their time on preliminary market research and securing leases in new markets.

The impact of the internationalisation of the Irish economy was also positive in terms of the number of foreign companies operating in Ireland, which account for approximately 25 per cent of GDP, 50 per cent of manufacturing employment, 75 per cent of manufacturing output and 85 per cent of merchandise exports.[6] This resulted in an extraordinary boost to business expectations and profitability in Ireland, most notably in the 30 per cent return on capital from US investment in the country, compared to 10 per cent in the rest of Europe. This enabled Ireland not only to attract the largest share of 20 per cent of US capital flows to Europe between 1993 and 2000, but also accelerated FDI from the EU, extending the non-inflationary phase of the employment boom to the end of the 1990s.[7]

The Irish Economic Boom of the 1990s

From 1993 until the global downturn in mid-2008, Ireland experienced rapid and sustained economic growth and was considered one of the fastest growing economies worldwide. The key to this growth was the huge FDI inflows, which increased by 1034 per cent from US$2.6 billion in 1996 to approximately US$26.9 billion in 2003. Ireland also became a net exporter of FDI capital flows, with outflows of €12.7 billion exceeding inflows by €3.6 billion in 2004. These international business activities not only made the Irish economy much more dynamic than ever before but also accelerated its integration in the global economic system.

While the beneficial effect of Irish economic growth was notable across the entire economy, developments in the industrial and financial sectors were most exceptional. The concentration of between one-third and one-half of Ireland's FDI inflows in Dublin's International Financial Services Centre (IFSC) boosted economic activities and increased the total value of Irish domiciled funds to US$500 billion (total funds serviced, including non-domiciled funds, reached US$768 billion) in 2005 from US$21 billion ten years earlier.[8] This provided the Irish Government with the capital needed for the implementation of national development programmes.

Inward investment also led to the creation of an export-oriented and high-skilled Irish industrial sector based on high technology manufacturing such as electronics, health care and pharmaceuticals. According to EI, thirteen of the top fifteen world pharmaceutical companies set up major operations in Ireland, and six out of the ten of world's top selling drugs are produced in Ireland, with annual exports exceeding €35 billion and over 17,000 people directly employed. The information and communication technology (ICT) sector also hosted seven of the world's top ten ICT companies such as IBM, Intel, Hewlett Packard, Dell, Oracle, Lotus and Microsoft, with annual exports exceeding €21 billion and direct employment of around 45,000 people.

More generally, the socio-economic impact of Irish economic growth was profound during the 1990s.[9] This was notable in the rate of unemployment, which fell from 16 per cent in 1993 to 3.5 per cent in 2001. Ireland was very successful in accommodating labour market changes, and in particular in involving effective use of the previously unemployed, women and immigrants.

Ireland was also successful in maintaining the social partnership introduced in 1987, which was accompanied by peaceful industrial relations so that the share of wages in gross domestic income declined sharply and the share of capital income rose to an unprecedented level. The share of labour income as a part of GDP fell to 42 per cent in 1998 from 52 per cent in 1986. Together with other measures, including wage moderation, this resulted in impressive business profitability and created a powerful incentive for domestic and foreign firms to do business and create jobs in Ireland.[10]

Ireland also exhibited an enhanced productivity performance that was created and sustained by its policy-welcoming attitude and favourable industrial policy towards FDI.[11] It is argued that South Korea was the only country that experienced faster productivity growth than Ireland among the Organisation for Economic Co-operation and Development (OECD) countries since 1975, but Irish productivity, which averaged 3.3 per cent per annum, exceeded that of most other countries and even challenged US productivity levels.[12] This was partly caused by the continued shift of economic activities and employment from the primary sector to the secondary and tertiary sectors, thus alleviating pressure from the Irish primary sector, which now employs only 9 per cent of Irish workers, compared to 40 per cent in 1960.

Also, Irish productivity was enhanced by tax and education policies supportive of business investment, stable and transparent legal and administrative systems, incentives to invest in peripheral regions, and improvements in transport and communication infrastructure. Irish corporate tax, which stands at a single corporate tax of 12.5 per cent for the entire corporate sector since 2003, has been among the lowest and most attractive to local and foreign companies. Investment in secondary and post-secondary education in the 1970s and 1980s provided solid support for the labour market, while the supply of well-educated young workers, and availability of short and more applied courses in the education system helped productivity as well.[13]

Ireland's Economic Relations with Egypt

Since Ireland's accession to the European Economic Community (EEC) in 1973, Irish–Egyptian economic relations have developed through a number of collaborative policy frameworks within the Euro-Mediterranean framework. The EEC's Global Mediterranean Policy of 1972 provided a regional platform for bilateral trade relations between Cairo and Dublin. The EC–Egypt Cooperation Agreement of 1977 was incomprehensive and thus economic relations centred mainly on the trade of basic goods and commodities, particularly the export of Irish beef to Egyptian markets. This limited scope of co-operation has changed since the mid-1990s, when both the Irish and the Egyptians became increasingly eager to integrate in the global economy and take advantage of the growing trends of globalisation, the ongoing process by which regional economies, societies and cultures have become increasingly integrated, and regionalisation, where there is a strong regional focus on developing networks and ties.

The political and economic changes that occurred after the fall of the Berlin Wall and the collapse of Communism in East and Central Europe provided another opportunity for Ireland and Egypt to open up their economic systems and liberalise their trade and investment regimes. Although the two countries launched their own economic reform and liberalisation programmes, the Euro-Mediterranean Partnership, also known as the Barcelona Process of 1995 – which now includes all 27 member states of the European Union along with 16 partners across the Southern Mediterranean and the Middle East in discussions and negotiations over economic, political and cultural issues of common concern – served as a new platform for Egypt and Ireland to develop their economic, political and cultural relations.[14] The liberal and outward approach of Irish investors was seen in practical terms in Egypt in the early stages of the Irish economic boom, with an investment worth US$250,000 made in a textiles factory in the Egyptian free (trade) zones in 1994. Since then, Ireland has emerged as a new European investor in Egypt, with total FDI stock worth US$46.2 million accumulated in non-petroleum sectors by 2008. The pattern of Irish FDI is not dramatically different from that of other EU investors. Ireland has invested 86.5 per cent of its total FDI in two large investments in Egypt, amounting to US$15 million and US$25 million in 1997 and 1999, respectively. This level of investment placed Ireland ahead of Austria,

Greece, Portugal, Sweden and Finland as major European investors in Egypt between 1994 and 2004.[15]

In the past decade, Irish and Egyptian officials and business leaders have been active in their attempts to develop bilateral ties and build institutional channels that are capable of fostering business relations.[16] The London-based Egyptian British Chamber of Commerce has regularly held conferences and workshops to bring together business communities in Egypt and Ireland and inform them of the available business opportunities. Such efforts have led to a notable Irish contribution to the flagship Smart Village Pyramids project, which in 2003 established Egypt's first business park dedicated to information technology. This project was followed by the setting up of an Egyptian information technology marketing support office in Dublin in the same year. This office created the brand 'Software from Egypt' on behalf of nine of Egypt's leading offshore software developers.

Irish investment has also been notable in infrastructural projects such as power stations, and biopharmaceutical and oil-related industries. As Ireland does not produce oil, there are numerous opportunities for greater co-operation in Egypt's petroleum and natural gas sectors, and related industries such as biochemicals and petrochemicals.[17] Egypt's comparative advantages in a number of key industries such as textiles and clothing may stimulate the interest of Irish firms in investing in Egypt, an opportunity that would not only attract substantial amounts of Irish capital flows but would also allow Egypt to foster links with successful Irish firms that could be useful for providing insights into rapid economic development.

The 'Irish Catch-Up Model' and Egypt's Economic Future

Why is the Irish model of economic development important for Egypt? The simple answer is that the dynamics and the nature of the Irish economic approach and policies, as well as the latter's implementation, have differed considerably from the approach of Egypt, and are also potentially transferable to the current Egyptian economic context.

Unlike Ireland, a lack of openness and consistency in Egypt's economic reforms minimised the success of liberalisation programmes of the 1970s and the 1990s, while the country was unable to capitalise on its political and economic ties with Europe and the US to improve its economic and social conditions. It is also apparent that Egypt's economic policies, which are characterised as being semi-capitalist, centrally planned, socially oriented, planned for the short-term and inconsistent with the norms of economic liberalism, differed greatly from Ireland's policy approach towards free trade and investment. The nature of Egypt's economic liberalisation between 1974 and 2004 highlighted the failure of the Government to attract substantial amounts of FDI, develop an export oriented policy or balance a mix of policies based on export orientation and import substitutions.

During the 1990s, Egypt and Ireland were marked by similarities and differences in their economic policies and reforms. They introduced comprehensive programmes of economic reform and liberalisation and strengthened ties with major trading partners, particularly in Europe and the US. The initiation and implementation of these programmes were successful but their final outcomes differed considerably. Ireland managed to transform itself from one of Europe's poorest countries into the Celtic Tiger, a step that marked the country's final transition from a developing to fully developed economy.

Meanwhile, Egypt's attempt at economic reform, aimed at restoring the country's credibility after the financial crisis of the late 1980s, succeeded in improving its macroeconomic indicators, but until 2007 failed to bring Egypt's real GDP up to 7 per cent per annum, the level needed to sustain economic growth and create sufficient jobs for the 635,000 people entering the labour market every year.[18]

However, largely because it has adopted a more investment-intensive focus in the last five years, Egypt has made a remarkable recovery in its economic growth, with real GDP averaging 7 per cent in 2008 for the second consecutive year, the highest recorded level since the early 1980s. FDI inflows also reached a record high, getting to US$11 billion in 2007 compared to US$237 million in 2003. Egypt also narrowed its trade deficit with the EU, its main trading partner, with Egyptian exports increasing from US$1.3 billion in 2003 to US$9.2 billion in 2008; while the trade deficit slightly increased in the EU's favour from US$4.4billion in 1999 to US$5.1 billion in 2008. Non-oil exports also surged by 53 per cent year-on-year, while tourism, a major economic sector, recorded a 4.5 per cent increase in terms of visitor numbers.[19]

This is an outstanding performance that indicates the capacity of Egypt to become a potential economic success.[20] The possibility of achieving this depends, however, largely on the capacity of the country to sustain the current rate of economic growth over the next decade, while developing and implementing a comprehensive set of industrial, financial, fiscal, tax and education policies that are conducive to a significant increase in FDI inflows and an improvement in the country's social and economic conditions.

Egypt is now at a crossroads. Government officials are trying hard to move the country on from its past experience of underperformance and a lack of sustainability in economic growth by looking to associate the country with a group of leading emerging markets. Egypt's success in achieving advanced economic development status hangs on its ability to seek the means to boost its current phase of economic growth and to benefit from the lessons of those other countries that have successfully achieved this.

The first and foremost factor, as far as the lessons that the Irish experience can teach Egypt are concerned, is the importance of immediate and full liberalisation of trade and investment regimes that allows Egypt to integrate into the global economic system and improves its competitiveness in domestic and global markets. This will enable Egypt to benefit tremendously when internal and external economic conditions become favourable. As events in Ireland have shown, though the economic boom did not take place until the 1990s, it was the positive policy approach towards free trade and investment, which began in the early 1950s, that contributed to this boom when the global economic conditions became favourable in the US and the EU.

Egypt's wider public policy agenda should also be shaped by the need to develop a market-oriented economy, while maintaining an outward-oriented economic system. Egypt should capitalise on the large number of bilateral and multilateral investment agreements, which exceeded a hundred agreements in 2007, in order to accelerate technological innovation and diffusion in the domestic economy. This may allow specialisation to take place by reaching the relevant economies of scale, guarantee access to international markets and strengthen the competitiveness of domestic firms by subjecting them to stimulating international competition.

Also, the introduction of new fiscal policies and structural reforms to tame inflation, and the launch of privatisation programmes and new business legislation can help the jump to a more market-oriented economy capable of supporting the influx of FDI, which increased above the Government's own expectations over the past two years.[21] The new policies may create the basis for a more competitive domestic market and make Egypt even more attractive to foreign investors. What is most needed now is the promotion of export-oriented FDI projects that are capable of enhancing Egypt's exporting capability and of speeding up the pace of the development process, especially in finance and manufacturing, through the transfer of knowledge and technology from globally competitive companies to the country's private and public sectors.

Egypt should make an effective utilisation of its inward and outward FDI flows as major sources of gross domestic capital formation. The Irish experience provides an exceptional model for a country such as Egypt with capital scarcity and inefficient allocation of national resources to overcome its limited natural and physical resources. Ireland has not only been able to attract huge amounts of foreign capital flows but also to diffuse them effectively into the national economy, making the country a global manufacturing and financial services cluster. This now seems possible in Egypt as the country's investment policies have become FDI-friendly in key sectors such as manufacturing, telecommunications and information technology.

The Egyptian Government needs to realise that economic growth should go hand in hand with socio-economic development and that the former has to be reflected in the living standards and conditions of its people. Such a realisation could help Egypt to avoid a repeat of the hugely embarrassing and tragic food crisis of March 2008, which saw several people die at a time of high economic growth approaching 8 per cent.

Given all this, Egypt could learn from what the Irish did right in the 1990s.

FDI plays a pivotal role in job creation. The successful emulation and implementation of key aspects of Irish employment policy can be useful to Egypt, which is currently struggling to accommodate around 635,000 graduates and new entrants into the labour market every year. Although unemployment is a major challenge for the Egyptian Government, the country seems to exhibit a positive trend in allocating FDI in labour-intensive industries such as manufacturing, infrastructure and tourism.[22] It is now the responsibility of the Government to seek appropriate policies, like many of those adopted in Ireland in the past decade and a half, to ensure that an aggregate supply can accommodate non-inflationary aggregate demand expansion, with the objective of reducing its unemployment rate of 10 per cent by almost half.

The FDI Factor, Ireland and the Credit Crunch

The globalisation of the Irish economy that led to the subsequent economic boom of the 1990s made the country vulnerable to external shocks such as the global financial and economic crisis that originated in the US with the subprime mortgage crisis. Ireland was among the first to be hit by this crisis.

This was evident in Ireland's housing sector, and its crash had wider repercussions for the broader economy, with many construction companies slashing jobs and major multinationals – Pfizer, Procter & Gamble, Motorola, Vodafone and Allergan – making substantial job cuts in recent times.

From a FDI perspective, the impact of the global economic slowdown and recession in major developed economies has led to a sudden decline of 20 per cent in global FDI flows in 2008 from its historic record of US$1.8 trillion in the previous year. The impact of this decrease was felt intensely in Ireland, whose inward investment fell by 120.1 per cent compared to the average fall of 33 per cent in developed countries in the same period.[23]

The divestment of US$6.1 billion from the Irish economy since the start of the credit crunch was primarily due to giant technology and pharmaceutical companies such as Intel, Microsoft, Amgen and Wyeth, with the latter company shelving plans to build a US$1 billion manufacturing plant in Cork in 2008. All of these companies had not only been responsible for pumping huge amounts into the local economies where they operated but also added to the Celtic Tiger brand as a major recipient of FDI.

Egypt was less affected than Ireland by the global financial crisis. This has been due largely to the low level of dependency on foreign investment in economic development and the limited integration of the Egyptian economy into the global economy. Egypt's share of inward investment declined by only 5.6 per cent, from US$11.6 billion to US$10.9 billion in 2008, while the country's GDP remained above 7 per cent for the second consecutive year. Although this is likely to decrease below 5 per cent for 2009 and possibly 2010, Egypt's ability to attract inward investment will continue to grow as long as the country remains committed to economic liberalisation and free market economy.

The Irish experience over the last two years, like the Asian financial crisis of 1997, shows that it is too risky to be overly reliant on foreign investment without consolidating national fixed capital formation and strengthening the foundations of the national economy. It also shows that it is essential for the country to diversify the sources of capital flows by equally targeting foreign investment from the Arab states, Europe, the US and Asian emerging markets. These factors can reduce the risk of sudden external shocks to the national economy and maintain the pace of economic growth at sustainable rates.

Conclusion

During the 1990s, Ireland showed an extraordinary ability to achieve high rates of economic growth, raise its living standards to well beyond the European average and transform itself from one of Europe's poorest countries into the Celtic Tiger. Despite the recent downturn, this achievement is exceptional by all economic and social standards and could serve as an exemplary model for many developing countries. The Irish experience shows that FDI plays a pivotal role in economic growth, and thus remains a key factor in a nation's economic development.

However, this depends largely on the ability of a government to utilise FDI inflows in increasing the country's domestic capital formation in order to overcome capital scarcity and limited physical and human resources, and to translate these investments into socio-economic development, particularly employment generation.

Not all the factors responsible for the Irish economic boom can be emulated. What is crucial and what should be considered seriously by all countries is the importance of adopting a liberal and pragmatic policy approach towards free trade and investment. The Irish experience has shown that a liberal and outward-looking economic system helped Ireland to attract more capital investments and achieve high levels of economic growth when the internal and external economic conditions became favourable during the 1990s.

Although Egypt has made a remarkable recovery in its economic growth in recent years, the Irish catch-up model can still provide lessons and insights for policy-makers on how to achieve sustainable economic growth and improve the country's socio-economic conditions. If Egypt is to become a potential economic tiger it should aim at promoting, attracting and utilising FDI in its economic development process, increasing its gross domestic capital formation and improving its economic, productivity and employment performances as bases for the country's future sustainable economic growth.

CHAPTER 9

Ireland, Israel and the Challenges of Innovation and Entrepreneurship

Yanky Fachler

Innovation policy is closely connected with economic growth, and any developed country wishing to compete in the modern world must make the promotion of entrepreneurship and innovation a national priority.[1] Innovation and entrepreneurship lead to new companies that produce jobs and wealth, and the diffusion of technology into industry gives rise to productivity increases.[2] Innovation also nurtures a culture of devising new and better products, processes and services, of embracing the rapid pace of technological change, and of encouraging the convergence of seemingly different technologies.[3]

Across the globe, cutting-edge innovators and entrepreneurs are leading the charge towards a culture of transforming ideas into economic opportunities.[4] These individuals know that only innovative, entrepreneurial, adaptive and zestful companies will survive the inevitable shake-out of the current global downturn. As business strategy guru Gary Hamel succinctly states, the challenge facing the business world is to innovate or become irrelevant.[5]

Within the broader context of the global race towards greater competitiveness, two countries stand out for their enthusiastic pursuit of policies aimed at encouraging entrepreneurship and innovation: Ireland and Israel. Politicians and pundits, captains of industry and business commentators, and economists and industrialists frequently dwell on the similarities – and the differences – between the Irish and the Israeli economies. For at least the last two decades, there have been sufficient parallels between Ireland and

Israel to ensure that leaders at all levels of the economy – government ministries, employers' organisations, trade unions and chambers of commerce – in each country have been looking to see if there is anything to be learned from the experience of the other.[6]

A useful starting point for any discussion on the comparison between Ireland and Israel, and the lessons of the Irish experience for the latter, is the period in the mid-1980s when both economies were suffering as the result of disastrous fiscal policies. From the early 1980s, the Israeli economy was experiencing constant upheaval. Finance ministers came and went, and while in office they often reversed their predecessors' policies. The result was rampant inflation which grew from an average of less than 10 per cent per year in the mid-to-late 1960s to nearly 500 per cent by the end of the first half of 1985. In July of that year, the Israeli National Unity Government adopted a comprehensive emergency programme for stabilisation and recovery. Within a few months of the adoption of this programme, in which the Histadrut Labour Federation – the major trade union body in Israel which was founded in 1920 and developed into one of the most powerful institutions in the state in subsequent decades – agreed to a wage freeze, inflation was down to a manageable 1–2 per cent a month.[7]

The situation in the Ireland of the early 1980s was not much better. Unemployment had reached 20 per cent, the national debt was 130 per cent of gross domestic product (GDP), there was negative migration and the tax burden stood at 60 per cent. In 1986, Ireland's National Economic and Social Council (NESC) devised a strategy that pulled the country out of stagnation, high taxation and debt. The *Programme for National Recovery* was a social partnership agreement between the Government, employers and employees for a wage freeze, budget cuts and the diversion of state resources to reduce the external debt burden.[8]

The remedial measures taken by both countries broadly succeeded. With similar populations and almost identical levels of per capita income, Ireland and Israel both turned the corner in the direction of soaring growth rates, strong domestic demand and rising asset prices. By the 1990s, both countries were being described as the two most dynamic economies on Europe's cluttered periphery.[9]

The rapid economic growth experienced by Ireland earned the Irish economy the title Celtic Tiger. During the period of Ireland's so-called 'economic miracle', the country was transformed from one of Europe's poorer countries into one of its wealthiest. A significant factor has been the openness of the Irish economy, its strong links to the US, and its membership of the EU. Between 1990 and 1995, the Irish economy grew at an annual average rate of 4.8 per cent, and between 1995 and 2000 it averaged 9.5 per cent. Growth rates then remained in the 4–6 per cent range, a level three times higher than the average for the original fifteen members of the EU. On a per capita basis, Ireland succeeded in attracting huge inward investment in both absolute terms and as a percentage of GDP. Ireland has consistently topped the 30-member Organisation for Economic Co-operation and Development (OECD) economic growth tables, often by a substantial margin.[10]

A combination of factors contributed to this sudden emergence of Ireland on the world economic stage: the establishment of flexible business practices, the reduction in red tape across the economy, fiscal discipline and low corporate taxes to inward investors.[11] Other factors include an English-speaking workforce; a youthful population; a rapidly expanding labour supply; substantial inward investment inflows; the strategic deployment of EU structural and cohesion funds; the pursuit of pragmatic and innovative government policies; and a social partnership approach to economic development. The Celtic Tiger led to soaring levels of disposable income, plummeting unemployment, reduced public debt, the initiation of major infrastructure projects, a reversal of the net emigration pattern that had been such a feature of Irish life for decades, and a dramatic reduction in days lost to industrial disputes.[12] In the first years of the twenty-first century, Ireland was consistently in the top five countries in the AT Kearney/ Foreign Policy Globalization Index. In 2002, 2003 and 2004, Ireland was in first place. In 2005, Ireland was in second place, in 2006 in fourth place, and in 2007 in fifth place.[13]

In Israel, too, the late twentieth century and the early twenty-first century saw the economy soar. World-beating technologies had their geneses in Israeli research and development (R&D): Disk-on-key technology, Internet Protocol (IP) telephony, Zip compression, the ingestible pill-size camera, modern drip-irrigation technology and ICQ instant messenger are just some of the Israeli breakthroughs.[14] Leading multinationals such as Microsoft, Berkshire-Hathaway, Motorola, Intel, Hewlett Packard, Siemens, Samsung, General Electric, Philips, Lucent, AOL, Cisco, Applied Materials, Winbond, IBM and Johnson & Johnson run core R&D activities in Israel.[15] In 2008, both Moody's Investor Service[16] and the Standard & Poor Rating Service[17] lifted Israel's key ratings to reflect the country's proven resilience in the face of global and local economic and political shocks. According to Dow Jones VentureSource, the top four economies, after the US, in attracting venture capital for start-ups in the first quarter of 2008 were: Europe (US$1.53 billion), China (US$719 million), Israel (US$572 million) and India

(US$99 million). Israel, with 7 million people, attracted almost as much venture capital for start-ups as China with its population of 1.3 billion.[18]

In 2007, Israeli companies occupied the first, second and third spots in the Deloitte Touche 'Fast 500' list of the fastest growing firms in the technology, media and telecommunications industries in Europe, the Middle East and Asia.[19] When INSEAD, the European graduate business school renowned for its entrepreneurship studies programmes, announced that it was establishing an international academic research centre in Israel, only the second campus outside France, it cited Israel's vast and long-term success in entrepreneurship and business initiatives.[20] A global analysis of university biotechnology transfer and commercialisation ranked the Hebrew University in Jerusalem in twelfth place among the world's top universities, based on the number of patents and their impact on biotechnology developments, scientific research and technology cycle time. This was ahead of Yale, Oxford and Johns Hopkins University.[21]

But while the trajectories towards the successes of the Israeli and Irish economies were similar, the policies that helped each country achieve such dizzy heights were very different. In Israel's case, the Government made a strategic decision to develop a domestic industrial sector. Ireland, which could almost be described as pre-industrial in the 1980s, saw little chance that a domestic industrial sector could lead the country out of its economic doldrums. The Irish Government therefore opted to woo EU and US multinationals.[22]

While both countries realised that to become more competitive they would need to focus on science and technology, Ireland's policies were driven primarily by the need for job creation. Ireland successfully wooed multinationals to open manufacturing plants, but much of the annual high-tech exports came from US companies which did not embed in the local community. The software was developed in the US, and Ireland was used primarily as a distribution hub. Because Irish companies tended to seek applications for technologies developed elsewhere, there was relatively little accompanying added value or technological innovation.[23]

Israel's policies were driven by a very different priority: the need for self-reliance in the high-tech defence industry. Ever since the French placed an arms embargo on Israel following the 'Six Day' Arab–Israeli War of 1967, the country has made a priority of creating new industries, with an emphasis on home-grown new product innovation. Generations of engineers cut their teeth on defence projects while doing their military service. When they left the army, they diverted their skills to commercial projects.[24] Thomas Friedman, who examined the new globalised world of the twenty-first century in his best-selling *The World Is Flat*,[25] describes Israel as a country that is 'hard-wired to compete in a flat world'.[26]

While Ireland was a pacemaker in the art of attracting inward financial investment, Israel has also had its successes. A recent example was the US$4 billion sale in 2006 of an 80 per cent stake in Israeli toolmaker Iscar Metalworking to American investor Warren Buffett's Berkshire Hathaway. This was the largest ever buy-out of an Israeli company, and the first non-US acquisition ever for Buffet's investment company. Both in Israel and abroad, this acquisition was seen as a seminal event that placed Israel firmly on the international map for future investments, the more so because it was a traditional business, not a hi-tech industry, that had been sold.[27]

But what makes the Iscar sale so noteworthy is that, even while Israel's political and business leaders were celebrating this breakthrough investment, they were looking over their shoulders at Ireland. When then acting Prime Minister Ehud Olmert praised the deal as providing great momentum in the Israeli economy, he felt strangely under pressure from another small country thousands of kilometres away. 'Israel is in a very competitive place compared to other places in the world,' he said, 'including Ireland'.[28] Earlier, Ireland also loomed large on the horizons of then Israeli Finance Minister Benjamin Netanyahu (the current prime minister) during his tenure between 2003 and 2005. He predicted that, within a decade, Israel would rise up the global GDP per capita table from twenty-ninth place to a place in the top ten. When it was pointed out to him that, even with a 5 per cent per annum increase, it would take a minimum of fifteen years to reach such lofty heights, Netanyahu responded by saying that Ireland had almost tripled its per capita GDP in just a dozen years.[29]

Following Netanyahu's strong endorsement of the Irish economy as a model for Israel, Isaac Herzog, then Labour Party whip, and Amir Peretz, then chairman of the Histadrut Labour Federation, embarked on a fact-finding mission to the Emerald Isle (where Herzog's late father, former President of Israel Chaim Herzog, grew up) in 2007. They were very impressed by Ireland's social partnership, with its high level co-operation between government and employers, workers and social organisations.[30] In October 2007, a high-level delegation representing Israeli employers and trade unions visited Ireland to study the model of social partnership in consultation with senior politicians and civil servants. In fact, between 1999 and 2008, nineteen high level Israeli delegations made official visits to Ireland.

Envious glances have not been the monopoly of the Israelis. Ireland, too, has begun to look at Israel as a model to emulate, with eight senior Irish delegations making official visits to Israel over the last decade. Two books published in Ireland in the early twenty-first century both tackled the challenges facing Ireland as it comes to the end of the Celtic Tiger era and looks to find ways of sustaining its economic achievements. Both books suggest roadmaps for the Irish economy, and both books make an explicit link between the Irish and Jewish Diasporas. In *The Best Is Yet To Come*,[31] Marc Coleman suggests that Ireland should emulate Israel's leverage of the Jewish Diaspora if it wants to see the economic boom sustained. In *The Generation Game*,[32] David McWilliams rightly predicts that the Irish economy was extremely vulnerable and that the phenomenal boom of the previous decade was about to end. He examines whether Ireland has the potential to reinvent itself, and whether Ireland's 70 million-strong Diaspora might be the key to the country's future economic success. Drawing on the example of Israel and the Jewish Diaspora, McWilliams argues that Irish exiles could inject vibrancy and enthusiasm into Ireland's cultural scene, while opening up economic opportunities all over the world. Clearly, then, decision-makers in both countries believe that they have something to learn from the other. What can Ireland teach Israel, particularly in the area of entrepreneurship and innovation?

By many objective criteria, Ireland serves as a very obvious role model for Israel. In the 2007 *Global Entrepreneurship Monitor (GEM) Report*,[33] which measured prevalent rates of entrepreneurial activity in 23 high-income countries, Ireland ranked third with a 16.8 per cent rate of overall entrepreneurial activity among the adult population. Israel had the lowest score of the 23 high-income countries, with 7.4 per cent. In every other category in the *GEM Report*, Ireland scored higher than Israel, whether in terms of nascent entrepreneurial activity, number of new business owner-managers, early-stage entrepreneurial activity or number of established business owner-managers.

If we compare per capita GDP, Ireland has scored consistently higher. Different sources generate slightly different figures, but the general trend is the same. According to the International Monetary Fund (IMF), Ireland was in seventh place globally in 2007, while Israel was in thirty-second place.[34] According to the World Bank, Ireland was in fifth place globally in 2007, while Israel was in twenty-seventh place.[35] According to the CIA's *World Factbook*, Ireland was in ninth place globally in 2007, while Israel was in thirty-sixth place.[36] And even if Israel's per capita GDP is disproportionately low because many Arab and ultra-Orthodox citizens of Israel do not participate in the workforce – because of the structure of the labour market and discrepancies in the skill sets and available work in the case of the former, and due to the Government's, at times grudging, willingness to fund the Orthodox community's religious study through hand-outs and subsidies – Israel clearly scores worse than Ireland.[37]

Ireland is very proud of its entrepreneurial spirit. In 2006, responding to claims by a former assistant director general of the Central Bank, Michael Casey, that there is 'something in our national psyche that stops us being good entrepreneurs', then Irish Minister for Enterprise, Trade and Development Micheál Martin reacted strongly. Entrepreneurship was alive and well in Ireland, said the Minister, quoting the 2006 Yearbook published by *Irish Entrepreneur* magazine, which listed more than 300 small and medium enterprises (SMEs) that doubled their net worth between 2002 and 2004. The Minister pointed out that, in 2005 alone, Enterprise Ireland (EI) had invested in 75 high potential start-up (HPSU) companies that would create 1,460 jobs. While agreeing that entrepreneurship was a key ingredient in Ireland's economic success, Martin attacked Michael Casey's negative view of Ireland's track record as fundamentally mistaken. 'We are very fortunate to have a positive and supportive culture for entrepreneurial endeavour, and this is translating into the emergence of many high quality, high growth potential businesses. The challenge now is to go on to make Ireland the most entrepreneurial country in the world.'[38]

In any country, starting a new business, which is a key parameter for examining a country's entrepreneurial spirit, involves considerable runaround and bureaucratic hassle. In Israel, starting a business takes two and a half times longer (34 days) than starting a business in Ireland (13 days). On average, four procedures are required to start a business in Ireland, while five are required in Israel. In terms of the ease of doing business, Ireland ranked eighth in 2007 and 2008, while Israel ranked twenty-sixth in 2007 and twenty-ninth in 2008. Obtaining a business licence in Ireland requires less than the world average, while in Israel it takes more than the average.[39]

Notwithstanding reports in the Irish media[40] that a global study conducted by researchers at the Hebrew University of Jerusalem found that Ireland is among the most heavily regulated countries in the world, Ireland scored very highly in the Heritage Foundation's 2008 Index of Economic Freedom.[41] According to the index, Ireland was the world's third freest economy, up from fourth place five years before that. Ireland ranked first out of 41 countries in the European zone. Even though Israel climbed the Index of Economic Freedom table from sixty-third place in 2002 to forty-sixth place in 2007, it is still far below Ireland.

In terms of business freedom, Ireland was ranked in fourth place globally in the 2009 Heritage Foundation Index, compared to Israel's placing at forty-second. The two countries are fairly evenly matched when it comes to trade freedom, with Israel just edging out Ireland, 86.6 per cent to 86 per cent, but Ireland is well ahead in terms of fiscal freedom. Israel has a very low score of 35.1 per cent for freedom from government, with Ireland at a respectable 65.5 per cent. Israel lags behind Ireland in monetary freedom (81.8 per cent to 84.9 per cent) and in investment freedom (80 per cent to 90 per cent). On other measures too, Israel scores lower than Ireland: property rights (70 per cent to 90 per cent); freedom from corruption (59 per cent to 74 per cent); and labour freedom (64 per cent to 80.4 per cent).

- Overall freedom to start, operate and close a business is another measure examined by the index. This freedom is 'strongly protected' by Ireland's regulatory environment, compared to 'relatively well protected' by Israel's regulatory environment.

The issue of excess bureaucratic red tape in Israel is a real one. In November 2007, OECD Secretary General Angel Gurría addressed the Prime Minister's Conference for Export and International Co-operation in Tel Aviv.[42] He predicted that Israel's new status as a full OECD member would translate into better policy performance in key areas like trade, investment and competition. But he also warned that Israel must confront red tape in key areas of doing business, like dealing with licences, employing workers or registering property.

According to Daniel Doron, the director of the Israel Centre for Social and Economic Progress,[43] several factors are preventing the Israeli economy from scoring higher in international league tables. The intervention of government in the Israeli economy can often choke entrepreneurship and growth, while the concentration of economic and political power spawns costly anti-competitive and inefficient monopolies. The anti-productive public sector employs every third person in the country, while the welfare regime consumes a third of the Government's budget.

On the face of it, therefore, Israel would seem to have some catching up to do in the areas of economic freedom and entrepreneurship. But are there areas where Ireland can draw inspiration from Israel, particularly in the field of innovation? *Ha'aretz* journalist Efrat Neuman answers this succinctly: 'No end is in sight for the chorus of hallelujahs voiced by Israeli politicians for Ireland. Surprisingly, the Irish seem to think they could take a page from the Israeli playbook.'[44]

The page in question is all about the Israeli attitude to innovation. On a visit to Israel, Microsoft founder Bill Gates said that the kind of innovation going on in Israel is critical to the future of the technology business. Israel, he said, along with the US, was fairly unique in creating new products, patents and copyrighted software. He added that Israel had a greater concentration of talented high-tech manpower in comparison to other countries – almost to the extent of Silicon Valley.[45] Angel Gurría has described Israel as a 'powerhouse in the field of information technology and software.'[46]

As we have seen, Ireland scores highly in several global league tables. Yet, despite making the promotion of a competitive enterprise environment an overt national priority, despite its well-educated population, its sophisticated and able institutions, and its pro-science and technology policies, Ireland was ranked only twenty-second in the World Economic Forum's 2007–8 Global Competitiveness Index,[47] compared to Israel's spot at seventeenth. In the critical area of innovation, Israel was in fifth place while Ireland was in nineteenth. In technological readiness, Israel was in fourteenth place, Ireland in twenty-fifth.

In the Networked Readiness Index, contained in the World Economic Forum's annual *Global Information Technology Report 2007–2008*,[48] Israel remained in eighteenth place for the fourth consecutive year, ahead of Japan, France and New Zealand. Ireland was in twenty-third place. The report also measured capacity for innovation, in terms of whether companies obtain technology exclusively from licensing or imitating foreign companies, or by conducting formal research and pioneering their own new products and processes. Israel was in tenth place, while Ireland was in twenty-fourth.

In several key areas of the report there is a considerable gap between the respective positions of Israel and Ireland. Israel was in first place for computers per capita, while Ireland was in twentieth place. Israel was in third place on the availability of scientists and engineers, while Ireland was in fifteenth place. In quality of scientific research institutions, Israel was in third place while Ireland was in sixteenth. Israel was in seventh place for company spend on R&D, compared to sixteenth place for Ireland. In technology absorption at the individual company level, Israel was in fifth place, while Ireland was in twenty-third place. In availability of latest technologies, Israel was in fourth place, Ireland in thirty-third. Israel was in eighth place for university–industry research collaboration, compared to Ireland in eighteenth place. Israel was seventh in terms of government procurement of advanced technological products, compared to Ireland in twenty-fifth place. In terms of the extent to which entrepreneurs with innovative but risky projects can generally find venture capital in their own country, Israel was in fifth place while Ireland was in ninth.

Two of the biggest gaps between the two countries were in quality of competition in the internet service provider (ISP) sector (Israel third place;

Ireland sixty-eighth) and educational expenditure (Israel fourth place; Ireland forty-third). Israel spent almost double per capita than the expenditure in Ireland.

The only two areas where Ireland significantly outscored Israel are the length of time required to start a new business (Ireland was in twenty-fourth place with 13 days; Israel in seventy-eighth place with 34 days), which was mentioned above, and in terms of value of high-tech exports, which is skewed greatly in Ireland's favour because of a huge proportion of foreign-owned exports within the national export figures.

The question to be asked is why does Israel seem to enjoy an entrepreneurial and innovative edge? One clue is provided by Sol Gradman, chairman of Israel's High-Tech CEO Forum.[49] He argued that Israel's high-tech advantage is based on a greater readiness to take risks, an entrepreneurial character and one of the world's highest proportions of engineers per population. According to Gradman, who was a guest speaker at the annual conference of the Irish Software Association in 2005, one of the dangers facing Ireland, and one the country is currently experiencing, is that the reliance on foreign technology can leave a vacuum when the multinational high-tech jobs start disappearing. As easily as multinationals can be attracted to Ireland, they can leave in search of greater profits elsewhere. If inward investment is not based on local entrepreneurship, the advantages can rapidly melt away.

Gradman's comments are borne out by the thousands of jobs that have been lost in recent years as multinationals reduced or eliminated their Irish workforce: 1,500 jobs at Seagate (1998), 800 jobs at Motorola (2000), 360 jobs at Matsushita Kotobuki (2000), 900 jobs at Gateway (2001), 400 jobs at Xerox (2001), 170 jobs at Intel (2001), 325 jobs at Dell (2001), 375 jobs at Solectron (2002), 120 jobs at Skilloft (2004), 220 jobs at SerCom Solutions (2005), 250 jobs at Quantum (2005), 200 jobs at Hewlett Packard (2005), 330 jobs at Motorola (2007), 150 jobs at Analog Devices (2007) and 220 jobs at Dell (2008).[50] Other multinationals that have shed jobs include Pfizer, Procter & Gamble, Thompson Scientific, SerCom Solutions and Symantec. Revealingly, when Intel was shedding 16,000 employees around the world, including in Ireland, 700 new employees were recruited by Intel's R&D centres in Israel.[51]

Israel avoided this kind of scenario by making it government policy to embed multinationals in the home-grown industries. The likes of Intel, IBM and Motorola have a major presence in Israel, but much of their activities are in R&D rather than manufacturing. Israel has consistently invested in its own high-tech, high-skill, science-based industries. Twenty-four per cent of the workforce holds a university degree. In terms of patents owned per head of population, Israel has more US-registered patents than China, India and Russia combined.[52]

Although Ireland's high-tech exports dwarf Israel's, 70 per cent of Israel's total industrial exports are high-tech, the highest proportion in the world. Israel has more companies listed on the NASDAQ Stock Market than any other country outside the US and Canada. Israel's incubation programme is regarded as one of the best of its type in the world, with thousands of Israeli high-tech companies reaching second stage financing. A key difference between Israeli companies and Irish companies is that the latter are less willing to take risks and less willing to give up equity. Urging Ireland to become more sophisticated in both production and innovation, McWilliams has suggested that Ireland should mimic Israel and take a closer look at the highly successful 'technology greenhouses' that have helped thousands of Israeli high-tech companies gain second stage financing.[53]

Although Ireland has been somewhat slow in recognising that it needs to give research activities greater commercialisation impetus, EI is making up for lost time through a policy of transforming SMEs and accelerating their development by making them more market focused and innovative. To achieve this, EI initiated the seeding and funding of hundreds of new high-potential start-up companies, and hundreds more productivity and competitiveness projects. According to EI's Frank Ryan, the goal is 'to see an R&D department in every company in our portfolio.'[54]

Having worked for many years in Israel as well as Ireland, I have often asked myself whether the 'can-do' attitude and spirit of improvisation is more embedded in the Israeli DNA than in the Irish DNA. Does Ireland's flame of innovation flicker too dimly?

My work with enterprise agencies throughout Ireland has brought me into direct contact with thousands of people who have toyed with the idea of starting their own business. In recent years especially, it has been intriguing to count how many non-Irish nationals have attended my Start Your Own Business courses for current and aspiring businessmen and entrepreneurs in towns and cities across Ireland. The newcomers see entrepreneurship as a fast-track route to financial independence. While some of the native Irish people at these events are undoubtedly driven by a genuine entrepreneurial urge to start their own business, many of them attend such courses because they have been, or fear that they may be, made redundant.

The glowing endorsement of Ireland by the *GEM Report* notwithstanding, it is possible to discern subtle negative nuances in the Irish approach to entrepreneurship. Many people in Ireland still harbour suspicions about the world of business. In previous generations, Irish people faced the prospect of no regular employment. Having and holding a job became an achievement in itself, one that was not lightly thrown away in favour of starting a business. Until relatively recently, the idea of opting out of the world of employment in order to savour the delights of the world of self-employment was seen as something of an aberration.[55]

Although the Celtic Tiger undoubtedly changed the face of the business scene, an undercurrent of suspicion of maverick entrepreneurs seems to persist until the present day. This was manifested in a very public manner when then Taoiseach Bertie Ahern made a statement in the Dáil in 2006 about the proposed management buyout of Aer Lingus initiated two years earlier by three Aer Lingus executives led by CEO Willie Walsh. Using distinctly anti-entrepreneurial language, Ahern claimed that 'management wanted to steal the assets for themselves through a management buyout, shafting staff interests'. When the head of a government describes a management buyout as stealing assets, he is sending out a very confused and negative message to the investment community.[56]

When Professor Danny Breznitz of the Georgia Institute of Technology in Atlanta met with leading figures in the Irish economy in 2007, he expressed his concern that the Irish system is weak at turning ideas into products. Not enough research was being carried out in Ireland, he said, and Ireland seemed slow at making research pay. One reason for this, according to Breznitz, was that the Government had to give the funding and the supports needed to help entrepreneurs to succeed. This would require changes in the financial system. The venture capital market was too timid and needed to be willing to take more risks. Another reason cited by Breznitz was a lack of self-confidence.[57]

This strikes at a key differentiator between Ireland and Israel. Beyond government policies, what is the secret behind Israel's ability to extract so much entrepreneurial and innovative thinking from its people? What makes Israel able to draw on seemingly endlessly renewable sources of ideas? Why has Israel earned a global reputation for its 'can-do' attitude to innovation and entrepreneurship?

Israel's business culture encourages individual imagination, and appreciates the contribution of the non-conformist.[58] Self-confidence is certainly part of the equation. But a critical factor at play here is Israel's special brand of innovative entrepreneurship that can be best described as *chutzpah*. With its origins in Aramaic, the word chutzpah migrated through Hebrew to Yiddish, was part of the cultural baggage carried by the millions of Jewish refugees who arrived in the US to escape the pogroms of Eastern Europe, and is now an integral part of the English language. Chutzpah essentially describes a mindset that says that anything is possible. It is the mindset that refuses to accept no for an answer and that thrives on confounding the odds. The chutzpah mindset means having the guts to leave your comfort zone, to defy conventional wisdom, to be prepared to rethink fundamentally the things around us, and to attempt things no one has ever tried before.[59]

It is chutzpah that drives Israel's maverick entrepreneurs and innovators. They have learned to harness, leverage, embrace, exploit and adopt chutzpah – and it shows. When the anonymous successful Irish venture capitalist quoted by McWilliams said that he intended to make the Irish high-tech sector 'more Israeli',[60] he probably meant that the Irish should display more chutzpah.

In December 2008, the Irish Government announced that venture capital funds of €500 million would be available for investment in start-ups. Commentators saw this as a direct imitation of the Israeli model. McWilliams commented that this was the kind of funding that helped make the entrepreneurial spirit so ingrained in Israel. Describing Ireland's high-tech sector as being 'on a respirator', Michael Hennigan, the editor of *Finfacts*, pointed out that the Israeli fund was set up in 1993 with just US$200 million, and today holds US$10 billion worth of investments.

But what about the reverse scenario? Does Israel still regard the Irish economy as a model worth emulating? Or has Israeli enthusiasm waned in the aftermath of the meltdown of the Irish economy since the onset of the global credit crunch? As noted above, after Ireland's Celtic Tiger economy grew by almost 90 per cent in a decade, a long line of Israeli officials (averaging almost two delegations a year) made a pilgrimage to marvel at a model they wanted to emulate. But then Ireland's debt-fuelled economy collapsed faster than most other European economies, Irish government bonds were rated as the riskiest in the EU and the possibly criminal activities of several Irish banks were revealed. It did not escape the notice of Israeli observers that the surge in start-ups in Ireland's building sector during the construction boom served to mask the perilous state of domestic entrepreneurship. There was very little venture capital investment in Ireland, compared to what was channeled into commercial property overseas.

Analysts Omri Zegen and Yariv Mann from the Reut Institute, the Tel Aviv based non-partisan and non-profit policy group that advises the Israeli Government, have suggested that, while Ireland may once have served as a role model for Israel, other models for accelerated economic growth are now also worth pursuing. They quote a comparative study into the operational characteristics of national economic councils in Europe that indicates that every state effectively adopts its own unique model of partnership, not necessarily based on the Irish model.[61]

Conclusion

Even in the current climate, both the Israeli and Irish economies have pockets of expertise that the other can emulate. Israel can learn from Ireland that integration and interdependence, underpinned by fiscal discipline and geopolitical stability, are critical factors in attracting foreign investment. Ireland can learn from Israel that long-term economic success needs a solid R&D foundation that can deliver cutting-edge technological innovation and world-beating entrepreneurship.[62]

Moreover, other emerging nations can certainly learn powerful lessons about entrepreneurship and innovation from Ireland and Israel. Barry O' Leary, the CEO of Ireland's Industrial Development Agency (IDA), claims that Ireland remains the most FDI-intensive economy in Europe.[63] Ireland's goal is to continue to reposition the country to ensure that it is viewed as one of the foremost innovation-led and knowledge-based economies of choice globally for mobile investment. A World Economic Forum (WEF) report on Israel's ICT sector, with special reference to education investments, immigration, investment incentives and maintenance of a ratio of R&D investment to GDP, concluded: 'Israel's experience and impressive success in this area...is worthy of study and emulation by countries with similar aspirations.'[64]

Whether the global economy happens to be in buoyant or recessionary mode at any given time, the business world continues to evolve at a ferocious pace. Any government wishing to stimulate economic development and to remain competitive in the global marketplace needs to stimulate capital investment, support education and move priorities from low productivity to higher productivity industries. In short, governments must encourage a spirit of entrepreneurship and innovation.

CHAPTER 10

The Celtic Tiger and the Chinese Dragon: Modelling the Irish and Chinese Economic Miracles

Liming Wang, Chang Liu and Francis Kane

If someone had predicted that Ireland, which in 1990 had a 15 per cent unemployment rate and the poorest economic record in Europe, would in the year 2003 have the highest growth rate in the developed world, that individual would have been called a lunatic.

James Flannery,
Director of the W.B. Yeats Foundation and
Winship Professor of the Arts and Humanities at Emory University

That is a sleeping dragon. Let him sleep! If he wakes, he will shake the world.
Napoleon

Introduction

It may come as some surprise to many Chinese and Irish people, but there is vast scope for comparison between China and Ireland. In short, we have far more in common with each other than is generally acknowledged.[1] From the perspective of both the humanities and the social sciences, startling evidence for particular commonalities between Ireland and China can be found. But it is on economics that this chapter concentrates, and its key focus is on the economic transformation of the two nation-states.

Throughout the 1990s and beyond, China and Ireland enjoyed sustained high economic growth, and in gross domestic product (GDP) growth terms were the respective 'star performers' of East and West.[2] This chapter seeks to identify and compare key factors in the dramatic economic metamorphosis of these two countries. While not claiming to outline a model for miraculous transfiguration, we would nevertheless hope that our analysis is of interest to other economies around the world.

The global economic crisis that began in 2008–9 was particularly calamitous for Ireland as it arrived on the back of a 'home grown' property and construction bubble, the bursting of which plunged the country into a recession more quickly and for a longer period than other EU economies. China, on the other hand, has appeared to recover its pattern of high economic growth following a temporary slowing down, which saw unemployment rise, particularly in export-related sectors of the economy, even though recession was avoided. Nevertheless, fears remain that inflation is causing a price bubble in the Chinese economy too. Although future trends are hard to predict, an increasing number of economists are interested in the lessons which may be learned from China's economic policies.[3] This chapter concludes with a look at the challenges which lie ahead for these two great navigators of history, China and Ireland, both of whom became fully independent republics in 1949.[4]

Chinese and Irish antiquity also has relevance for our analysis. Our ancestors began to globalise in the depths of antiquity and settled throughout the world without military conquest. To this day, what it means to have a Chinese or an Irish identity goes beyond citizenship of a particular nation-state. Our cultures and social history form part of the fabric of many societies around the world[5] and, as shall be seen, overseas compatriots with feelings of attachment to their ancestral motherlands have contributed greatly to the wealth of China and Ireland in recent times.

Economic Boom

Ireland

The term 'Celtic Tiger' is widely recognised as portraying the spectacular performance of the Irish economy through the 1990s and beyond; the 'Tiger' part of that expression is distinctly Asian, and arose due to Irish growth figures reflecting those of the East. Irish real national income per head jumped from 65 per cent of the EU-15[6] average at the beginning of the 1990s to above parity by the beginning of the new millennium. Unemployment tumbled from a high of 17 per cent in the late 1980s – a level double the EU average – to a historic low of 4 per cent – half the EU average – by the end of the

1990s. Budget deficits were transformed into surpluses, the government debt-to-GDP ratio was slashed, and the population at work increased by an astonishing 50 per cent. The average economic growth rate was 6 per cent in the period 1995–2007. Per capita GDP rose to 40 per cent above that of the four biggest European economies (Germany, the UK, France and Italy) to the second highest in the EU behind Luxembourg. By 2007, Ireland's GDP per capita had surpassed that of the US.

China

Meanwhile, following economic reform and opening-up policies from 1978 onwards, China has also undergone enormous change. No longer a poor and isolated nation, but rather completely transfigured into a mighty engine of growth in the world economy, China has achieved an average economic growth rate of 9.6 per cent for the last 25 years, something quite simply unparalleled in modern history. Hundreds of millions of human beings have been lifted out of poverty. A staggering drop from 53 per cent of the population in 1981 to 8 per cent in 2001 remained below the poverty line.[7] Figure 10.1 compares the GDP growth rates of Ireland and China from 1991 to 2007.

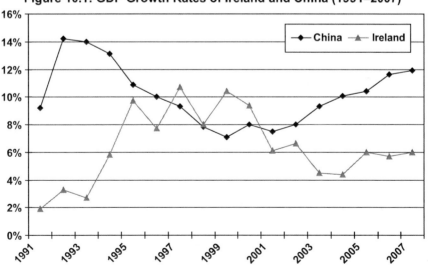

Figure 10.1: GDP Growth Rates of Ireland and China (1991–2007)

Factors Contributing to Chinese and Irish Economic Success

Various factors have been identified as contributing to Ireland's economic miracle: low corporate tax rates and related foreign direct investment (FDI) incentive policies, a well-educated workforce, ethnic ties with the US, and geographical and language advantages. Since the 1970s, universal secondary level education and increasing state investment in all levels of education have helped create a highly educated and productive workforce. In the early 1980s, the Irish Government reversed the previous pattern of lax domestic fiscal policy. Key to this was the capacity to offer an extremely low corporate income tax rate as an incentive for FDI. Ireland's entry in 1973 to the EU made Ireland – an English-speaking country on the western fringe of the EU – an inviting gateway to the European market for US-based multinationals. It also allowed Ireland to become a beneficiary of EU policies that provided financial assistance to its less-well-off members. Direct grants in the form of structural funds from the EU were used for sorely needed infrastructure investments in the Irish economy. Over the years, the aggregate level of this funding has amounted to tens of billions of US dollars.

As for China, after decades of state control over all productive assets, the Government embarked on a major programme of economic reform in 1978. It encouraged the formation of both rural enterprises and private businesses, increased investment in infrastructure, liberalised foreign trade and investment, relaxed state control over the prices of many goods, provided generous tax incentives for foreign investors, and there was also higher investment in education and industrial production.

Other factors that contribute to China's robust economic growth include strong state leadership; constant economic reform and improvements in the effectiveness of macroeconomic management; the unleashing of domestic private entrepreneurship; the large size and growth potential of domestic markets; macroeconomic stability and consistency across reform policies; an increasing availability of managerial and scientific personnel; and huge local networks of inter-firm supply chains. China and Ireland may also have simultaneously benefited from what has become known as the 'demographic dividend', referring to the positive boost to the economic environment created by a shift to a relatively higher proportion of the population being of working age. China and Ireland have experienced similar changes in the dependency ratios of their populations over recent decades. The year 1979 was particularly significant for both countries, as the legalisation of contraception was introduced and birth control finally became legal in Ireland; in China, the one-child policy of population growth control first became compulsory. This will be looked at later in this chapter.

Attracting Foreign Direct Investment

Looking at the two countries in terms of their economic development, it is clear that inward FDI has played a very significant role. Since the late 1950s, Ireland has adopted a stance of closer integration into the international economy, and a major milestone was EU membership in 1973. Given the low levels of domestic investment capital available, FDI was essential. Ireland benefited from the increased scale of global FDI from the late 1950s by having established a more fiscally and financially welcoming environment than other European countries. Vernon's product cycle can be appropriately applied to Ireland, as it became a low-cost manufacturing base within Europe for maturing US enterprises, which were already exporting new products to the growing European market.[8] Ireland became an attractive base for operations with its original tax-holiday incentives designed to make it an export platform. Crucially, economic success in China has also benefited greatly from inward direct investment flows from abroad. China has experienced phenomenal growth in FDI, which generated US\$82.7 billion by the end of 2007. China has been the biggest FDI recipient among developing countries over the past seventeen years. Positive assessments of the contribution of FDI to GDP growth at both the Chinese national and mega-regional levels have been widely reported.[9]

Table 10.1 shows the results of surveys conducted by the Swiss-based International Institute for Management Development and published as the *World Competitiveness Yearbook*. It can be seen that Ireland is perceived as the top country in the world in relation to two key indicators: its image abroad as encouraging business development and offering attractive investment incentives to foreign investors. China closely follows in the third and fourth positions in the two surveys.

Trade Openness

International trade in goods and services is a principal channel of economic integration. It is argued that trade liberalisation may indirectly affect poverty by influencing economic growth. In the published literature, the trade–growth–poverty relationship involves two critical linkages that have been at the centre of heated debate over the past ten years: whether trade is good for growth (the trade–growth linkage) and whether growth is good

Table 10.1: Business Development and Investment Incentives of Ireland and China Compared to Other Major Economies

The image abroad of your country encourages business development		Investment incentives are attractive to foreign investors	
Country	Values*	Country	Values
Ireland	8.82	Ireland	8.59
Netherlands	8.09	Netherlands	7.78
Germany	7.41	China	7.20
China	7.06	United Kingdom	6.85
United Kingdom	7.06	USA	6.84
Japan	7.05	Belgium	6.52
USA	5.94	Germany	6.12
Belgium	5.81	France	5.92
France	4.46	Japan	4.94

* Rankings out of ten.
Source: Institute for Management Development (IMD), *World Competitiveness Yearbook*, 2007, Switzerland: IMD, 2007.

for the poor (the growth–poverty linkage). Concerning the trade–growth linkage, a range of studies have found that trade is one of the most important driving engines for long-run economic growth.[10] In the case of Ireland, its economy has been described as being among those countries with the greatest exposure to international trade in the world. In the 1990s alone, Ireland's trade-to-GDP ratio increased by over 50 per cent. The AT Kearney Foreign Policy Globalization Index of 2004 ranked Ireland as the third most globalised country in the world in terms of trade.

China's sustained economic boom, on the other hand, has often been ascribed in the past to the success of its free trade and export-oriented policies, especially after accession to the World Trade Organization (WTO) in 2001, which has further accelerated the country's integration into the global economy. According to the National Bureau of Statistics, China's foreign trade ranked third worldwide in 2007, from twenty-ninth in 1978. From 1978 to 2007, China's share of the world's total trade increased from 0.8 per cent to 7.7 per cent. Thus, the trade-to-GDP ratio, meaning imports plus exports/GDP (often called the 'trade openness ratio'), reveals some similarities in the degree of trade openness in Ireland and China, with a convergence in the figures over the last five years.

Figure 10.2 compares the trade openness ratios of Ireland and China from 1991 to 2007. The data indicates that Ireland had an extraordinarily high trade openness ratio with a value higher than one for a full decade from the early 1990s. The figures are not overly surprising when under-

Figure 10.2: Trade Openness Ratios of Ireland and China, 1991–2007

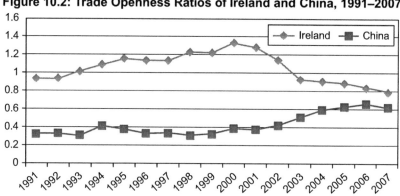

stood in the context of Ireland's economy being small, with open trade regimes also operating in its neighbouring countries. Furthermore, given the high degree of US-based multinational involvement in the Irish economy, Ireland imports many intermediate products and components which are manufactured into final products and then exported at higher value. The costs of these intermediate products are not taken into account when GDP is calculated, only the value added of the final export products.

After 2003, the trade openness ratio of Ireland dropped below 1 to 0.8, and the trend thereafter is noticeably downward. In contrast, China's trade openness ratio has maintained an upward trend from 0.36 in 1991 to over 0.6 in 2007. Considering the fact that China is a very large and relatively self-sufficient country, recent figures are high indeed, justifying the identification of trade openness as another common factor in the high growth of the two economies.

Preferential Tax Policies towards Foreign Investment Enterprises (FIEs)

At the initial stage of attracting FDI, both Ireland and China adopted strategies to cut taxes for foreign firms investing in the two countries. In Ireland, low rates of corporation tax are a prominent feature of industrial strategy. From the late 1950s, tax incentives were targeted toward manufacturing exports; these were consolidated in 1981 into a 10 per cent tax rate on all manufacturing, while corporation tax on other activities was set at a much higher rate. These preferential tax policies proved to be successful in attracting multinational enterprises (MNEs) to target Ireland rather than elsewhere. A rate of 10 per cent was extended over time to embrace other industries, including software manufacture, by the early 1980s. In 1987, it was further extended to include internationally traded financial services.

These policies proved highly successful and, by the end of the 1990s, the International Financial Services Centre (IFSC) in Dublin comprised some three hundred firms employing over ten thousand people.

The Chinese Government adopted a similar strategy to attract foreign investments by offering preferential tax conditions from the 1980s onwards. For example, foreign investors can enjoy tax breaks and rebates in the special investment zones (IZs) located in China's south-eastern coastal belt. The most common tax break that a foreign enterprise investing in an investment zone may receive is a 50 per cent discount on corporation income tax. This effectively means a reduction from 30 per cent to 15 per cent on corporation income tax (CIT).[11] Furthermore, if the foreign invested project also brings with it technology that is regarded as 'advanced technology' by the Chinese authorities, then a further three years' reduction by half (i.e. three years at 7.5 per cent) can be negotiated. Also, if a foreign enterprise (FE) has an export value of more than 70 per cent in a certain year, then the FE may receive a preferential CIT rate of 10 per cent for that year.

Another benefit that a FE investing in a IZ may receive is a tax rebate. There are two types of refund that can be negotiated in terms of tax: if the FE reinvests the profits that it has made in China back into its own enterprise or other enterprises in the IZ, and these enterprises commit to operate for a further five years, then such enterprises will receive a 40 per cent rebate on CIT on the total investment amount. If the reinvestment of profits is made into an export-orientated or high-technology enterprise, then the FE shall receive a full rebate for the entire amount of CIT paid on the amount of the reinvestment. This approach played a key role in attracting FDI flows to China.

Recently, due to EU restrictions on tax incentives to foreign investments among its member states, Ireland has had to increase its corporation income tax to 12.5 per cent. Nevertheless, this figure, at 26 per cent, is still much lower than the average corporate tax rate in the EU. Interestingly, something similar is now happening in China. After three decades of very generous tax preferences towards foreign investors in China, the Chinese Government has also recently decided to increase CIT to foreign investors. It can reasonably be anticipated that this might affect FDI flows to China, but the latest data indicates that this policy adjustment has not, in fact, curbed foreign investors' interest in the country.[12]

Ethnic Ties with Overseas Investors

Scholars have identified Ireland's ethnic ties with the US, the product of a longstanding Diaspora, as a key factor in the Irish economic boom. US relations with Ireland have long been based on common ancestral ties and shared values. Due to Irish immigration, some 44 million American citizens now identify themselves as having some degree of Irish descent, as have more than half of the individual presidents of the US (including most of those in the period we are interested in: Presidents Ronald Reagan, Bill Clinton and the recently elected Barack Obama). These relations have broadened and matured, given the significant US role in Ireland's economic success.

As of year-end 2006, the stock of US FDI in Ireland stood at US$84 billion, more than double the US total for China and India combined (US$31.2 billion). Currently, there are approximately 620 US subsidiaries in Ireland, employing roughly 100,000 people and spanning activities from manufacturing of high-tech electronics, computer products, medical supplies and pharmaceuticals to retailing, banking, finance and other services. In 2005, US firms accounted for 61 per cent of Ireland's total exports of €89 billion. In more recent years, Ireland has also become an important research and development (R&D) centre for US firms in Europe. Meanwhile, the majority of FDI flows to mainland China come from Hong Kong[13] and Taiwan,[14] two regions that also have very close ethnic ties with mainland China.

In 1985, the Pearl River Delta (in Guangdong Province), the Minnan Delta (in Fujian Province) and Hainan Island were designated as the three largest open regions able to offer investment incentives to foreign investors. Most of the investments that these regions received were from Hong Kong and Macau (under Portuguese rule until 1999), where most people speak Cantonese, the language of Guangdong Province. For example, during the period to 1993, the Pearl River Delta received one-third of the cumulative utilised FDI in China, with Hong Kong providing over 80 per cent of this, and thus Guangdong Province has been the destination for over 40 per cent of Hong Kong's FDI into mainland China. Table 10.2 shows the major investors investing in Ireland and China: the US is the top investor in Ireland, while Hong Kong and Taiwan are the top two investors investing in mainland China.

'High-Tech Focused' Industry Strategy

Though Ireland and China began by promoting export-platform inward foreign investment into the manufacturing sector at the initial stage of opening up, both countries followed this with a more 'high-tech focused' industry strategy. In the case of Ireland, based on the concept of moving up the value chain, the Irish Government developed a greater capacity for

Table 10.2: Major Investors in Ireland and China

Origin of IDA Supported Companies in Ireland by the End of 2005			Top 10 Source Countries to Mainland China by the End of 2005		
Origin	Number of Companies	Total Employment	Origin	Amount (100 million US$)	Share of total (%)
US	470	95,515	Hong Kong	2,889.48	46.42
Germany	122	10,782	Taiwan	621.19	9.98
UK	111	7,356	United States	543.85	8.74
Rest of Europe	201	16,504	Japan	534.45	8.59
Asia Pacific	39	2,991	Korea	313.18	5.03
Rest of the World	37	2,339	Singapore	289.56	4.65
			United Kingdom	132.87	2.13
			Germany	115.17	1.85
			France	74.7	1.2
			Holland	69.67	1.12

Source: for data on Ireland: Forfás, *Annual Employment Survey 2006*, Dublin: Forfás, 2006; For data on mainland China: Ministry of Commerce, *FDI in China*, Beijing: Ministry of Commerce, 2006.

strategic planning about targeting specific forms of investment. From the late 1970s and early 1980s, the Irish industry strategy shifted from process and assembly operations to a concentration on newer and more high-tech industries. As Hardiman comments, this strategy is entirely consistent with the sort of technical upgrading strategy pursued in the 'Asian Tiger' countries of Singapore, Taiwan, South Korea and Hong Kong. Specifically, the areas targeted by the Irish Government included the following: microelectronics, office equipment, pharmaceuticals, chemicals and biotechnology.[15]

The view of the Irish authorities is that, by attracting one 'blue-chip' firm, a magnet is created to attract the presence of related or complementary firms. By the end of the 1990s, almost all of the largest international firms in information and communication technology (ICT) and in pharmaceuticals had a presence in Ireland, including firms such as Microsoft, Intel, Hewlett Packard, IBM and Motorola, among others. The creation of a high-tech industrial cluster in Ireland yields an agglomeration economic effect which attracts an increasing number of related firms to gather together. This agglomeration effect has assembled a concentration of both up- and down-stream firms in Dublin, Cork and Galway, including both production and service firms.

On the other side of the globe, the Chinese Government also realised the importance of developing its high-tech sector. China initiated a fifteen-year medium- to long-term plan for the development of science and technology. The nation aims to become an 'innovation-oriented society' by 2020 and a world leader in science and technology by 2050. Under this plan, China wants to develop indigenous innovation capabilities, leapfrog into leading positions in new science-based industries, increase R&D expenditures to 2.5 per cent of GDP by 2020 (up from 1.34 per cent in 2005), increase the contribution to economic growth from technological advances to 60 per cent, limit dependence on imported technology to 30 per cent and become one of the top five countries in the world in the number of patents granted. During the period 1993–2003, China's R&D expenditures grew faster than any other nation, pushing up its share of world R&D investment from 3.6 per cent to 9.5 per cent. During the same period, the EU's share of world R&D investment declined from 28.5 per cent to 25 per cent and the US's share dropped from 37.6 per cent to 36.1 per cent.

Meanwhile, from 1984 to 2002, the Chinese Government set up 49 national level Economic and Technology Development Zones (ETDZs).[16] A national level ETDZ is a relatively small piece of land set aside in coastal cities and other open cities inland. It attaches great importance to improving the hard and soft investment environment and adheres to a policy of 'mainly developing high-tech industry, focusing on industrial projects, absorbing foreign funds and building up an export-oriented economy' to strive for fast and sound development. Serving as 'windows and bases' in the fields of opening-up, capital attraction, export enlargement, high-tech development and regional economy promotion, it now becomes a powerful engine in developing the regional economy and industry structure. Indeed, the ETDZs have scored great achievements and have become the hot spots for foreign investment and the main export locations. Furthermore, to stimulate the development of advanced technologies in a wide range of fields, for the purpose of rendering China independent of obligations to foreign technologies, the Chinese Government launched the 863 programme.[17] Regarding intellectual property rights and the use of intangible assets for manufacturing and trade, Ireland has the highest imports of royalties and licence fees of any territory in the world, amounting to an extremely high US$2,748 per person in 2005.[18] The value of these services is worth three times more to Ireland than that of the next highest territory, which is Hong Kong. Thus, Ireland and China are the top two importers of royalties and licence fees in the world.[19]

Investment in Education

Another common factor behind the Irish and Chinese economic boom lies in both governments' efforts to invest in education. Dating back to the 1960s, the Irish Government recognised that changes to the occupational structure of society associated with the growth of manufacturing would place significant demands on education and training systems. Therefore, it invested heavily in education. According to the 2005 Organisation for Economic Co-operation and Development (OECD) report,[20] Ireland was amongst a small group of countries where spending per student in primary and secondary level education rose by 30 per cent or more between 1995 and 2002. In this period, Ireland's GDP grew particularly rapidly, spending on these sectors grew about half as fast, while investment in third level education kept pace with GDP.

The OECD report shows more Irish people than ever before have now attained third level education. Ireland is also rated second in the number of science graduates per 100,000 employed people aged 25–34. The report also shows that Ireland is among the countries where more young people (those born in the 1970s) have completed secondary education compared with those born in the 1950s. The OECD states that Ireland is among a small number of countries to make 'remarkable improvement' in the category of upper secondary education attainment, relative to the population.

The results of these efforts have been positive. According to an annual survey of global executives carried out by the Swiss-based International Institute for Management Development, Ireland was ranked second out of 60 OECD and medium-income developing countries in terms of how well the overall educational system meets the needs of a competitive economy, and fifth in terms of how well university education meets these needs. Gunnigle and McGuire found that executives of ten major US multinational firms admitted that education and skill levels rank second in importance to the corporation tax regime in drawing these firms to Ireland.[21]

The Chinese Government also realised the importance of developing education to support national economic development. Since the 1990s, when China made higher education a priority, the proportion of graduates from senior secondary schools who go on to pursue higher education has risen significantly, from nearly half in 1995 to 75 per cent by 2006. The gross enrolment ratio in tertiary education rose from 6 per cent in 1999 to 20 per cent in 2005, more than India's 11 per cent and Vietnam's 16 per cent.

To improve provision of third level education, the Chinese Government launched the '211 Project'[22] from the early 1990s. Project 211 is, as of 2007, a project initiated in 1995 by the Ministry of Education of the People's Republic of China (PRC) involving the 106 key universities and colleges in China. The project aims at cultivating an educated elite for national economic and social development strategies. The project sprang from the realisation in the mid-1990s that China's 30 elite universities at that time fell below international research standards.

Inclusion in the project means that universities have to meet scientific, technical and human resources standards and must offer advanced degree programmes. Other major education investments include Project 985,[23] which provides extra funding for world-class Chinese universities in the twenty-first century. This project is also conducted by the Chinese Ministry of Education. Most of these universities and research institutions are located in China's south-eastern coastal belt, and thus serve as the major suppliers of the educated labour force for those multinationals operating in the region.

Demographic Dividends

Many economists take a 'population neutral' view which holds that population growth has little direct impact on economic growth. While Harvard researchers Bloom and Canning concur, they urge reconsideration of the relative proportions of working people to their dependants (children and old people) in a population (the 'dependency ratio'), claiming that, with the right government policies in place, a declining dependency ratio may contribute to increases in GDP per head. Their recent studies into the age structures of the Chinese and Irish populations present a persuasive case that economic growth in China and Ireland has happened against the backdrop of a remarkable demographic phenomenon: a bulging of the working-age populations over the last few decades which has created a window of growth opportunity for both nations.[24] This 'wave of relative youth' can be ascribed to a certain extent to government intervention in China and Ireland, and it is at the very least a curious coincidence that these interventions and their subsequent effects on the dependency ratio happened within a year or two of each other. Historically, there was a sudden drop in the fertility rates of both populations after 1980: as mentioned, Ireland legalised contraception and China had just adopted nationwide population control measures, in particular the one-child policy. One effect has been a temporary swelling of the workforce proportionally, with fewer dependants than before. Over time, it is well attested that there will be a slowing down of this factor as the lag in the population works itself through the decades. Indeed, in Ireland's case, 2005 was identified as the last year of the demographic 'sweet spot',[25] while China is expected to feel some of the effects of an ageing population after 2010.

In recent years, the United Nations has begun to champion the link between economic development policies and the dependency ratio,[26] while at the same time warning that the global population is already ageing, causing a reversal of previously favourable dependency conditions, with the proportion of the world's population over 65 years of age now rising fast. In Figure 10.3, a dependency ratio comparison graph is plotted for Ireland and China for the period 1960 to 2006.

Figure 10.3: Dependency Ratio Comparison Graph for Ireland and China, 1960–2006

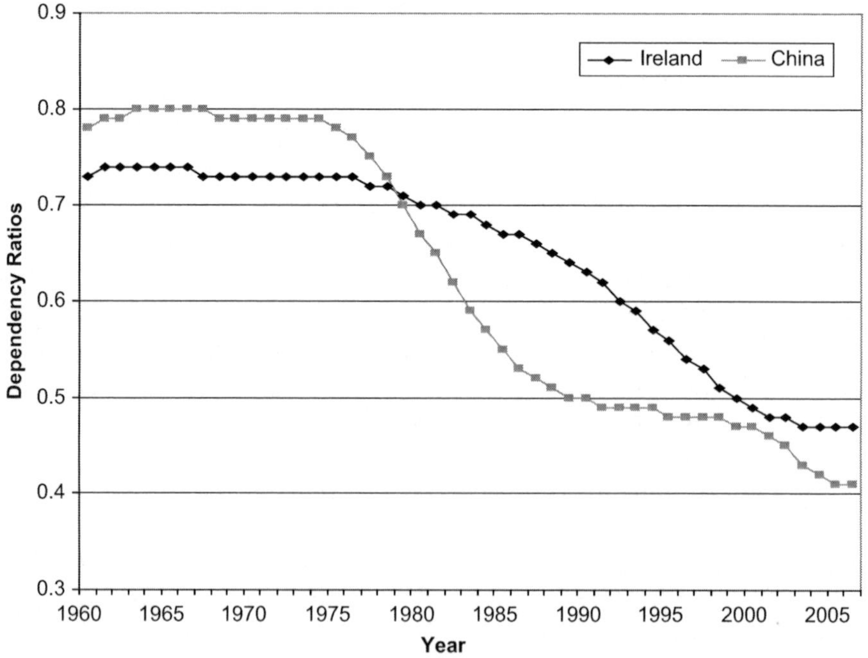

When Irish children born in the 1960s hit the workforce, there were not so many children in the generation just behind them. Ireland was suddenly free of the enormous social cost of supporting and educating and caring for a large dependent population.

In the case of China, the Chinese Government introduced the one-child policy in 1979 to alleviate social and environmental problems. The one-child policy has been implemented via a system of incentives for compliance, such as preference in educational opportunities, health care, housing and job assignments, and disincentives for lack of compliance, such as fines and loss of access to education and other privileges. The policy is based on universal access to contraception and abortion. Eighty-seven per cent of all married women use some form of contraception (including sterilisation). Most women accept the method recommended by the family planning worker. Reliance on long-term contraception keeps the abortion rate low (25 per cent of Chinese women of reproductive age have had at least one abortion, as opposed to 43 per cent in the US).[27]

The original intent of the one-child policy was economic – to reduce the demand on natural resources, maintain a steady labour supply and reduce unemployment caused by surplus labour. Although there have been negative effects,[28] the case for the one-child policy in helping to stimulate China's economic development appears strong: from 1978 to 2003, the rate of population increase declined from 12.5 per cent to 6 per cent, while at the same time China's GDP per capita increased from less than US$250 to US$1,090, with the Chinese GDP annual rate of increase at an average of 9.6 per cent from 1978 to 2003.

Table 10.3 summarises the factors behind the economic booms of Ireland and China identified above.

Major Challenges Ahead

The 'butterfly effect', an expression coined by Nobel Laureate Professor Edward Lorenz to illuminate his brilliant mathematical modelling of chaos

Table 10.3: Common Factors Behind Economic Booms

Ireland	China
Opening policy, EU membership	Open door policy, WTO accession
Low corporation tax rate	Tax preferences towards FIEs
State efforts to attract FDI	State Efforts to attract FDI
Focus on high-tech sector	Economic and Technology Development Zones (ETDZs)
Irish diaspora: overseas Irish investment	Overseas Chinese investment
Heavy investment in education: integration with the country's FDI-oriented development strategy	Heavy investment in education: 211 Project; 863 Project; 985 Project
Legalisation of artificial contraception	One-child policy became compulsory in 1979

Source: L. Wang, 'Red Hot Dragon', Business & Finance, Asia Supplements, vol. 43, no.18, 2007, pp. 8–11.

theory, describes how minute changes in the initial conditions of a complex system like the weather can push the whole system in a certain direction and, through further knock-on effects, lead to massive consequences in that system later. That same expression can be used to describe how the global financial and economic crisis progressed from subprime mortgage bad debts in the US to a credit crunch and then a banking crisis, with free market developed economies suffering particularly badly. In short, there has been an economic meltdown of extraordinary proportions and unknown future effects. The Celtic Tiger roars no more while the Chinese Dragon, awake and arisen, finds itself returning to the centre of a shaken world. Notwithstanding the urgent need of both countries to deal as effectively as possible with the crisis, there are major challenges ahead which strike us as fundamental to delivering future prosperity, as well as protecting all that has been achieved thus far.

The current economic crisis has highlighted Ireland's dependency on the US economy. An estimated 90 per cent of Ireland's exports depend on US firms,[29] suggesting that Ireland has a type of conduit economy which enjoys considerable benefits when healthy economic conditions exist in the US, but suffers severely when times are bad there. In the longer term, a key challenge concerns the lack of competitiveness of the Irish economy. Both salaries and prices are high in relation to the rest of the world, and Ireland's attractiveness to foreign investors, even those from the other side of the Atlantic, is not what it once was. There is also the challenge of maintaining high employment levels for Ireland's highly educated young people. The fear is that Ireland's youth may return to the pattern of emigration that blighted the country for so long up to the Celtic Tiger years; in the twelve months to April 2009, Ireland experienced a small net emigration for the first time since 1995. Rising unemployment may also have unprecedented effects in Ireland due to the migration to the country of a proportionally high number of people from other EU states, most notably from Eastern Europe. Since 2004, the number of new arrivals in Ireland has amounted to a staggering 15 per cent of the entire population, following Ireland's decision to open its doors to the movement of workers from countries like Poland.

This enlightened policy reaped economic rewards in terms of high growth up to 2007, but sharp increases in dependency would place further pressure on an already struggling economy. Ireland's unemployment rate rose from 4.5 per cent in August 2007 to 12.4 per cent in August 2009.[30] The free movement of labour is theoretically a very positive development within the EU, allowing a more dynamic and fluid labour market to evolve, but for Ireland, with such a small population, there could be severe economic and social impacts if long-term unemployed new migrants choose to stay in the country on welfare. Ireland's small population also places it in a vulnerable position as regards credit and financing.

The crash in property prices and the end of the construction boom has left the banks with 'toxic assets', that is, debts on loans that the Irish Government plans to buy in an effort to get the banks lending again. This taxpayer-funded bail-out plan avoids nationalisation and involves the creation of a National Asset Management Agency (NAMA). For NAMA to work, the market will need to recover strongly. Irish governments of the future will find it economically necessary to reduce public spending and raise taxation. A return to high growth cannot be expected, even in the mid-term, and the model of Ireland's economic miracle must now include the sober conclusion that the huge inflation of property prices up to 2007 in a country with no real shortage of land was unfortunate. How Ireland deals with its current economic problems will provide a measure of the real achievement of the Celtic Tiger years. A return to modest growth would protect that achievement.

The challenges facing China remain as huge as one might expect for an enormous country with a massive population. With respect to the current global economic crisis, we believe they hinge on two crucial relationships which are of enormous importance to the development of China's real economy in the future: exports and economic growth on the one hand, currency appreciation and inflation on the other. China's domestic demand is of increasing importance to its economic growth in a world where demand for its exports is not growing as fast as it once was, although it should be pointed out that China's GDP growth in the twenty-first century has not depended as heavily on exports as is commonly assumed. There is a danger, however, that speculative capital inflows to China as a result of the appreciating yuan (CNY) will trigger a vicious circle of increased money supply, leading to inflation and rising interest rates. So China needs to stimulate domestic demand further and promote confidence without overexposing itself to 'get rich quick' speculators.

Looking beyond the immediate crisis, China faces a widening gap between the rich and the poor and between the wealth of rural and urban households. Damage to the natural environment is another enormous problem which must be tackled, given the rapid rises in production and consumption over the last 30 years. In September 2009, the Chinese leadership signalled its stance on protecting the environment by pledging a curb in carbon emissions and a commitment to invest in green energy, including the planting of vast forests and the generation of 15 per cent of the country's energy from renewable sources within a decade.[31] China's contin-uing integration into the world economy will to some degree depend on its ability to resolve, not only its environmental problems, but also the diffi-culties posed by damaging corruption and illegality in business, as well as a lack of rigorous protection of intellectual property rights in many parts of the country.

Nevertheless, China has made such great strides forward over the period of time this chapter has focused on that there is good reason to believe that the general direction of its economy will remain upward, onward and for-ward. Economic forecasts remain cautiously optimistic for China, given its relative isolation from the problems of the credit crunch and its very large reserves. The Chinese Government was able to announce a stimulus pack-age equivalent to some €500 billion towards the end of 2008 and, by summer 2009, with GDP growth forecasts at 8 per cent to 9 per cent for 2009 and higher for 2010, there is strong evidence that China is the first major world economy to recover from the downturn.

China's Government has also been able to ensure that credit continues to flow in the economy due to its management and regulation of the bank-ing system, but with free-flowing credit comes the risk of bubbles in the equities and property markets, as well as high inflation. China's banking sector has suffered previously from non-performing loans, leading to gov-ernment recapitalisation. There are concerns that a massive loan growth of 164 per cent in the first eight months of 2009, compared with the same period in 2008, representing CNY8,185 billion (translating as more than a trillion dollars of credit), cannot be sustained and that 'growth could falter as lending returns to a more sustainable level'.[32]

China's top banking regulator, the China Banking Regulatory Commis-sion, is likely to insist that the banks ensure they have enough reserves to cover bad loans and that the diversion of loans into speculative stocks and property investments be closely monitored and even discouraged. In other words, China faces risks to its economic miracle that may strike readers as reminiscent of the difficulties Ireland has faced. China is not immune from the vicissitudes of the world economy and globalisation has certainly led to an increase in global economic interdependence. Fortunately for China, its problems, whilst manifestly great, are not such that they are predicted to induce serious social instability. In brief, China's rise should continue.

The Celtic Tiger is no more, but what now stands in its place is a new Ire-land, barely recognisable to the one that existed throughout most of the last century. The Red Dragon has awakened and is shaking the world, and it shows itself to be a mighty beast of many colours, including green.

Ireland's economic engagement with China has been slow off the mark compared with other Western countries.

McWilliams warns: 'If you have a weakness, China will make it weaker.'[33] Although Ireland should maintain and continue to cultivate its economic relationship with the giant economy to the West, the time is now right to look to China as the emerging economic superpower of the East. We believe that China presents an opportunity for Ireland. Increased engagement with China by the Irish economy could offer a more balanced and diverse strategy for the challenges ahead. Civilisation in Ireland and China began some five thousand years ago. It's about time we got to know each other better.

CHAPTER 11

Irish Catch-Up Success and Reflections on Vietnam's Economic Reforms

Khuong Minh Vu

Introduction

The year 1986 marked a turning point in economic development in both Ireland and Vietnam. Both countries faced critical economic challenges and both responded with unprecedented reforms that have led to remarkable achievements for each country over the past two decades. In terms of per capita income (in dollars, as measured in purchasing power parity (PPP)) rankings, Ireland rose 21 places from nearly the bottom of the developed group in 1986 to the fourth highest place – after only Luxembourg, Norway and the US – in 2006, while Vietnam rose 17 places from ninety-fifth to seventy-eighth place over the same period (see Table 11.1).

In economic development, no country can provide a perfect model. However, there are countries whose development models and success can provide powerful reflections and insights that make some other countries think harder about the past, current and future paths of their development. In this spirit, Ireland's economic 'catch-up' appears to be a valuable model for Vietnam to reflect on and learn from as it prepares for the next phase in its economic development. Specifically, this chapter sets out Ireland's economic achievements in terms of a framework (based on the core factors of free market policy stance, good governance and human capital), or even a 'recipe' that other countries can follow on a pragmatic basis.

Although Ireland and Vietnam are dissimilar in their levels of development and population size,[1] what Ireland did right in its economic catch-up

Table 11.1: Change in per Capita Rankings* of Ireland and Vietnam: 2006 vs 1986

Country	Group Rank			World Rank		
	1986	2006	Change 1986–2006	1986	2006	Change 1986–2006
Developed economies (24 countries)						
Luxembourg	1	1	0	1	1	0
Norway	2	2	0	2	2	0
United States	4	3	1	4	4	0
Ireland	23	4	19	26	5	21
Switzerland	3	5	-2	3	7	-4
Iceland	7	6	1	7	8	-1
Canada	5	7	-2	5	9	-4
Netherlands	9	8	1	9	10	-1
Austria	8	9	-1	8	11	-3
Denmark	6	10	-4	6	12	-6
Australia	10	11	-1	10	13	-3
Sweden	11	12	-1	11	14	-3
Belgium	13	13	0	13	15	-2
United Kingdom	18	14	4	18	16	2
Finland	17	15	2	17	17	0
Germany	14	16	-2	14	18	-4
France	12	17	-5	12	19	-7
Japan	15	18	-3	15	20	-5
Greece	19	19	0	19	21	-2
Italy	16	20	-4	16	22	-6
Spain	21	21	0	23	23	0
New Zealand	20	22	-2	20	24	-4
Israel	22	23	-1	24	25	-1
Portugal	24	24	0	29	27	2
Developing East Asia (9 economies)						
Singapore	2	1	1	22	3	19
Hong Kong, China	1	2	-1	21	6	15
South Korea	3	3	0	38	26	12
Malaysia	4	4	0	49	35	14
Thailand	5	5	0	71	50	21
China	8	6	2	93	64	29
Indonesia	7	7	0	79	74	5
Philippines	6	8	-2	75	75	0
Vietnam	9	9	0	95	78	17

*per capita GDP in PPP $ (2005 price level).
Source: 105 economies with data available for the world rankings; data from World Development Indicators (WDI).

during the 1990s can offer relevant lessons for Vietnam. The two countries have much in common in terms of the economic issues they have faced, including the following. In 1986, both countries were the poorest in their peer groups. In terms of per capita gross domestic product (GDP), Ireland ranked twenty-third in the group of 24 developed nations, while Vietnam was at the bottom of the group of 9 developing East Asian economies (see Table 11.1). Both countries had historically suffered severe economic problems caused by economic mismanagement. For each country, the reform initiated at the depth of its crisis (in the late 1980s) has improved the people's standard of living substantially and enhanced their appreciation of reform. High levels of emigration in the past also made the Irish and Vietnamese more open to the world and better able to embrace opportunities brought about by globalisation in recent decades.[2] As laggards in development, both Ireland and Vietnam had received generous international aid for development. This source of aid accounts for nearly 3 per cent of the gross national product (GNP) for Ireland (largely from the European Union) and about 4 per cent of the GDP for Vietnam.[3] Both countries have great potential in terms of human capital, which is characterised by homogeneity, industriousness, adaptability and embracing of change. Finally, the Irish model has never relied on unique factors, such as a visionary leader or highly paid public servants, as seen in the development of Singapore. Therefore, the lessons from what Ireland did right are perhaps more transferable to other countries than those of other economic models such as the Nordic model.

Economic Reforms in Ireland and Vietnam

Ireland

In 1986, Ireland's economy was in a severe crisis. GDP shrank by -0.43 per cent from the previous year and the unemployment rate hovered at 17.4 per cent. As a percentage of GDP, government debt reached 114.5 per cent, the fiscal deficit exceeded 10 per cent and the current deficit was about 4.2 per cent.[4] Amidst the doom, the recently elected Taoiseach Charles Haughey, with the support of all the major players in the political–economic arena, launched a push for decisive economic reforms based on a strategic framework laid out by the National Economic and Social Council (NESC) in its report *Strategy for Development 1986–90: Growth, Employment and Fiscal Balance*, written in October 1986.[5] These reforms were the basis for a miraculous recovery. Over the twenty-year period of 1986–2006, Ireland's per capita GDP increased sharply, with its global rank ascending from twenty-sixth to fifth place (see Table 11.1).

Vietnam

In 1986, Vietnam was among the poorest countries in the world with a per capita GDP of US$203. After ten years of stagnation with the socialist development model, which began after the country was officially reunified in 1976, Vietnam fell into deep economic trouble. The country suffered formidable challenges, from severe food shortages to hyperinflation. For instance, the annual per capita food output fell from 304 kilogrammes (of paddy rice equivalent) in 1985 to 301 kilogrammes in 1986 and to 281 kilogrammes in 1987,[6] while inflation soared from 90 per cent in 1985 to 455 per cent in 1986.[7] The crisis provided a strong catalyst for Vietnam to embark on its unprecedented economic reforms marked by the Sixth Party Congress of the Communist Party of Vietnam held in December 1986.

The reforms, ranging from granting land use rights to farmers, to legalising the private sector, to opening the economy to the world and modernising the financial sector, have brought about remarkable results. The country achieved annual growth rates averaging 7.5 per cent for GDP and over 20 per cent for exports for the period 1986–2006. As a result, Vietnam's per capita GDP rank in the world rose by seventeen places from ninety-fifth in 1986 to seventy-eighth in 2006 (see Table 11.1).

However, Vietnam's per capita GDP was still below US$1,000 in 2008, and the road to prosperity seems to be narrower and bumpier ahead. Inflation, labour strikes, a deteriorating education system, corruption, pollution and an infrastructure deficit have become increasingly serious problems hindering further growth of the country. Learning lessons from what Ireland did right should not only shed light on the challenges currently faced by Vietnam, but may also suggest a means for Vietnam to advance towards a more robust and sustainable path of development. The next section sets out Ireland's economic achievements in the form of a framework or 'recipe' that other countries like Vietnam can use as a benchmark in gauging their own progress.

Determinants of Ireland's Catch-up Success

The literature on the Irish accomplishment has provided insightful views, which are not always in agreement, regarding the factors that explain Ireland's remarkable economic growth performance since 1986.[8] An examination of Ireland's success suggests a policy framework that includes three premises and ten execution concepts critical to the implementation of a catch-up endeavour (see Figure 11.1).

Figure 11.1: Three Premises and Ten Execution Concepts Critical to the Implementation of a Catch-Up Endeavour

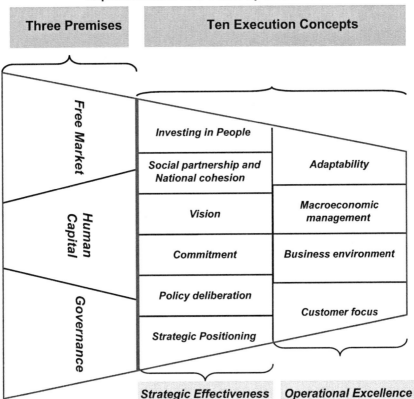

The three premises are a *free market*, which requires a faithful respect for the free market principles; *governance*, which necessitates the critical role of good governance in development; and *human capital*, which regards human capital as the country's most valuable competitive advantage and the major engine of development endeavors.

Free Market

Ireland's respect for the free market premise is evidenced by its vigorous efforts to foster market freedom, promote private entrepreneurship and reduce the size of government.

In terms of market freedom, Ireland rapidly rose in the global rankings, from twenty-fourth place in 1996 to seventh place in 2006 to third in 2008.[9]

In private entrepreneurship, Ireland has also ascended to the top positions in the rankings for the Organisation for Economic Co-operation and Development (OECD) countries. In 2007, it was ranked second among 'established entrepreneurs' and third among 'new firm entrepreneurs'.[10] Ireland decisively brought down the share of total government expenditures in GDP from 51.6 per cent in 1986 to 39.9 per cent in 1990 to 34.4 per cent in 2005.[11] In addition, the relative share of Ireland's public sector employment in the labour force was also reduced to a much lower level relative to Norway, Sweden, France, Finland and Belgium.[12]

Governance

This is a crucial determinant of the long-term performance of economies. Good governance encourages productive activities by all of the players in the economy, and therefore fosters economic development.[13] The conventional wisdom about good governance, however, is biased towards the traditional indicators of institutional quality, which include regulatory quality, transparency, government effectiveness and control of corruption, while overlooking the powerful role of the factors fostered by catch-up endeavours, such as commitment and pragmatism. For a country that initiates its catch-up endeavours following a crisis caused by many years of mismanagement in a flawed economic model, commitment and pragmatism are arguably the most critical factors that determine the effectiveness of the intended pathway to prosperity and the duration of success. This point can be well illustrated by looking at the dynamics of per capita rankings for selected OECD countries. As shown in Table 11.1, over the period 1986–2006, Ireland rose 21 places from twenty-sixth to fifth place. How could this have happened? Figures 11.2 and 11.3 provide insights into this.

Human Capital

Human capital has been determined by growth literature to be 'the main engine of growth'.[14] Ireland's success provides a good and distinctive example of this conclusion.

First, it shows that both aptitude (traditionally measured by educational attainment) and attitude are vital to successful development. While it takes a long time to increase the aptitude of a population, it can dramatically change its attitude regarding the circumstances that necessitate profound reforms towards gaining a clear vision that is deeply shared. Second, leveraging the country's human capital should be a top priority for a government

Figure 11.2: Governance in Ireland, Finland and France
Institutional Quality

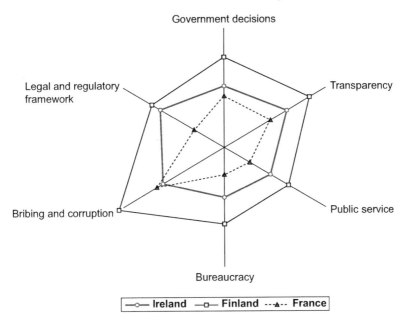

Commitment and Pragmatism

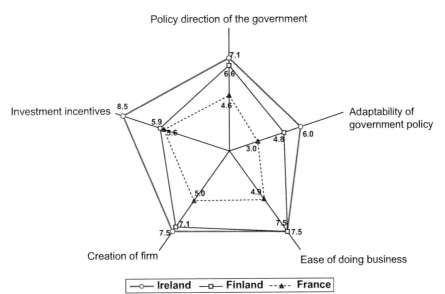

Figure 11.3: Human Capital in Ireland, Finland and France
Education and Aptitude

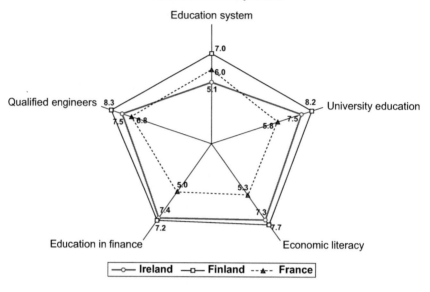

Culture and Attitudes

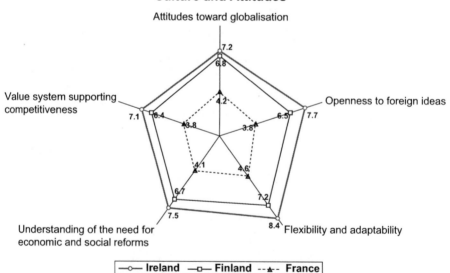

in its endeavour to foster economic development. To that end, in the late 1980s, the Industrial Development Agency (IDA), Ireland's agency in charge of attracting and developing foreign direct investment (FDI) into Ireland, switched 'the focus of attention away from tax incentives and finance' and towards human capital by promoting a young, educated, flexible and innovative working population. This refocus was successful, as pointed out by McSharry and White:

> Whether by design or good fortune, the business leaders associated Ireland with the very asset – human capital – they regarded as critical to success: bright, educated young people. And these were just the qualities that served to distinguish Ireland from her European competitors in the battle for industrial development.[15]

The IDA leveraged Ireland's human capital, not only from the domestic supply, but also from the Irish Diaspora population. A notable example is the case where the IDA convinced Intel to choose Ireland over competing countries as a location to invest in a large-scale microchip plant, despite Ireland's lack of experienced engineers in this field:

> [To eliminate this weakness, the IDA located] Irish engineers who were working abroad and had relevant experience in the semi-conductor industry. Within five weeks, over 300 Irish engineers, mainly in the US, had been identified and individually contacted; each of them had between three and seven years' experience in the production of volume semi-conductors. The final report handed to Intel had the positive finding that over 80 per cent of the expatriate engineers would return to Ireland if given a good career opportunity with a quality company. This report was crucial in satisfying Intel that Ireland could satisfactorily host an advanced microchip plant.[16]

Placing the primary focus on its human capital, Ireland's development strategy emphasises that its 'future prosperity requires the creation of high quality, high value-added employment and the pursuit of growth policies which will lead to increased quality employment.'[17]

Ten Execution Concepts

In order to suggest a way in which the tenets of the Irish catch-up model can be implemented and benchmarked in a clear and pragmatic fashion, we outline ten execution concepts that build on the above-mentioned three premises. They can be divided into two categories: *strategic effectiveness* (six concepts) and *operational excellence* (four concepts). The six strategic effectiveness concepts include vision, commitment, policy deliberation, social partnership and national cohesion, investing in people, and strategic positioning. The four operational excellence concepts are macroeconomic management, business environment, adaptability and customer-focus.

While the ten execution concepts are interconnected and important to the success of a development endeavour, the six strategic effectiveness concepts are crucial to long-term success and the four operational excellence concepts are vital for short- to medium-term accomplishment.

Six Strategic Effectiveness Concepts

Vision

For a robust and sustainable catch-up endeavour, a country needs to have a clear and inspiring vision for its future. Ireland set the vision to transform itself into 'a world-leading society that is rich in creativity, learning and personal and social well-being.'[18]

The NESC, which includes representatives from government, trade unions, employers, farmers, non-government organisations (NGOs), and independent experts, has argued that vision is the power that took Ireland from the past to the future.[19]

Commitment

Without a deep commitment to catch-up, a nation will not achieve such success, regardless of the greatness of its potential or the breadth of its opportunities for catch-up.

A deep commitment to catch-up enables a nation, not only to come together at difficult moments, but also to go decisively beyond conventional practice to pursue its dream.

Ireland is an excellent example of this hypothesis. At the height of its crisis in 1986, the key players in society, including government, opposition parties, labour unions and employers, set aside disputes and rivalries to endorse unprecedented measures that laid the foundation for the country's profound reform. This deep commitment allowed the Government to make painful but necessary decisions to cut the budget deficits and reduce public sector employment.[20] In a comparison, Sautet remarks that New Zealand also looked to make substantial reforms, but that it failed to 'become a growth dynamo like Ireland because the reforms implemented did not go beyond OECD standard practice'.[21]

Policy Deliberation

Policy deliberation plays a crucial role in ensuring a high quality government decision-making process and in enhancing the society's support for change.

The NESC played a central role in the country's policy deliberation process and it undertook a strategic, long-term analysis of Ireland's position and problems, which has enabled it to make outstanding contributions to the country's success.[22]

Social Partnership and National Cohesion

Social partnership was a distinctive feature of the Irish development model and became 'the backbone of the Irish economic policy'.[23] Ireland's social partnership was initiated with the first *Programme for National Recovery* (PNR) in 1987 when the country was in crisis. The PNR was negotiated on the basis of the NESC's report *A Strategy for Development 1986–1990*, which formulated an agreed strategy for Ireland 'to escape from its vicious circle of real stagnation, rising taxes and exploding debt'.[24] The PNR, which is now in its seventh renewal, laid the foundation for a highly productive partnership between the Government, labour force and employers, and played an important role in enabling Ireland to recover quickly from the crisis and rapidly move forward. Particularly, thanks to the PNR, labour strikes ceased to be a general problem in the two decades since 1987.[25]

The social partnership approach has been extensively applied in other countries in various formats and with varying focuses to enhance a society's productivity and coherence. For example, the Area-Based Partnership (ABP) initiatives, which were first introduced in Ireland in 1991, have led to concerted efforts at the local level to promote job creation and community development.[26]

The Irish model also emphasised national cohesion through economic development. In 2002, Ireland launched its National Spatial Strategy, a twenty-year strategy designed to enable every region in the country to reach its potential through strategic and well-coordinated investment programmes. This strategy, therefore, will not turn regions against one another, but create competition according their own strengths and their complementing of, and linkages with, other regions. Even since the downturn in the Irish economy in recent times, this programme has continued to promote the objective of balanced regional development.[27]

Investing in People

Ireland's attention to investing in people dates back to 1967 when Ireland introduced free secondary education nationwide and provided free school transport in rural areas.[28] Since 1986, the focus on investing in people has been even stronger and more strategic. Over the period 1986–2005, the share in GDP of the sectors serving people (including education, health care, recreational, cultural and sporting activities) rose from 10.9 per cent to 15.1 per cent, while the share for public administration, defence and compulsory security fell from 6.3 per cent to 3.6 per cent.[29] Ireland has also vigorously stimulated an enterprise culture through entrepreneurship initiatives, even in primary schools, 'to enable people to become more competent decision makers and active participants in their local communities'.[30]

Strategic Positioning

Ireland is a small economy that has long been open to the world, especially since it joined the European Economic Community (EEC) in 1973. However, in 1986, the NESC realised that the country's integration and development strategy was ineffective due to a number of factors, including:

- The narrow focus of promotion efforts that attracted FDI in only a limited number of manufacturing industries.
- The lack of incentive for FDI firms to upgrade their operations beyond manufacturing toward higher value-added stages, such as research and development, product design, applications engineering, marketing and market research, and distribution.
- The neglect of development of indigenous firms.
- The failure to establish stronger linkages between FDI sectors and the remainder of the economy.[31]

Based upon these conclusions, Ireland painstakingly revised its development strategy with a strategic positioning characterised by three features: deeper integration, high value-added and quality employment, and broad-based industrial growth.[32] The new strategy was hugely successful. The trade-to-GDP ratio went up from 100 per cent in 1986 to 150 per cent in 2006, after peaking at 184 per cent in 2000; the FDI stock rose from US$36.6 billion in 1986 to US$156.6 billion in 2006.

Over the period 1986–2005 (for which data is available), Ireland's manufacturing sector's value-added component rose by 4.8 times, while in an advanced economy like Finland the increase in this measure was only by 2.3 times. The share of the value-added component in manufacturing sector output in Ireland improved from an average of 34.4 per cent over the period 1986–90 to 34.8 per cent for 2001–5. In Finland, this figure declined from 33.8 per cent to 31.6 per cent. Ireland also achieved notable success in its growth strategy beyond manufacturing. Ireland's financial service sector's value-added component rose by 265.7 per cent over the period 1995–2005 with its share in GDP jumping from 17.3 per cent to 25.8 per cent. For comparison, in Finland this sector grew by only 125.6 per cent over the same period, with its share in GDP climbing slightly, from 18.8 per cent to 20.7 per cent.[33]

The Four Operational Excellence Concepts

Macroeconomic Management

Since 1986, Ireland has markedly improved its macroeconomic management. The government budget turned from chronic deficits (-10.3 per cent of GDP in 1986) to surpluses (+4.7 per cent in 2000). Over the same period (1986–2000), government debt reported as a percentage of GDP dropped from 114.5 per cent to 39.1 per cent and the unemployment rate fell from 17.4 per cent to 4.3 per cent.[34]

Business Environment

As assessed by the OECD, 'by the end of 1997, Ireland was one of the less regulated OECD countries in terms of barriers to entry and entrepreneurship, market openness, and labor markets.'[35] In the 'ease of doing business' rankings published by the World Bank, Ireland was consistently in the top tier, ranking eleventh in 2005, tenth in 2006, eighth in 2007 and seventh in 2008. The most attractive features of Ireland's business environment are 'starting a business', 'protecting investors', 'paying taxes', 'closing a business', and 'getting credits'.[36]

Infrastructure, however, remains one of Ireland's major disadvantages and it is interesting to note that Ireland has recently been better organised in solving this problem.

In 2004, Ireland committed twice the EU average to public investment, with a total capital expenditure of about €5.6 billion (4.9 per cent of GNP), a rise of 177 per cent from €2 billion in 1997.[37] In 2005, Ireland launched 'Transport 21', which aims to deliver a world-class transport system to Ireland. This expenditure is the largest investment ever made in Ireland's transport system, with €34 billion being invested over the period 2006–2015.[38] Ireland has also been identified as one of the world's leading users of the private sector to solve the infrastructure deficit problem, especially with regard to transport and waste treatment.[39]

Adaptability

In the face of constant, rapid and unpredicted changes in the external environment, adaptability is important as it permits a government to lower the costs of overcoming new challenges and to seize emerging opportunities.

It is worth noting that the adaptability of the Irish Government's policies has been driven by policy studies. For example, the 'Culliton Report', *A Time for Change*, produced by the Industrial Policy Review Group in 1992, which sharply raised awareness of the importance of a competitive business environment to the development of enterprise, had considerable influence on policy regarding investment in infrastructure and human capital.[40] To better address the new challenges pointed out by the report, the IDA was reorganised in 1994 into three agencies: IDA Ireland, responsible for attracting and nurturing FDI; Enterprise Ireland (EI), in charge of the development and promotion of the indigenous business sector; and Forfás, the national policy and advisory board that is accountable for enterprise, trade, science, technology and innovation.

Customer Orientation

Strong customer orientation is one of the most prominent features of the Irish development model. A good example is provided by the support to foreign investors from the IDA, as guided by its mission statement: 'We will carry out our mission with integrity, professional excellence and responsiveness to all with whom we come in contact.'[41] It is important to note that, in attracting FDI, the IDA has not resorted solely to financial incentives, but has tried to provide investors with the services needed to help them make better and more informed decisions, and improve the efficiency of their operations. Achieving a high level of investor satisfaction enabled Ireland to obtain greater investments from each established investor towards higher value-added activities.[42]

Reflections on Vietnam's Reforms through the Lens of the Irish Catch-Up Model

Two major concerns have arisen with regard to Vietnam's economic progress. The first is that Vietnam's growth has been below potential, as evidenced by its inferior performance relative to China, which Vietnam has followed as a development model (see Figure 11.4A). It is even more disconcerting that Vietnam's growth path has been identical to that of

Indonesia, which had been praised by the World Bank[43] as a high-performing nation before it collapsed when the Asian financial crisis erupted in 1997 (see Figure 11.4B). The second is the deterioration in the country's fundamental conditions for high economic growth. Inflation rose to 12.6

Figure 11.4: (A) Vietnam's Growth in Comparison to China's (per capita GDP) (B) Per Capita GDP Growth Path since the US$200 Level

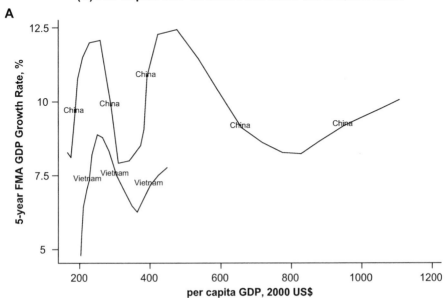

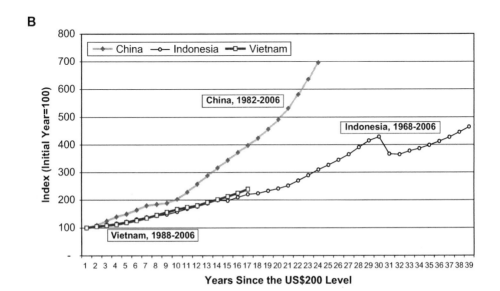

per cent in 2007 and to over 20 per cent in 2008. Corruption, labour strikes, crime, environmental pollution and infrastructure bottlenecks have become formidable problems, and economic growth is expected to substantially slow down. As such, it is now vital, even at a time when the Irish economy itself is experiencing a severe downturn, that Vietnam employs the policy framework constructed from the Irish 'catch-up' model to investigate what may have gone wrong with Vietnam's own reforms.

Vietnam's Compliance with the Three Premises

Free Market

Vietnam's economic reform, initiated in 1986, has gradually been moving towards a market economy. This transition has enabled the country to transform its economy in the right direction. However, the Government has not fully embraced free market principles, as is evidenced by its designation that the state-owned sector takes the leading role in the economy and its aggressive expansion of government employment and application of very inefficient policies. As Perkins observes:

> Vietnam's government-directed approach in creating state-owned conglomerates, [...] appears to be little more than a repackaging of existing arrangements without a change in business behavior. [...] It is hard to see what contribution these new, larger units will make to Vietnam's international competitiveness.[44]

Furthermore, Vietnam has accelerated its expansion of public sector employment relative to the economy over time, which is in a sharp contrast with not only the Irish model but also the pattern observed for China (see Table 11.2).

Governance

Vietnam's efforts to upgrade the quality of its governance are alarmingly inadequate.

Corruption has become a chronic and severe problem. In the global corruption perception rankings, published by Transparency International, Vietnam's rank has been worsening over time: seventy-fourth in 1998, seventy-sixth in 2000, eighty-fifth in 2002, one hundred and second in 2004, one hundred and eleventh in 2006, and one hundred and twenty-first in 2008.[45] Vietnam's government effectiveness is not only low, but is

**Table 11.2: Employment Growth in 1995–2000 and 2000–2005:
Vietnam vs. China**

Sector	Vietnam		China	
	1995–2000	2000–2005	1995–2000	2000–2005
The Economy [E]	13.9%	13.6%	5.9%	5.2%
The Public Sector (Government, Party, and SOEs) (P)	15.2%	22.9%	-21.1%	-17.0%
Public sector expansion (+) or reduction (-) relative to the economy (P-E)	+1.3%	+9.3%	-27.0%	-22.2%

Source: Author's calculations from national statistics (Vietnam: Statistical Yearbooks 2001–2006, Establishment Census 2002; China: Statistical Yearbooks 2005 and 2006).

declining. This decline is a cause for concern because it is in contrast to the patterns observed in China and India (see Figure 11.5).

Human Capital

Human capital has not been effectively mobilised in the drive for economic development in Vietnam.

Vietnam has focused mainly on its abundance of cheap labour and lax environmental controls to attract FDI. However, labour strikes have recently become a serious problem and the country faces a shortage of skilled

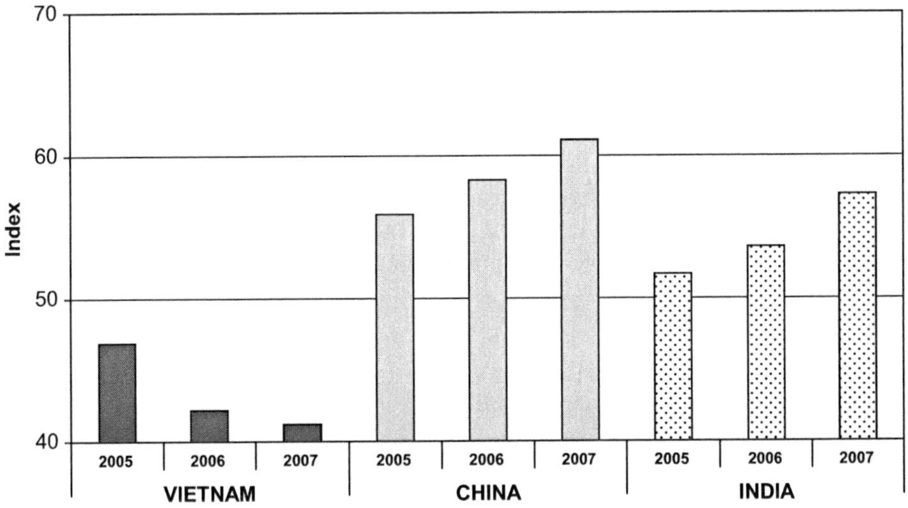

Figure 11.5: Government Effectiveness in Vietnam, China and India

labour.[46] On the other hand, the Government is plagued by ideological loyalty and corruption and has made little effort to recruit or promote people of high integrity and competence. The exploitation of connections and bribery are common in government as the means to get recruited or promoted.[47]

Vietnam's Application of the Ten Execution Concepts

Strategic Effectiveness Concepts

Vision

Vietnam has set its objective to 'become an industrialized country by 2020'.[48] This aim, however, does not have a clear direction for development and does not provide a strong moral purpose to motivate the people.

Commitment

Lacking a clear vision, a nation's commitment tends to be shallow. In its reforms, Vietnam has taken 'a cautious economic stance' and is not willing to take 'risks in order to achieve higher economic growth'.[49] A vivid example was Vietnam's refusal to sign a trade agreement with the US in September 1999. A US trade official noted: 'When you compare this to the effort put forward by China during trade negotiations, [...] it shows how Vietnam is simply not convinced about opening up.'[50] Perkins further commented: '[This] is clear evidence of the reluctance of many officials, even in the top leadership, to accept the kind of industrial policy that is likely to be the most appropriate for their country.'[51]

Policy Deliberation

Vietnam has been avoiding policy deliberation. All of the important decisions made by the Government are made by the communist party leadership without public consultation with outside experts and public discussions. The decisions made at the national level are made by the politburo, while those at the local level are made by the local leadership committee of the party.[52] There have also been serious concerns about the quality of government decisions. Many, including the decision on the Dung Quat refinery project – the first such project of its type in Vietnam, which was initiated in the 1980s and has made slow progress in coming to fruition since then, despite a number of attempts to re-launch it and bring in new partners – the demolishing of the existing national assembly hall to build a new one, and the merging of Hanoi (the capital) with Ha Tay province, have been strongly criticised.[53]

Social Partnership and National Cohesion

Vietnam has made significant efforts to mobilise resources and social support to alleviate poverty and help the poor, especially in remote areas. However, social partnership in the country is weak and driven by the instructions of the party. On the other hand, the country's development policy does not enhance national cohesion. The Government has merged and split provinces without strategic consideration. The number of provinces has risen from 40 to 64 since 1990.[54] More importantly, the provinces compete against one another for government subsidies and foreign investment.

Investing in People

Compared to nations with comparable per capita income, the Vietnamese have an appreciably better education level.[55] However, during the reform period, the country neglected to invest in its people. The education system has deteriorated in its training quality and moral values. For example, a recent survey by the Ministry of Education of 1,827 students at 12 universities and colleges shows that 85 per cent have cheated on exams, 42 per cent have plagiarised, and 36 per cent have begged or bribed professors for good grades.[56] Society has also paid the price for the heavy financial burden borne by students, especially at the primary and secondary levels.[57]

Strategic Positioning

Vietnam's lack of strategic positioning has severely limited development. According to a recent report by the Industrial Policy and Strategy Institute (IPSI), the think tank of Vietnam's Ministry of Trade and Industry, the share of the value-added component in gross industrial output (VA/GO) has declined substantially from 42.5 per cent in 1995 to 38.45 per cent in 2005, to 29.63 per cent in 2006 and to 26.3 per cent in 2007.

Operational Effectiveness Concepts

Despite this, Vietnam has performed relatively well on the four operational excellence concepts.

Macroeconomic Management

Since 1986, Vietnam has had impressive success in stabilising the macro-economic environment. The annual inflation rate was brought down from 455 per cent in 1986 to an average of 6.3 per cent for the period 1996–2006. The exchange rate of local currency per US dollar has been depreciating over time, but in a controllable pattern, from VND11,015 (per US dollar) in 1995 to VND14,514 in 2000, to VND16,054 in 2006 and to VND16,806 in October 2008, while foreign reserves have risen consistently from US$1.379 billion (equal to two months of imports) in 1995 to 23.872 billion (equal to eight months of imports) in 2007. The country's fiscal and trade deficits have been kept at low levels. As a percentage of GDP, the average level for the period 1996–2006 was -2.2 per cent for the fiscal balance and -1.8 per cent for the trade balance.

Business Environment

Vietnam has come a long way in its transition from a command economy to a market economy since 1986. The business environment has significantly improved, especially since 2000, when the enterprise law was put in place. Vietnam's freedom score rose from 44.3 to 49.8 in the Index of Economic Freedom in 2007, with business freedom rising from 40 to 60 and trade freedom from 51 to 62.8 over the same period. Currently, Vietnam's economy is the one hundred and forty-fifth freest in the 2009 Index. Its score has improved somewhat, reflecting moderate improvements in three of the ten categories. The country is now ranked thirty-second out of forty-one countries in the Asia–Pacific region, and its overall score is lower than the world average.[58] In addition, in the World Bank's 'ease of doing business' rankings, Vietnam was ranked ninety-ninth in 2006 and ninety-first in 2008.

Adaptability

Vietnam has been adapting rather well to changes in the external environment over the course of its reform from a closed economy in the late 1980s to one of the most open economies in the world, with the trade-to-GDP ratio reaching 154 per cent in 2006. In addition, Vietnam is one of the top performers among developing countries in attracting FDI, as the FDI stock exceeded US$40 billion or over 60 per cent of GDP in 2007.[59]

Customer Orientation

The Government has become more customer-oriented in its dealings with foreign investors. A notable example is the Government's success in attracting Intel's investment of US$1 billion to build its largest chip assembly-and-test plant in Ho Chi Minh City in 2006.[60]

Conclusion

This chapter has investigated Ireland's economic catch-up from the late 1980s through to the early part of this century, and proposed a framework that other countries could use as a benchmark in trying to emulate Ireland's long-term success. The model consists of three premises about the fundamental role of free market, governance and human capital in economic development, and ten execution concepts, which can be divided into six strategic effectiveness concepts and four operational excellence ones. In this model, the three premises and six strategic effectiveness concepts are crucial to building a foundation for long-term prosperity, while the four operational excellence concepts are vital for short- and medium-term growth.

Vietnam has performed rather well according to the four operational effectiveness concepts, which has resulted in its impressive economic growth over the past two decades. However, the country's inadequate upholding of the three premises and poor implementation of the six strategic effectiveness concepts have considerably lessened its capability to rapidly advance toward prosperity.

Using the Irish catch-up policy framework as a benchmark, Vietnam's economic reforms have performed poorly in upholding the three premises and applying the six strategic effectiveness concepts. However, the country has performed fairly well in implementing the four operational excellence concepts. These findings explain why Vietnam has achieved impressive results in economic growth since 1986 and why its foundation for long-term growth has weakened over time. Based upon this performance, the country is expected to face more formidable challenges during its next stage of development.

CHAPTER 12

The Elephant and the Tiger: India and Ireland in a Globalised World

P.S. Raghavan

Though set in vastly different socio-economic contexts and far apart in scale and magnitude, Ireland's Celtic Tiger phenomenon and India's economic resurgence over the past two decades had some striking parallels and some important contrasts.

In 1991, India was in a similar predicament to that in which Ireland found itself in the late 1980s – with a stagnant domestic economy, a high level of unemployment, a severe balance of payments deficit and rising debt-servicing obligations. In response to this crisis, India's then Finance Minister Dr Manmohan Singh (now prime minister since 2004) introduced far-reaching reforms, dismantling restrictions on industrial production and imports, enabling expansion of the private sector and liberalising the foreign direct investment (FDI) regime.

These reforms had a dramatic impact. From 1991 to 2003, the Indian economy – in those days often likened to an elephant because of its size and sluggishness – grew at an average annual rate of over 6 per cent. Organisation for Economic Co-operation and Development (OECD) figures show that, in the five fiscal years 2004 to 2008 (ending 31 March each year), the gross domestic product (GDP) growth was 8.5 per cent, 7.5 per cent, 9.4 per cent, 9.6 per cent and 9 per cent respectively.

Ireland underwent a similar transformation – starting from a higher economic base, of course. Over the decade from 1990 to 2000, the economy grew at an annual average rate of over 6 per cent, with the period from 1995 to 2000 seeing much higher growth rates. After a brief dip in 2001 and 2002, the economy continued to grow at a rate of about 5 per cent until 2007.

A surge in FDI and a strong export performance attended the Celtic Tiger years in Ireland. At its peak in 2000–5, Ireland attracted in excess of US$20 billion each year. India's FDI record was far more modest – in an economy about six times as large as that of Ireland, annual FDI ranged from US$4 billion to US$6 billion during this period.

India's exports of goods and services were about 20 per cent of GDP; Ireland's exports, relative to its GDP, were about four times as much. In India, as in Ireland, the services sector experienced robust growth. The services sector contributed nearly 65 per cent to GDP in Ireland in 2007; in India, the proportion was about 55 per cent. Services exports also increased strongly. By 2008, services constituted about 40 per cent of total exports in both countries. Banking, financial, insurance and business consultancy services formed a significant proportion of Ireland's services exports, while India's services exports were dominated by computer and related information services.

From 1990 to 2007, the contribution of industry to GDP fell from 30 per cent to 25 per cent in Ireland; in India, it increased from 25 per cent to 29 per cent. Particularly over the last few years, manufacturing has shown a declining trend in Ireland, its share of GDP falling to about 12 per cent in 2007. In India, manufacturing capacity has continued to expand, its contribution being 16 per cent of GDP in 2007. Over the past decade or so, India has emerged as a design and production base for a wide range of industrial products.

Rapid growth did not significantly alter the aggregate savings pattern in India. The savings rate remained at its traditional level of around 30 per cent, continuing to generate most of the resources required for domestic investment.

The real estate sector rode the crest of the economic boom in both countries. Its rise was particularly steep in Ireland. By 2007, the contribution of the building construction industry to GDP was, by some estimates, over 20 per cent. While the construction industry in India was second only to agriculture in employment generation, its contribution to GDP in 2007 was a more modest 5 per cent.

Both countries benefited from their young populations and the quality of their educational institutions, the combination of which produced, in each country, a growing pool of young, technically qualified individuals from which the expanding high-technology knowledge industry could draw.

The Diasporas of both countries played an important role in each – with remittances, mobilising inward FDI, and returning in significant numbers to their countries of origin to occupy the managerial positions being created by the expanding economies.

There was, of course, a considerable gap in the levels of development of the two countries. The size of India, its economic disparities, social challenges and infrastructural problems meant that its growth was variegated, with significant regional variations. The Indian Government had, therefore, to constantly temper its pro-growth policies with a developmental agenda, seeking to address the rising aspirations of India's poor for upward economic mobility. The banks, dominated by the public sector, were tightly regulated; developmental lending was an essential part of their credit portfolio. Government expenditure on infrastructure, health and education raised an estimated fifteen to twenty million people out of poverty each year, constantly increasing the consumption demands of India's billion-strong population. Many of these factors cushioned India against the impact of the global financial crisis of 2008–9 and the subsequent economic downturn.

Historically, India and Ireland have had an extraordinarily diverse interaction, disproportionate to their relative sizes and to the geographical distance between them. This should have reinforced the mutual desire to exploit the complementarities in their economic trajectories.

Ireland's India connections date back to the nineteenth century, when hundreds of Irish missionaries set up educational, health care and social help institutions across the length and breadth of British India. At another level, numerous Irish soldiers, civil servants, doctors and engineers were recruited for the British colonial administration in India. Many of them made distinguished contributions to social and economic projects in India.

At yet another level, a political affinity developed in the late nineteenth century between the Irish Home Rule movement[1] and India's freedom movement.[2] The Indian National Congress and the Irish nationalist movement maintained close contact through the twentieth century. The profile of this association was considerably enhanced by the mutual admiration of Eamon de Valera[3] and Jawaharlal Nehru.[4] The mutual influence is evident in Part IV of the Indian Constitution – the Directive Principles of State Policy – which is drawn from Article 45 of the Irish Constitution.

On India's independence in 1947 and Ireland's declaration of a republic in 1949, the leaders of the two countries declared their desire to translate the extraordinary political solidarity into strong bilateral trade links. However, given the different levels of development of the two countries, their distinct domestic preoccupations and the geographical distance between them, the practical scope for promoting this political agenda was somewhat limited.

Bilateral trade and economic relations languished at insignificant levels in the four decades from the 1950s to the 1980s. The political relationship remained cordial and, particularly after Ireland's accession to the United Nations in 1955, Irish neutrality and India's policy of non-alignment during World War II provided the basis for co-operation in the international arena on issues of development, disarmament, decolonisation and opposition to apartheid.

The economic resurgence of the 1990s in both countries reignited mutual interest in intensification of business links. Irish President Mary Robinson's state visit to India in 1993 was an indication of this. In her speech at the presidential banquet in Delhi, she acknowledged that bilateral trade had hitherto been at 'a very low level' and that conditions were now more conducive to expanding economic relations through joint ventures and increased trade. A flurry of business exchanges followed, starting with an exploratory visit to Ireland in 1994 by a delegation of the Confederation of Indian Industry (CII). Irish Tourism and Trade Minister Enda Kenny led a 30-member Irish delegation to India soon after in 1995. Several Memoranda of Understanding (MoUs) were concluded during that visit, involving CII, the Irish Trade Board, the Irish Business and Employers Confederation (IBEC), Export Import Bank of India, and a number of Irish-owned telecommunication, technical services and computer software companies.

In the Information Technology (IT) sector, synergies were quickly established. The Irish company Kindle Banking (Software) Systems made India its base for Asia in 1998. Other Irish IT companies discovered the competitive advantage of outsourcing to India. The offshore call centre business – pioneered by Ireland in the early 1990s – was rapidly slipping away to lower cost countries like India, forcing Irish businesses up the business process outsourcing (BPO) value chain. Particular efforts were made to establish links between Irish-owned and Indian IT companies, through a trade delegation to India in 2000 led by the Irish Minister for Enterprise, Trade and Employment Mary Harney, during which an MoU was concluded between India's National Association of Software & Services Companies (NASSCOM) and the Irish Software Association.

Other links were created in the IT industry, but they escaped significant attention since they were between branches of multinational corporations in both countries. By the end of the 1990s, almost every IT multinational corporation (MNC) which was present in Ireland had also established a base in India. The expanding Indian operations of the IT MNCs included provision of IT products and services to their European branches. In the complex MNC web of supplies, payments and transfer pricing, transactions are not necessarily reflected in the trade statistics of the country of origin or final destination. Visa data showed that there were regular exchanges of personnel between the Indian and Irish branches of IT MNCs – a trend that has strengthened further in recent years.

Another development that has largely flown under the radar is the significant increase since the early 2000s of technically qualified Indian personnel in the Irish economy. The rapid expansion of the Irish economy in the 1990s created demand for skilled manpower – particularly in the health care and IT sectors – that could not be met from within Ireland. In 2000, the Irish College of Anaesthetists went on a special mission to India (and Pakistan) to recruit anaesthetists to meet a sudden shortage. Similar recruitments were made from India of radiologists, physiotherapists and nurses, as well as doctors of some specialised disciplines. A steady stream of IT professionals and engineers continued to swell the Indian population in Ireland. In most years between 2000 and 2008, the largest number of work permits issued to applicants from outside the European Economic Area (EEA) was to Indians. This demand for Indian professionals continued to increase even after 2004, when a wider pool of technically qualified personnel from the new European Union (EU) countries became available to Ireland. The Indian population in Ireland grew from an estimated 2000 in the year 2000 to nearly 25,000 by 2008.

In October 1999, the Irish Government launched an 'Asia Strategy' for 'long-term development of foreign earnings in Asia'. Notwithstanding the growing (even if not yet intense) India–Ireland economic engagement, as well as the historical affinities, the strategy did not include India as a focus country. Its focus was restricted to East Asia and Southeast Asia. It was only during the mid-term review of the strategy in 2004 that India was included as a priority country in Ireland's Asia Strategy.

In an emphasis of this new thrust, Taoiseach Bertie Ahern led the largest ever Irish trade mission to India in January 2006, with three cabinet ministers and over ninety Irish business representatives. The six-day visit, covering New Delhi, Bangalore and Mumbai, was packed with meetings, workshops and presentations. It was reported that €35 million worth of contracts were concluded during the visit. A number of MoUs were concluded by business representatives on the trip. By far the biggest achievement of the visit, however, was that it provided a broad exposure to Indian and Irish businesses of the huge opportunities for collaboration. This infusion of awareness imparted a strong impetus for business exchanges.

India–Ireland bilateral merchandise trade increased by about 15 per cent in 2007. Trade in services was estimated to have grown by about 20 per cent.

New investment initiatives were launched in both directions in IT, pharmaceuticals, food processing, electrical machinery, mechanical engineering and the building materials industry. The Irish export promotion agency Enterprise Ireland (EI) opened an office in New Delhi in 2006, and the inward investment promotion agency, the Industrial Development Agency (IDA), established a presence in Mumbai in early 2008.

On the whole, India–Ireland economic activity from 1990 to 2007 was distinctly below potential. Bilateral merchandise trade was only about €450 million in 2007 – well under 0.5 per cent of the foreign trade of either country. While the trade in services grew more briskly, its estimated level of €400 million in 2007 was still incommensurate with the opportunities. Two-way investment flows were equally below par. Ireland's 'educational exports' – the Indian students studying at its higher education institutions – were also below expectations in terms of numbers. By 2008, there were about twelve hundred Indian students in Irish universities – far from the target of four thousand Indian students by 2009, a target set in the mid-term Asia Strategy review of the Department of Foreign Affairs.

The fundamental reason for this underperformance was undoubtedly an awareness gap between potential collaborators on both sides. While multinationals created their own networks, Irish companies were less prepared to leave their comfort zone of business with the US, the UK and the rest of the EU. Equally, Indian corporates needed encouragement to look beyond their traditional contacts in the US, the UK and a few of the bigger EU economies. Perhaps the governments and business chambers in the two countries could have been more proactive in highlighting the opportunities.

The role of the Irish Diaspora in the Celtic Tiger phenomenon could certainly have been a useful case study for India in the early stages of its economic revival. In the early 1990s, immediately after the launch of its liberalisation programmes, there was a concerted effort to attract investments from non-resident Indians (NRIs) through high-yield India Development Bonds and mutual funds investing in Indian equity markets. While this effort produced satisfactory results, the spectacular Irish success in harnessing its Diaspora to persuade large foreign corporations to invest substantially in Ireland merited study and emulation.

Another useful case study for India (and other countries seeking FDI) would be the methodologies evolved by the IDA to identify potential foreign investors, to persuade them of Ireland's unique attractions, to tailor packages of incentives according to their unique needs and to guide them through the initial stages of their investment in Ireland.

Looking ahead, it could be argued that the present situation offers even more mutually beneficial opportunities for the two countries than the last two decades. The Indian economy in its current stage provides interesting openings for the Irish sectors which have been hardest hit by the recent downturn.

In India, the immediate impact of the global financial crisis in late 2008 was a withdrawal of funds by foreign institutional investors, a fall in external commercial borrowings, a decline in stock market indices and a contraction of credit flows. Exports dropped and the growth in industrial production fell accordingly. GDP growth had to descend from the giddy levels of recent years.

However, the intrinsic fundamentals of the economy and a governmental stimulus package ensured a reasonably orderly recovery. GDP growth in fiscal year 2009 (ending 31 March 2009) was 6.9 per cent, according to the latest revised estimates. Official projections are for growth of about 6.5 per cent in fiscal year 2010 and close to 8 per cent in fiscal year 2011. Inward FDI recorded a remarkable quantum jump in the past three years – after hovering between US$4 billion and US$6 billion between 2000 and 2005, it soared to US$23 billion, US$34 billion and US$33 billion in fiscal years 2007, 2008 and 2009 respectively. Foreign institutional investors (FII) have returned in strength to the Indian market, with net investments of US$10 billion in the first half of fiscal year 2010.

The Indian real estate sector continues its robust growth. The global crisis caused a correction in property prices, ranging from 10 to 20 per cent in various parts of the country, but this trend is already reversing. As a necessary corollary of India's development, the need for new dwelling units is projected to grow steadily – over the next 10 to 15 years, 80 to 90 million units are expected to be constructed. A requirement of about 370 million square feet of office and commercial space is projected just for 2009–10.

The construction industry will also benefit from the Indian Government's programme of massive investment in infrastructure. The plans include the construction of 7,000 kilometres of roads every year for the next 5 years, doubling the country's seaport capacity to 1,500 million tonnes, and developing 35 new airports in addition to upgrading 300 existing ones.

A number of Irish property developers, architects and engineering, procurement and construction (EPC) contractors have already entered the Indian market. The Quinn Property Group recently announced the opening of a 1.2 million sq. ft commercial complex in Hyderabad. The Irish multinational CRH has acquired a 50 per cent stake in a cement manufacturing company in Hyderabad. The building materials industry in India is doing well as a consequence.

The Indian telecommunications industry continues to be one of the fastest growing in the world. India added an average of 9.5 million new mobile phone customers every month in 2008. Irish companies providing niche IT services for the telecommunications sector are moving into this market.

The Indian banking sector provides yet another segment of opportunity for Irish IT companies. Because of conservative credit policies and prudent debt management, Indian banks emerged from the global financial turmoil with their assets largely secured and with reasonable levels of profitability. A major technical upgrade is now underway, seeking to extend the benefits of ATMs, mobile banking, real time settlement systems and electronic payment mechanisms to rural and semi-urban areas in India.

Education is an area of tremendous promise. Ireland has placed considerable emphasis on marketing higher education to Indian students. With 50 per cent of India's 1.2 billion population under the age of 25, the increase in demand for quality higher education outstrips the pace at which additional capacity is being created in the country. The shortfall in capacity is precisely in areas in which Ireland is seeking to attract talent. Significant numbers of Indian students seek postgraduate programmes abroad in IT, science and engineering disciplines. This mobility is encouraged by the easy availability from Indian banks of educational loans with liberal repayment schedules. Loan repayments qualify for income tax deductions.

Ireland has so far been less successful in attracting Indian students than Australia (which has over 95,000 Indian students), the US (about 80,000) and the UK (about 30,000). A focused marketing strategy is required, which can deal more effectively with the competition and with nagging visa issues.

Closely allied to education is a collaborative relationship in science and technology. In 2008, the Irish Government published a strategy paper for a 'Smart Economy', in which Ireland would be the hub of innovation and commercialisation of new technologies in Europe. The increasing use of India by foreign corporate entities as a research and development (R&D) base illustrates the potential of research collaboration as a cost-effective stimulus for Irish innovation and research. A programme of cooperation in science and technology, concluded in May 2009 between the two governments, envisages such collaboration through joint research projects by institutions in India and Ireland.

Alongside the opportunity for investments in India's fast-growing economy is the potential for attracting Indian investment into Ireland. Indian investments in Ireland today include three pharmaceutical companies and manufacturing facilities for electrical transformers, substation automation and industrial fasteners. This is a small proportion of the Indian investment abroad over recent years. In fiscal years 2008 and 2009 alone, Indian companies have invested US$33 billion abroad. More and more Indian companies are seeking bases for their European operations. As it did with US investors in another era, the IDA would need to evolve methodologies sensitive to the Indian corporate ethos to persuade these companies that English-speaking Ireland, with its low corporate taxation and other incentives, would meet their requirements better than alternative locations. The correction in Irish property prices and the reduction underway in unit labour costs should reinforce the argument.

The picture, therefore, is that, despite a long history of affinity between the two countries, Ireland and India did not take full advantage of the synergies created by their rapid growth over the last two decades. The size of its economy, its internal dynamics and its relative insulation from the global financial crisis cushioned India against the impact of the global downturn. India's sustained economic growth, its expanding manufacturing base and its young, technically qualified population continue to offer opportunities for Irish businesses. It appears that Irish businesses (as distinct from foreign corporations based in Ireland) are now increasingly seeking to exploit these opportunities. This has imparted momentum to the activities of the Ireland India Business Association, launched in May 2008 when the downturn was already on the horizon. The two governments have demonstrated their greater commitment to fostering commercial links between Ireland and India.

The World after the Financial Crisis

The year 2010 will mark a crucial turning point in Irish and world history. Globally, the financial crisis is the first taste we have of how the world may evolve through the twenty-first century. In the next ten years, the developed world will engage in a period of rebuilding, while the developing world will simply be building.

In Ireland, 2010 will definitively mark the end of the economic 'miracle'. We now face a financial crisis that is bringing into open view a range of institutional weaknesses that make this period in our history and the debate on the way forward from here the most important since the early 1920s.

While the 'panic' phase of the global financial crisis is now over, the developed world faces the next decade burdened by high levels of debt at government, household and banking sector levels, not to mention looming contingent liabilities in the form of demographics-driven health care and pension costs.

It is possible that some developed world countries could regress in light of the pressures of the financial crisis, as countries like Argentina and Uruguay did in the last century. Ireland must move forward. Ireland is still a young nation with an adolescent economy. Only by understanding the nature of the changes that occurred through our 'great transformation' and by adopting a strategic view of how the world outside Ireland is changing can we establish a basis to move to the next phase in our development as a society and economy.

Large-scale reform and the sincere willingness of policy-makers to drive home change will provide the catalysts to spur this development. To paraphrase the words of US President Barack Obama's Chief of Staff Rahm

Emanuel, we should 'not let this crisis go to waste', and should use it as an opportunity to overhaul and redesign the institutions that will carry Ireland through the twenty-first century.

Many of our contributors reinforce this view in their essays. For example, writing from a Chinese perspective in Chapter 10, Liming Wang *et al.* argue that 'how Ireland deals with its current economic problems will provide a measure of the real achievement of the Celtic Tiger years. A return to modest growth would protect that achievement.'

So, What Did We Do Right?

Broadly speaking, the contributors to this book are drawn to Ireland because of the dramatic nature of its 'great transformation' and, it seems, because they perceive many of the policy actions undertaken in Ireland to be relevant to their own countries. For example, Ashraf Mishrif comments in Chapter 8 that, while the dynamics and nature of the Irish economic approach have differed from the approach of Egypt, they are also potentially transferable.

With few exceptions, the contributors divide Ireland's recent economic history into three parts – the long period of economic underachievement up to and including 1987, Ireland's economic 'catch-up' period from 1988 to 2001 ('what we did right') and Ireland's 'bubble' years from 2001 ('what we did wrong'). In the context of the current economic depression in Ireland, two strands that run through the contributions to this book are striking.

The first is that, despite the downturn, most of our contributors regard Ireland's catch-up period as worthy of ongoing study and as an example for other countries to follow. The second is that a range of contributors regard the bubble and subsequent collapse of the Irish economy over the past nine years with a sense of the inevitable. There is no sign here of the mixture of denial and bewilderment that colours the accounts of Irish policy-makers and commentators. Christophe Gillissen notes in Chapter 4 that the approach employed by Ireland had a dark side. In France, which has experienced speculative financial bubbles and crashes since at least 1720,[1] the speedy and shiny nature of the Celtic Tiger provoked suspicion.

The lopsided nature of Ireland's boom is also highlighted by other contributors as too risky and over-reliant on globalisation (Ashraf Mishrif, Chapter 8) while Liming Wang *et al.* (Chapter 10) note that 'Ireland has a type of conduit economy which enjoys considerable benefits when healthy economic conditions exist in the US, but suffers severely when times are bad there.'

Model or Miracle?

Many of the contributors regard the transformation of Ireland's economy more as a miracle to dissect and to selectively copy, than as an established socio-economic model in its own right. To some, such as Joseph Morrison Skelly, who writes here on the lessons of Ireland for Upstate New York (Chapter 2), Ireland's economic achievement represents less a model to be reproduced than an example of the need for initiative. However, Khuong Minh Vu (Chapter 11) goes as far as to distil and extract the transferable parts of the Irish experience into a recipe and actionable framework that other countries like Vietnam can follow.

What is very clear, however, is the extent to which Ireland has entered the political discourse and policy debate in a range of countries, from the way it captured the imagination of both sides of the Israeli political spectrum, to the manner in which it 'gained a pre-eminent place in Greek media and public discourse as the Government's favourite model for economic development', to quote Andreas Antoniades (Chapter 7). Indeed, both Jonathon Powell (Chapter 3) and First Minister Alex Salmond (Chapter 1) remark on the enormous change in the way other countries, most notably and importantly Britain, regard Ireland now compared to during the 1980s.

While the ingredients behind the Irish miracle may not yet represent a coherent, long-standing economic model in the same way as that of the Nordic countries, there is a very strong consensus amongst our contributors as to the factors that have driven Ireland's success and that are attractive to other countries. In the Introduction to this book, we grouped these factors under the banner of intangible infrastructure – the set of factors that develop human capability and permit the easy and efficient growth of business activity. This set encompasses factors like the democratic intellect referred to by First Minister Salmond, the notion of economic freedom highlighted by Joseph Morrison Skelly and the investment zones set up in China.

One of the very important challenges that faces Ireland now is to learn the lessons offered by other countries as it seeks to rebuild its economy. For instance, Yanky Fachler (Chapter 9) notes that, 'Ireland can learn from Israel that long-term economic success needs a solid research and development foundation that can deliver cutting-edge technological innovation and world-beating entrepreneurship.' A recent letter in the Irish media makes just this point. Instead of 'sinking money into property and money-juggling investment banking firms', it urges the Irish to follow the Israeli strategy of basing their economy 'on the solid and sound foundations of indigenous, well-capitalised high technology companies that work closely with universities and research institutes'[2] Ireland must also reorient its economy to a rapidly changing global economy and readjust itself to the spirit of the times. In undertaking this readjustment process, the ability to recall how we pulled ahead of other countries serves to point the way forward. For example, Ireland's economic success relative to its former peer group of Mediterranean countries like Portugal (Chapter 5) was based largely on much better and more persistent gains in labour productivity, a salutary observation in the context of the current debate in Ireland on labour costs.

In coming years we will likely see the emergence of a more multi-polar world with the countries once referred to as 'emerging' set to lead the way in terms of their contribution to global economic growth. The likes of China and Brazil have learnt the lessons of the emerging market crises of the late 1990s and enter this decade with strong balance sheets, high growth rates and fast-changing societies and consumer tastes.

As such, the large 'emerging' countries like China and India are on course to regain their former economic glories (in 1820 the two countries made up 48 per cent of the global economy, and International Monetary Fund (IMF) estimates put their combined economic weight at 28 per cent of the global economy by 2030). What is interesting in this book is that the Chinese and Indian contributors reproach Ireland for not making more of its links to their countries. For example, in Chapter 12, P.S. Raghavan points out that, 'despite a long history of affinity between the two countries, Ireland and India did not take full advantage of the synergies created by their rapid growth over the last two decades.'

Who Is Next?

At the same time, there are a large number of countries for whom the Irish experience – catch-up, asset price bubbles and the period of reform and recovery that we hope will follow this crisis – represents a valuable lesson. Countries like Taiwan, Indonesia, Vietnam (Chapter 11), Egypt (Chapter 8), the Baltic States, Romania (Chapter 7), Bulgaria, Columbia, Mexico and Chile, not to mention individual states in the US, have great potential but at the same time are at crossroads in terms of their socio-economic development.

Similarly, the current extensive nation-building efforts of Gulf states by developing significant external ties in the educational sphere, coupled with a regional strategy of 'Emiratisation', not to mention the financial crisis that recently hit Dubai, makes this a particularly timely moment for this dynamic and highly ambitious region to take stock of the Irish experience as it moves forward in its strategy of building up its strengths in numerous areas, from commercialisation and capacity building to private sector development and foreign direct investments.

Indeed, other emerging countries are potentially moving into bubble-type conditions, and need to be mindful not to replicate the ugly, chaotic and damaging economic bubble that Ireland experienced. Countries like China, which 'faces risks to its economic miracle that may strike readers as reminiscent of the difficulties Ireland has faced' (see Chapter 10), need to continue to aim for a more balanced and arguably less 'hot' economy.

In summary, what other countries should learn from Ireland is that intangible factors like education, economic openness, a friendly business climate and a purchase on the economic actors driving global growth (in Ireland's case, US multinationals) are necessary ingredients in spurring economic development. The benefit of Ireland's experience also suggests that strong institutions are necessary pillars of a strong economy and healthy public life, but importantly that these institutions need to be continually reinvigorated and reinvented. This did not occur in the later part of Ireland's boom.

Two other factors are important. One is to achieve a harmonious combination of local assets with international conditions, while at the same time putting in place local buffers to powerful international forces, such as the side effects of global interest rates and capital flows, for example. The other, again with the benefit of Irish hindsight, is to integrate economic policy-making with social, foreign policy and institutional elements of policy. As a final comment here, it goes without saying that once any country becomes the object of admiration by others and is spoken of as a 'model', then its economic glory has peaked and it is vulnerable to complacency.

What Must Ireland Do Now?

The next three to four years will, for most Irish people, be a period of painful adjustment, financially in terms of having to pay down debt and adjust to more modest incomes, and psychologically in terms of curbed expectations of lifestyle. This has been the case in the aftermath of many asset price bubbles through the twentieth century, and in particular a series of banking crises in the nineteenth century. However, the speed of the downshift in Ireland and the fact that this is arguably the first major economic boom–bust cycle we have experienced in centuries leads us to believe that our crash is in some way unique, and that we have little to learn from other nations.

What happened to Ireland's economy, society and public life in the past 25 years offers plenty of good as well as bad lessons to other countries, but the real change we must make is to be more open to the example and advice of others. History has shown repeatedly that nations and economies have emerged stronger from crises once they have undertaken serious reform and adapted themselves to the new world order. This is what Ireland must do in the next ten years. This is the key lesson of this book.

Notes and References

Introduction

1. 'The Rise of the Brand State', available from <http://www.foreignaffairs.com>, accessed August 2009.
2. J. Lee, *Ireland 1912–1985: Politics and Society*, Cambridge, Cambridge University Press, 1989, p. 521.
3. The Mississippi Scheme of 1721 was one of the original asset price bubbles. Scotsman John Law financially re-engineered the finances of the French state contingent on the promise of riches from the colonies. Law's scheme collapsed with considerable collateral economic damage to the French economy.
4. From a lecture given by Adam Smith in 1755, see <http://www.adam smith.org>.
5. *Report on Intangible Infrastructure*, London, Credit Suisse Research Institute, November 2008.
6. Cross-holding structures are common in Continental Europe (especially Germany) and in Asian countries like South Korea and Japan where companies and financial institutions hold significant and long-term equity and debt holdings in each other.

Chapter 1

1. 'Green Is Good', *The Economist*, 17 May 1997.
2. *Business and Finance*, vol. 44, no. 4, p. 18.
3. *Taking forward the Government Economic Strategy – A Discussion Paper on Tackling Poverty, Inequality and Deprivation in Scotland*, Edinburgh, Government of Scotland, 2008.
4. Holyrood is the Scottish Parliament and Scottish Parliament Building.

Chapter 2

1. See, for example, P. Kirby, *The Celtic Tiger in Distress: Growth with Inequality in Ireland*, Basingstoke, Palgrave, 2002.

2. 'The Growth Index', Public Policy Institute of New York State, September 2007, p. 1.
3. 'Could New York Let Upstate *Be* Upstate?', Public Policy Institute of New York State, May 2004, p. 1.
4. R. Pendall, 'Upstate New York's Population Plateau: The Third-Slowest Growing State', Brookings Institution, Center on Urban and Metropolitan Policy, August 2003, p. 2.
5. R. Pendall, M.P. Drennan and S. Christopherson, 'Transition and Renewal: The Emergence of a Diverse Upstate Economy', Brookings Institution, Centre on Urban and Metropolitan Policy, January 2004, p. 1
6. ibid, p. 14.
7. 'Could New York Let Upstate *Be* Upstate?', p. 1.
8. New York State Department of Labor, press release, 17 July 2008, available at: <http://www.labor.state.ny.us>, accessed 23 August 2009; New York State Department of Labor, press release, 18 December 2008, available at: <http://www.labor.state.ny.us>, 23 August 2009.
9. R. Pendall and S. Christopherson, 'Losing Ground: Income and Poverty in Upstate New York', Brookings Institution, Metropolitan Policy Programme, September 2004, p. 2.
10. Pendall *et al.*, 'Transition and Renewal', p. 4.
11. Pendall, 'Upstate New York's Population Plateau', p. 1.
12. 'The Growth Index', p. 1.
13. 'Could New York Let Upstate *Be* Upstate?', p. 8.
14. See, for example, M.J. O'Sullivan, *Ireland and the Global Question*, Syracuse, New York, Syracuse University Press, 2006, p. 81.
15. A. Barrett, J. Goggin, I. Kearney, *Quarterly Economic Commentary*, winter 2008, Dublin, Economic and Social Research Institute, December 2008.
16. Kirby, *The Celtic Tiger in Distress*, pp. 48–52.
17. D. O'Hearn, *Inside the Celtic Tiger: The Irish Economy and the Asian Model*, London, Pluto Press, 1998, p. 74; N.J. Smith, *Showcasing Globalization? The Political Economy of the Irish Republic*, Manchester, Manchester University Press, 2005, pp. 46 and 68.
18. O'Sullivan, *Ireland and the Global Question*, p. 59.
19. ibid., p. 66.
20. M. Slaughter, 'What Data Tells Us', *Wall Street Journal*, 27 March 2008.
21. 'Foreign Direct Investment: Bringing the Benefits of Globalization Back Home', Partnership for New York City, June 2008, p. 3.
22. Pendall *et al.*, 'Transition and Renewal', p. 11.
23. ibid., pp. 2–7
24. Pendall and Christopherson, 'Losing Ground', pp. 14–15.
25. Pendall *et al.*, 'Transition and Renewal', p. 5.
26. ibid., p. 12.

27. ibid., p. 10.
28. D. Seth, 4 February 2008, available at: <http://deepaksethspeak.blogspot.com>, accessed 23 August 2009.
29. ibid.
30. 'Could New York Let Upstate *Be* Upstate?', p. 9.
31. O'Sullivan, *Ireland and the Global Question*, p. 59.
32. Pendall *et al.*, 'Transition and Renewal', p. 7.
33. Pendall and Christopherson, 'Losing Ground', p. 15.
34. College of Nanoscale Science and Engineering, University at Albany, press release, 15 July 2008, available at: <http://cnse.albany.edu>, accessed 23 August 2009.
35. College of Nanoscale Science and Engineering, University at Albany, press release, 15 July 2008, available at: <http://cnse.albany.edu>, accessed 23 August 2009.
36. See, for example, C.A. Agostini, 'The Impact of State Corporate Taxes on FDI Location', *Public Finance Review*, vol. 35, no. 3 (May 2007), pp. 335–360.
37. M.A. O'Grady, 'Bogota Eyes the Irish Model', *Wall Street Journal*, 24 March, 2008.
38. S.A. Hodge, 'US States Lead the World in High Corporate Taxes', Fiscal Fact 119, The Tax Foundation, 18 March 2008.
39. 'A Fair Share – At Least!', Public Policy Institute of New York State, March 2003, p. 4.
40. ibid., p. 2.
41. 'How High Is the Upstate Tax Burden – and Why?', Public Policy Institute of New York State, August 2004, pp. 1–2.
42. Powell, 'Economic Freedom and Growth: The Case of the Celtic Tiger', *Cato Journal*, vol. 22, no. 3 (Winter 2003), p. 431.
43. ibid., p. 435.
44. ibid., p. 438.
45. ibid., p. 439.
46. ibid., p. 440.
47. 'Could New York Let Upstate *Be* Upstate?', p. 2.
48. 'How High Is the Upstate Tax Burden – and Why?', p. 2.
49. 'Could New York Let Upstate *Be* Upstate?', p. 11.
50. 'New York State's Economy in 2004: Which Way Out?' Public Policy Institute of New York State, April 2004, p. 3.
51. ibid., p. 3.
52. Pendall *et al.*, 'Transition and Renewal', p. 9.
53. 'Upstate *Now*', New York State Senate, available at: <http://www.nysenate.gov>, accessed 23 August 2009; M. Brandecker, 'Senate GOP Pushing for Upstate *Now*,' Legislativegazette.com, 29 January 2008, available at: <http://www.legislativegazette.com>, accessed 23 August 2009.
54. 'Could New York Let Upstate *Be* Upstate?', p. 2.

55. Office of Governor David Patterson, Press Release, 3 June 2008, available at: <http://www.state.ny.us/governor/press/press_0603081.html>, accessed 23 August 2009.
56. E.J. McMahon, 'Enough Is Enough: Why and How to Cap New York State's School Property Taxes', Empire Center for New York State Policy, March 2008.
57. Pendall *et al.*, 'Transition and Renewal', p. 7.
58. ibid., p. 10; Claudia H. Deutsch, 'Shrinking Pains at Kodak', *New York Times*, 9 February 2007.
59. Pendall *et al.*, 'Transition and Renewal', p. 5.
60. See, for example, J.D. House and K. McGrath, 'Innovative Governance and Development in the New Ireland: Social Partnership and the Integrated Approach', *Governance: An International Journal of Policy, Administration and Institutions*, vol. 17, no. 1, January 2004, pp. 29–58.

Chapter 3

1. Richard de Clare, also known as Strongbow, led the Norman invasion of Ireland in 1170.
2. The series included *Some Experiences of an Irish RM* (London, Longmans, 1899) and *Further Experiences of an Irish RM* (London, Longmans, 1908) by Edith Somerville and Violet Martin (under the name Martin Ross), depicting the life of a resident magistrate in the west of Ireland. The books were the basis for a well known TV series *An Irish RM*.
3. The Troubles refers to a period of conflict dating from the early 1960s to the signing of the Belfast Agreement in 1998, principally between the nationalist, mainly Catholic, community and the unionist, predominantly Protestant, community in Northern Ireland. The Troubles sprang from discrimination against the nationalist and Catholic community minority from the Protestant majority.
4. Earl Mountbatten of Burma was the last viceroy of the British Indian Empire in 1947 and thereafter the first governor general of the Union of India. In the 1950s he was First Sea Lord. He was a central figure in the British Establishment and a mentor to Prince Charles. He was killed in 1979 when the IRA bombed his boat at Mullaghmore, County Sligo.
5. The Great Famine (1845–1852) was a period of devastation in Ireland, when, against a backdrop of a lopsided land ownership system, a potato blight triggered mass starvation, disease and poverty which in turn intensified already bad social, political and economic problems. Death and emigration lead to a halving of the Irish population. Some historians point to the Famine as an act of genocide by the British, while others assess it as neglect and political mismanagement.
6. Refers to the support of British politicians for the cause of the Orange Order and Unionist political establishment in Northern Ireland.

7. Paul Hill, Gerry Conlon, Paddy Armstrong and Carole Richardson were convicted in October 1975 of the Guildford pub bombings. Statements from the Four were later found to be extracted through torture and coercion, and in some cases had been fabricated by police. The Four were released in 1989 and their convictions were quashed.

8. The Birmingham Six were six men who were wrongfully convicted in 1975 of the Birmingham pub bombings. The Six were freed in 1991 when their convictions were quashed by the Court of Appeal. Police were found to have had tampered with evidence and the confessions of the Six.

9. The Sunningdale Agreement was an initiative (in December 1973) to stem the Troubles in Northern Ireland by creating a power-sharing pan-community Northern Ireland Executive and a cross-border Council of Ireland. The Agreement fell apart largely because of Unionist opposition and a series of strikes.

10. The Anglo-Irish Agreement – signed on 15 November 1985 by Prime Minister Margaret Thatcher and Taoiseach Garret FitzGerald. The Treaty gave the Irish Government an advisory role in Northern Ireland's Government, though it also underlined that there could be no change in the constitutional position of Northern Ireland unless a majority of its population consented to join the Irish Republic.

11. On Bloody Sunday, 30 January 1972, twenty-seven civil rights marchers were shot by the British Army Parachute Regiment, resulting in fourteen deaths. Several inquiries were established to investigate the shootings, the most recent of which, the Saville Inquiry, is due to release its report in 2010.

12. In response to rioting and violence in Derry in December 1969, Jack Lynch stated on RTÉ that the Irish Government can 'no longer stand by and see innocent people injured', a statement that has often been misquoted as 'no longer stand idly by' and misinterpreted as one of belligerence.

13. The Good Friday Agreement is seen as bringing an end to the Troubles. It was signed on 10 April 1998 by the Irish and British Governments with the support of the main political parties in Northern Ireland. One of the key tenets of the Agreement was that any change to the constitutional status of Northern Ireland could result only from a majority vote by its electorate. A British–Irish Council, North–South Ministerial Council and, most importantly, a new Northern Ireland Assembly were established by the Agreement.

14. The practical aspects of the Agreement – Executive and Assembly – were suspended by the Irish and British Governments in 2000 owing to lack of progress on decommissioning of arms, but they were re-started in May 2000 on the commencement of decommissioning by the IRA.

15. The St Andrew's Agreement was struck in October 2006 between the Governments of Britain and Ireland and the main political parties in Northern Ireland to devolve political power to Northern Ireland (from London). The key components of the Agreement were the restoration of the Northern Ireland Assembly and broader support for the new Police Service of Northern Ireland.

Chapter 4

1. P. Joannon, 'Charles de Gaulle and Ireland', in P. Joannon (ed.), *De Gaulle and Ireland*, Dublin, Institute of Public Administration, 1991, p. 21.
2. J. Julienne, 'La France et l'Irlande nationaliste de 1860 à 1890: évolution et mutation de liens multiséculaires', *Études Irlandaises*, vol. 24, no. 1, 1999, pp. 123–136.
3. The Irish Question was a term, used predominantly in the nineteenth century, to describe the movement (in Ireland) for Irish political independence and was often used more broadly to describe Irish nationalism.
4. The Easter Rising took place over Easter Week 1916 and was largely based in Dublin. It was a revolutionary event that aimed to overthrow British rule in Ireland, though poor organisation and a lack of broad support meant that it was suppressed and most of the leaders of the Rising were executed. The Rising and its glorious failure sowed the seeds of the War of Independence that followed three years later.
5. I. McKeane, 'Journees Sanglantes/ Days of Blood: The French Press and the Easter Rising', in R. O'Donnell (ed.), *The Impact of the 1916 Rising among the Nations*, Dublin, Irish Academic Press, 2008.
6. J. aan de Wiel, *The Catholic Church in Ireland, 1914–1918*, Dublin, Irish Academic Press, 2003, pp. 312–321.
7. B. Ducret, 'La France et l'Irlande (1914–1923)', *Etudes Irlandaises*, IX, 1984, pp. 189–204.
8. *La Vieille-France*, 17 September 1919, quoted in G. Gavan Duffy, *La République d'Irlande et la Presse Française*, Paris, Délégation du Gouvernement élu de la République Irlandaise, 1919.
9. Guided by the principle that my enemy's enemy is my friend, Sinn Féin had made overtures to the German Government to help in establishing Irish independence. Help from Germany came in the form of arms, and the interception of a German U-boat laden with arms in 1916 led to the execution of Sir Roger Casement for treason.
10. A. Ghesquière, 'La représentation diplomatique française dans l'Etat libre d'Irlande (1920–1930)', in Eamon Maher and Grace Neville (eds), *France–Ireland: Anatomy of a Relationship*, New York, Peter Lang, 2004, pp. 225–237.
11. P. Rafroidi, 'Avant-propos', in Jacques Verrière et Jean Guiffan, *L'Irlande: Milieu et Histoire*, Paris, Armand Colin, 1970, p. 6.
12. *Les Cahiers du Militant*, No. 6: 'L'exemple de l'Irlande', Rennes, Les éditions du Parti national breton, n.d.
13. R. Faligot, *La Harpe et l'Hermine*, Rennes, Terre de Brume, 1994, p. 85.
14. D. Leach, *Fugitive Ireland: European Minority Nationalists and Irish Political Asylum, 1937–2008*, Dublin, Four Courts Press, 2009.
15. The Vichy Regime was the French Government from July 1940 to August 1944, headed by Marshal Philippe Pétain.

16. D. Keogh, *Ireland and Europe, 1919–1948: A Diplomatic and Political History*, Dublin, Gill & Macmillan, 1988, p. 185–189.

17. F. Mitterrand, 'L'Irlande et l'Europe', in James Dooge (ed.), *Ireland in the Contemporary World*, Dublin: Gill & Macmillan, 1986, p. 1–4.

18. R. Dumas, *Affaires Étrangères, vol. 1: 1981–1988*, Paris, Fayard, 2007, pp. 197–200.

19. *Irish Times*, 16 July 1996.

20. G. FitzGerald, *Reflections on the Irish State*, Dublin, Irish Academic Press, 2003, pp. 161–162.

21. Laurent Fabius, 26 October 2000, available at: <http://www.assemblee-nationale.fr/europe/c-rendus/c0124.asp>, accessed 20 August 2009.

22. The Nice Treaty, signed on 26 February 2001, reordered the structure of the European Union (following the Maastricht Treaty and the Treaty of Rome). The Treaty was initially rejected by Ireland (in a referendum in June 2001) but passed by Irish voters a year later.

23. M. Considère-Charon, *Irlande: Une Singulière Intégration Européenne*, Paris, Economica, 2002, pp. 102–103.

24. C. Gillissen, 'L'Irlande entre l'Europe et le Monde Anglo-Saxon', in Yann Bevant (ed.), *Passerelles et Impasses*, Rennes, Liv'Editions, 2007, pp. 75–85.

25. Remarks by Tánaiste Mary Harney at a meeting of the American Bar Association in the Law Society of Ireland, Blackhall Place, Dublin, Friday, 21 July 2000, available at: <http://www.entemp.ie/press/2000/210700.htm>, accessed 20 August 2009.

26. *Le Monde*, 1 October 2005.

27. *L'Express*, 5 July 2001.

28. *Les Echos*, 23 May 2007.

29. *Le Point*, 21 June 2001.

30. M. Albert, *Capitalisme Contre Capitalisme*, Paris, Seuil, 1991.

31. R. Boyer, 'Le Capitalisme Étatique à la Française à la Croisée des Chemins', in Colin Crouch and Wolfgang Streeck (eds), *Les Capitalismes en Europe*, Paris, La Découverte, 1996, pp. 97–137.

32. J. Stiglitz, *La Grande Désillusion*, Paris, Livre de Poche, 2002.

33. M. Considère-Charon, *Irlande: Une Singulière Intégration Européenne*, pp. 54–84.

34. *Le Figaro*, 2 June 1999.

35. *Les Echos*, 11 June 2001.

36. *Jeune Afrique*, 2 October 2005.

37. *Le Monde*, 24 January 2006.

38. Quoted in *Alternatives Économiques*, no. 173, September 1999.

39. *Le Monde*, 21 September 2007.

40. *Les Echos*, 22 February 2005.

41. I. Rufflé, 'Espace Libéral et Impasse Sociale: Á qui Profite la Croissance en Irlande?', in Y. Bévant (ed.), *Passerelles et Impasses*, pp. 181–194.

42. M. Förster and M. Mira d'Ercole, 'Income Distribution and Poverty in OECD Countries in the Second Half of the 1990s', *OECD Social, Employment and Migration Working Paper*, 22, OECD, 2005, p. 11.

43. A. Sapir, 'Globalisation and the Reform of European Social Models', *Bruegel Policy Brief*, vol 1, November 2005, p. 5, available at: <http://www.bruegel.org>, accessed 20 August 2009.

44. *Nouvel Observateur*, 9 June 2007.

45. C. Gillissen, 'L'Irlande et l'Union Économique et Monétaire', in C. Maignant (ed.), *Le Tigre Celtique en Question*, Presses Universitaires de Caen, 2007, pp. 41–53.

46. *Flash Eurobaromètre*, 151b, November 2003.

47. P. Brennan, 'Croissance Économique et Exclusion Sociale: Eléments du Problème', *Études Irlandaises*, vol. 24, no. 2, 1999, pp. 155–162.

48. E. Todd, *L'illusion Économique*, Paris, Gallimard, 1998, pp. 174–176.

49. Förster and Mira d'Ercole, 'Income Distribution and Poverty in OECD Countries', pp. 9–10.

50. *Growing Unequal? Income Distribution and Poverty in OECD Countries*, OECD, 2008.

51. D. Begg, address to the National College of Ireland on Social Partnership, 11 November 2002.

52. Central Statistics Office, 'National Income and Expenditure 2006', Dublin, Stationery Office, 2007, p. 2.

53. The Progressive Democrat party was established in December 1985 by a number of politicians who had split from Fianna Fáil and Fine Gael, the best known of which was Des O'Malley. The party had a liberal economic and social agenda. It is now disbanded.

54. I. Grosfeld and C. Senik, 'The Emerging Aversion to Inequality: Evidence from Poland 1992–2005', William Davidson Institute Working Paper, no. 919, April 2008, p. 16, available at: <http://www.wdi.umich.edu/files/Publications/WorkingPapers/wp919.pdf>, accessed 20 August 2009.

55. B. Tonra, *Global Citizen and European Republic*, Manchester, Manchester University Press, 2006.

56. S. Lemass, *Dáil Debates*, vol. 175, col. 938, 3 June 1959.

57. The European Constitutional Treaty 2005 aimed to create a consolidated constitution for the European Union. Following rejection of this Treaty by France and the Netherlands, it was replaced by the Treaty of Lisbon (signed on 13 December 2007) and that came into force on 1 December 2009 following a second Irish referendum.

58. C. Gillissen, 'Autopsie d'un Référendum: L'Irlande et le Traité de Lisbonne', in Y. Bevant et A. Goarzin (dir.), *Bretagne et Irlande: Pérégrinations*, Rennes, CRBC Rennes 2 / Tir, 2009, pp. 207–228.

59. *Le Monde*, 2 November 2008.

60. 'Making Choices – Shaping Futures: Why We Should Embrace the Nordic Model', address to the CORI social policy conference, 19 June 2008, available at: <http://www.ictu.ie>, accessed 20 August 2009.

Chapter 5

1. J. Braga Macedo, 'Converging European Transitions', *The World Economy*, vol. 23, no. 10, 2000, pp. 1335–1365; O. Blanchard, 'Adjustment within the Euro: The Difficult Case of Portugal', 2006, available at: <http://econ-www.mit.edu/files/740>, accessed 31 August 2009.
2. P. Honohan and B. Walsh, 'Catching Up with the Leaders: the Irish Hare', *Brookings Papers in Economic Activity*, vol. 1, 2000, pp. 1–77.
3. O. Blanchard and P. Portugal, 'What Hides behind an Unemployment Rate: Comparing Portuguese and US Labour Markets', *The American Economic Review*, vol. 91, no. 1, 2001, pp. 187–207.
4. P.R. Krugman and A.J. Venables, 'Integration, Specialization and Adjustment', *European Economic Review*, vol. 40, 1996, pp. 959–67.
5. K.H. Midelfart, H.G. Overman and A. J. Venables, 'Monetary Union and the Economic Geography of Europe', *Journal of Common Market Studies*, vol. 41, no. 5, 2003, pp. 847–68.
6. P. Pita Barros, 'Convergence and Information Technologies: The Experience of Greece, Portugal and Spain', *Applied Economics Letters*, vol. 9, 2002, pp. 675–80; F. Barry, 'Economic Integration and Convergence Processes in the EU Cohesion Countries', *Journal of Common Market Studies*, vol. 41, no. 5, 2003, pp. 897–921; M. Cassidy, 'Productivity in Ireland: Trends and Issues', *CBFSAI Bulletin*, Spring 2004, pp. 83–105.
7. Labour productivity growth in Portugal is matched by that of total factor productivity growth, which also declined after 1973.
8. J. Temple and H.J. Voth, 'Human Capital, Equipment Investment, and Industrialization', *European Economic Review*, vol. 42, 1998, pp. 1343–62.
9. D. Dollar and E.N. Wolff, 'Convergence of Industry Labour Productivity among Advanced Economies, 1963–1982', *Review of Economics and Statistics*, vol. 70, 1988, pp. 549–58; R.M. Sundrum, 'Growth and Employment in the Mature Economies: a Long-term Perspective' in J. Cornwall (ed.), *The Capitalist Economies: Prospects for the 1990s*, Aldershot, Edward Elgar, 1991.
10. Factor returns – the return (usually through regression analysis) attributable to a single factor or dependent variable.
11. 'Steady state' means that the observed behaviour of a system should continue into the future, and that the probability of this behaviour(s) being repeated through time will be constant.
12. Factor productivity growth refers to drivers of improvements in economic output that are not derived from changes in inputs.

13. For Portugal, see also M.M. Godinho and R.P. Mamede, 'Convergência e mudança estrutural no âmbito dos "países da coesão"', *Análise Social*, vol. 38, 2004, pp. 1069–90; A. Aguiar and M.M.F. Martins, 'O crescimento industrial', in P. Lains and A. Ferreira da Silva (eds.), *História Económica de Portugal, 1700–2000*, vol. 3, Lisbon, Imprensa de Ciências Sociais, 2005.

14. For example, due to the 1974 revolutionary legacy, Portugal's labour market is still partially dependent on constitutional legislation, making changes harder to introduce.

15. R. Färe, S. Grosskopf and D. Margaritis, 'Productivity Growth and Convergence in the European Union', *Journal of Productivity Analysis*, 25, 2006, pp. 111–141.

16. The cohesion group was the group of lower income countries that were recipients of relatively large amounts of aid.

17. Figure 5.2 also shows GNP data for Ireland. GDP growth rates overestimate the growth of the Irish economy because of overpricing of foreign-owned firms which had an increasingly large share of output.

18. Honohan and Walsh, 'Catching Up with the Leaders: The Irish Hare', pp. 1–77. The impact of net immigration was also felt in the quality of the Irish labour market, as levels of education and training were above the average of the Irish resident labour force.

19. This is not unlike what happened with the ECSC and EEC, which led to higher levels of trade but also to the implementation of public policies at European level.

20. The 1965 trade agreement followed the creation of EFTA, in 1959, by the UK and six other countries, including Portugal, and the French veto of UK accession, in 1961. The EFTA was geared mainly to industrial trade and Ireland was mainly an exporter of agricultural goods.

21. F. Gottheil, 'Ireland: What's Celtic about the Celtic Tiger?', *The Quarterly Review of Economics and Finance*, vol. 43, 2003, pp. 720–37.

22. Gross capital formation refers to net new investment (purchases less disposals) in fixed assets by households, governments and corporations.

23. F. Gottheil, 'Ireland: What's Celtic about the Celtic Tiger?', p. 727.

24. F. Barry, 'Peripherality in Economic Geography and Modern Growth theory: Evidence from Ireland's Adjustment to Free Trade', *The World Economy*, vol. 19 no. 3, 1996, pp. 345–65.

25. F. Gottheil, 'Ireland: What's Celtic about the Celtic Tiger?'. Rates of profit can be inflated by manipulation of internal pricing by multinationals, in order to take advantage of the low corporate profit tax in Ireland. In 1981, the tax on foreign earnings profits was raised from zero to 10 per cent, below most Western European countries.

26. The 1972 agreement led to a significant reduction of trade barriers to the extent that the 1985 Accession Treaty with the EC was concerned mostly with the reduction of tariffs across the Spanish border – and of course with agriculture, fisheries and the *acquis communautaire*.

27. Social overhead capital is capital spent on social infrastructure/public goods like hospitals and schools.

28. 'Creative destruction' is a phrase coined by the economist Joseph Schumpeter to describe the disruptive and often radical process of transformation that accompanies innovation. The internet could be an example here.

29. P. Lains, 'Structural Change and Economic Growth in Portugal, 1950–1990' in S. Heikkinen and J.L. van Zanden (eds.), *Explorations in Economic Growth*, Amsterdam, Aksant, 2004, pp. 321–40.

30. W. Baer and A. Nogueira Leite, 'The Economy of Portugal within the European Union: 1990–2002', *The Quarterly Review of Economics and Finance*, vol. 43, 2003, pp. 738–754.

31. Shift-share analysis aims to decompose changes in economic variables like demographics and employment across regions.

32. I consider here the modified shift-share analysis developed by M.P. Timmer and A. Szirmai, 'Productivity Growth in Asian Manufacturing: the Structural Bonus Hypothesis Examined', *Structural Change and Economic Dynamics*, vol. 11, 2000, pp. 371–92. The shift-share analysis used here has several limitations, including the fact that it measures average instead of marginal productivity and that it only takes into account labour inputs.

33. M. Cassidy, 'Productivity in Ireland: Trends and Issues', *CBFSAI Bulletin*, Spring, 2004, pp. 83–105.

34. P. Pita Barros, 'Convergence and Information Technologies: the Experience of Greece, Portugal and Spain', *Applied Economics Letters*, vol. 9, 2002, pp. 675–80.

35. Färe *et al.*, in 'Productivity Growth and Convergence in the European Union', look at the impact of efficiency, technology, and physical and human capital on labour productivity in a sample selection of European countries.

36. We use in this comparison the purchasing power parity (PPP) exchange rates implicit in total GDP. It should be taken into account, though, that Irish GDP is inflated due to overpricing of multinationals. That bias is probably larger at the end of the period amounting to about 15 per cent (see above). This implies that the decline in Portugal's relative labour productivity level is overestimated.

37. M. O'Mahony and B. van Ark (eds.), *EU Productivity and Competitiveness: An Industry Perspective. Can Europe resume the Catching-up Process?*, Luxembourg, Official Publications of the European Communities, 2003.

38. Barros also finds that the relationship between speed of convergence and ICT-intensity was not significant for the cohesion countries during 1971–1992. See P. Pita Barros, 'Convergence and Information Technologies: the Experience of Greece, Portugal and Spain', *Applied Economics Letters*, vol. 9, 2002, pp. 675–80.

39. It should be recalled that the analysis does not take into account the interaction between structure and labour productivity levels.

40. Human capital refers to the skills, values and knowledge base of a labour force that drive it to produce economic value. Human capital is developed through good education, training and health.
41. Due to a lack of data, it is not possible to relate physical and human capital inputs to productivity at the sectoral level.
42. J. Esteban, 'Regional Convergence in Europe and the Industry Mix: A Shift-Share Analysis', *Regional Science and Urban Economics*, 30, 2000, pp. 353–64.

Chapter 6

The author would like to thank Dr Ben O'Loughlin and Dr Vasilis Alevizakos for their useful comments on earlier drafts of this chapter.

1. See B. Papadimitriou, 'Real "Models"', *Kathimerini*, 16 April 2006.
2. See 'The Irish Miracle and the Greek Indecision', *Kathimerini*, 6 July 2003.
3. See A. Christodoulakis, 'The "Wreck" Accelerates the Privatisations', *To Vima*, 27 January 2002.
4. The law 3219/2004 amended PASOK's former development law 2601/1998.
5. See <http://www.mnec.gr>, accessed 22 September 2009.
6. See A. Karamitsos and A. Christodoulakis, 'The Market Applauds the Changes and Requests Further Benefits', *To Vima*, 6 July 2003; C. Zioti, 'Friendly Opening Towards Business', *To Vima*, 6 July 2003; D. Papadokostopoulos, 'Irish Model for Large Investments', *Kathimerini*, 2 July 2003; 'The Irish Miracle and the Greek Indecision', *Kathimerini*, 6 July 2003; D. Papadokostopoulos, 'The Path to Convergence Goes through Ireland', *Kathimerini*, 31 August 2003.
7. See B. Bakouri, 'The Irish Miracle...and the Greek Illusions', *Kathimerini*, 24 August 2003.
8. It should be mentioned here that these attempts were, at least partly, driven by various institutions and policy initiatives at EU-level (which, again, tried to diffuse the lessons from the Irish economic miracle within the EU).
9. Interview with Lina Giannarou, *Kathimerini*, 8 February 2004.
10. See Karamanlis' interview with Pari Kourtzidis. Pari Kourtzidis, 'Karamanlis vision', *Kathimerini* and *The Economist* (special edition), no. 13, January 2005.
11. Kostas Karamanlis' speech at SEV's Annual General Assembly, 26 May 2004, available at: <http://www.sev.org.gr/online/assemblies.aspx>, accessed 22 September 2009
12. See C. Korfiatis, 'Two "Schools" and Two Lines in the Industrialists' Syndicate', *To Vima*, 30 May 2004; A. Kapsilis and A. Kovaios, 'How Were the Economic Models of Ireland and Sweden Created?', *To Vima*, 30 May 2004; 'The Irish Model of Development – Discussing the Greek Economy in SEV, Karamanlis presented Five Basic Directions', *Kathimerini*, 27 May 2004.
13. Z. Tsolis, 'Mr Alogoskoufis Clearly Prefers Dublin', *To Vima*, 16 April 2006.

14. See, for instance, his interview in *Ta Nea*, 10 May 2005, available at: <http://digital.tanea.gr/> , accessed 22 September 2009. See also his speeches to the Greek Parliament on 13 April 2006, available at: <http://democracy.pasok.gr>, accessed 22 September 2009.

15. Indicative of the row this dismissal generated in PASOK was *Eleftherotypia's* front-cover title 'Swedish Gym in PASOK', 8 April 2006. Also the articles by P. Sokos and G. Karelias in the same issue of the paper.

16. See P. Sokos, 'Floridis...Dismissal Model', *Eleftherotypia*, 7 April 2006.

17. Kostas Karamanlis, speech at the ND National Summit for Local Governance, 7 April 2006, available at: <http://www.nd.gr>, accessed 22 September 2009.

18. George Alogoskoufis, speech at the panel on World Economic Situation and Prospects 2006, organised by the foundation for Economic and Industrial Research (IOBE) and United Nations Regional Information Centre (UNRIC), 11 April 2006, available at: <http://www.alogoskoufis.gr/omilies.php>, accessed 22 September 2009.

19. ibid.

20. See 'Models Catwalk', *Eleftherotypia*, 13 April 2006; C. Korai, 'Clash of Models – Karamanlis' Assault against PASOK, with Ireland against Sweden', *Eleftherotypia*, 13 April 2006; D. Tziordas, 'ND with a Compass in Hand', *Eleftetherotypia*, 16 April 2006; P. Mandraveli, 'The Silk Models...', *Kathimerini*, 14 April 2006; T. Oikonomopoulos, 'Weather-vane', *Kathimerini*, 14 April 2006.

21. ibid. See also analyses in the special section of *To Vima*: 'The Clash of Models – Ireland or Sweden', 16 April 2006, pp. A18–23.

22. See, for instance, C. Korai, 'Clash of Models'; D. Tziordas, 'ND with a Compass in Hand'; Interview with M. Papaioannou (PASOK) in *To Vima*, 16 April 2006; Interview with T. Pagalos (PASOK) in *Elefterotypia*, 23 April 2006.

23. See, for example, Dan Flinter, 'How to Become Ireland', interview in *To Vima*, 9 October 2005; interview with Michael Ahern in *Kathimerini*, 16 April 2006.

24. C. Mega, 'The Greek Chaos and the Swedish Model', *Eleftherotypia*, 16 April 2006; C. Kopsini, 'There is also the "Doing-Nothing Model"', *Kathimerini*, 12 April 2006.

25. See the press release at: <http://www.mnec.gr/en/press_office/Deltia Typou/dt/Ministry_Conf_press_release.html>, accessed 22 September 2009.

26. See, for instance, A. Hemikoglou, 'The Neoliberal Tiger that Became a Little Cat', *To Vima*, 28 February 2009; G. Tsiaras, 'The Irish Dream that Became Nightmare', *To Vima*, 18 April 2009.

27. Z. Tsolis, 'Apart in the "Miracle", Together in the (Economic) Nightmare', *To Vima*, 9 April 2009.

28. The full content of these laws is available at: <http://www.mnec.gr>, accessed 22 September 2009.

29. For a recent review of the Greek economy, see Vassilis Monastiriotis, 'Greece: Economy', in *Central and South-Eastern Europe 2009 – Europa Regional Surveys of the World Series*, London, Routledge, 2009.

Chapter 7

1. This is the label attached to the Slovak economic potential and was inspired by the Tatra Mountains, which are on Slovak territory.

2. Interview with the BBC ahead of Estonia's accession to the EU on 1 May 2004, available at: <http://news.bbc.co.uk/1/hi/world/europe/3623515.stm>, accessed 7 October 2009. Estonia was the first former Soviet country to introduce a low rate of corporate taxation, similar to that introduced in Ireland in 1991. In contrast with Ireland, Estonia had a flat rate for income and corporate tax.

3. In comparing Romania to Ireland, Jonathan Scheele, the chief of the European Commission in Bucharest, suggested that Romania could have its own 'Dacic Tiger' economy. Dacia was the ancient name for Romania before its territory was conquered by the Roman empire. See <http://www.zf.ro/opinii/va-urma-romania-exemplul-irlandei-2964556>, accessed 7 October 2009.

4. In 1989, living standards in Eastern Europe were at best half of that of their neighbours in developed Europe, while those with the toughest communist regimes like Romania were slipping into poverty. As recently as 2001, Romania's per capita GDP represented a mere 30 per cent of the EU average per capita GDP.

5. Shock therapy economic policies refer to the very sudden introduction of new policy regimes, structures or the dismantling of old ones (such as price controls or tax structures). In the past twenty years this approach has been practised in a number of emerging economies, such as Russia in the late 1990s, in the context of deep economic and political dislocation.

6. Eight former communist states joined the EU in May 2004: Czech Republic, Estonia, Hungary, Latvia, Lithuania, Poland, Slovakia, Slovenia with Romania, and Bulgaria following suit in January 2007.

7. Romania's GDP contracted for three years in a row: in 1997 by -6.1 per cent; by -5.4 per cent in 1998; and by -3.2 per cent in 1999. Unemployment at year-end was 8.9 per cent in 1997, 10.3 in 1998 and 10.5 in 1999, and was most probably much higher than the official data which did not account for those in the grey economy or those of working age who had left the country.

8. According to Ireland's Reception and Integration Agency, Romanians formed the second largest group of asylum seekers in the country in 2000, see <http://www.reintegration.net/ireland/index.htm>, accessed 7 October 2009; by 2006, it was estimated that 30,000–40,000 Romanians were living in Ireland, see <http://www.bbw.ro>, accessed 7 October 2009.

9. EBRD Transition Report, 2008.

10. EBRD Transition Report, 2002.

11. R. Dornbusch, 'Credibility, Debt and Unemployment: Ireland's Failed Stabilization', NBER (National Bureau of Economic Research) Working Paper no. 2785, 1988.

12. The EBRD has published an annual Transition Report since the inception of the transition from socialism to market economics in Eastern Europe.

13. R. Dornbusch, 'Credibility, Debt and Unemployment: Ireland's Failed Stabilization'.

14. See <http://www.9am.ro/stiri-revista-presei/2005-12-20/privatizare-bcr-cum parata-de-erste-bank.html>, accessed 7 October 2009.

15. Estimates place the number of civil servants in Romania at approximately 1.2 million, or circa 26 per cent of the active labour force. The public administration was slightly reduced over the past 20 years.

16. Official estimates show the number of pensioners in Romania as of March 2009 at 5,512,697.

17. The Washington Consensus was a creation of the late 1980s for the countries undergoing reform then. It prescribed a set of specific economic measures by IFIs such as the IMF, the World Bank and the US Treasury Department for developing countries experiencing difficulties.

18. Another factor that led to a decrease in Romania's population was a negative rate in population growth. Negative birth rates were not a problem in Ireland in the 1980s, as was the case in Romania.

19. *Warsaw Business Journal*, 21 February 2005.

Chapter 8

1. P. Fortin, 'The Irish Economic Boom: What Can We Learn?', *International Productivity Monitor*, no. 3, Fall 2001, pp. 19–32.

2. *Al-Ahram* (Cairo), 8 December 2006.

3. P. Fortin, 'The Irish Economic Boom', p. 19.

4. D. Flinter, 'The Transformation of the Irish Economy: the Role of the Public Policy', CIT Working Paper 052112, Clemson University Centre for International Trade, 21 December 2005, pp. 5–7.

5. F. Barry, 'Irish Economic Development over Three Decades of EU Membership', unpublished paper, August 2003, p. 1.

6. P. Fortin, 'The Irish Economic Boom', p. 27.

7. ibid., p. 27.

8. C. Boland *et al.*, 'The Dublin International Financial Services Cluster, Microeconomics of Competitiveness', Harvard Business School, 5 May 2006, pp 15–21.

9. K. Mcloughlin, 'The Endangered Celtic Tiger', *Socialism Today*, issue 98, February 2006.

10. P. Fortin, 'The Irish Economic Boom', p. 26.

11. Comprehensive analysis on this issue can be found in F. Ruane and H. Gorg, 'Reflections on Irish Industrial Policy towards Foreign Direct Investment', Trinity Economics Paper Series, Policy Paper no. 97/3.

12. P. Fortin, 'The Irish Economic Boom', pp. 19–21.

13. ibid., p.23
14. R. Miller, 'Business Dominates Middle East Agenda', *Sunday Business Post*, 4 February 2007.
15. A. Mishrif, *European Union Direct Investment into Egypt 1972–2004*, unpublished Ph.D. thesis, King's College London, 2006, p. 223.
16. 'Ministers of Investment and Foreign Trade Discuss with the Irish Trade Minister Increasing Bilateral Cooperation in Trade and Investment', *Al-Ahram*, 7 November 2007.
17. M. Naguib Abo Zaid, 'Would Ireland Be the Fifth Power in the European Economy?' *Al-Ahram*, 6 December 2006.
18. A. Mishrif, 'British Direct Investment and Employment in Egypt', unpublished paper, 2008, p. 15.
19. A. Mishrif, *Investing in the Middle East: The Political Economy of European Direct Investment in Egypt*, London, I.B. Tauris & Co, 2010, p. 45.
20. A. Mishrif, 'Egypt: the Up-Coming Economic Tiger', *Al-Ahram*, 14 October 2007.
21. A. Dubsky, 'Egypt on the Rise', ArabianBusiness.com, 1 March 2007, available at: <http://www.arabianbusiness.com/>, accessed 20 August 2009.
22. A. Mishrif, 'British Direct Investment and Employment in Egypt', p. 15.
23. 'Assessing the Impact of the Current Financial and Economic Crisis', UNCTAD, January 2009, pp. 5 and 22.

Chapter 9

1. UNCTAD, available at: <http://www.unctad.org>, accessed 17 August 2009.
2. D. Ahlstrom, 'Strategy for Success', *Irish Times*, 11 June 2007.
3. W.H. Schacht, 'The National Council for Science and the Environment, Industrial Competitiveness and Technological Advancement: Debate Over Government Policy', Brief for US Congress, September 2000.
4. Y. Fachler, *Fire in the Belly*, Cork, Oak Tree Press, 2001.
5. G. Hamel, *The Future of Management*, Cambridge, Mass., Harvard Business School Press, 2008.
6. H. Sher, 'Trail of the Tiger', *The Jerusalem Report*, 30 May 2005.
7. D. Gottlieb, 'Inflation and Policy Response – The Israeli Case: 1970–1989', *Price Dynamics*, 1992, pp. 71–91.
8. See <http://www.nesc.ie>, accessed 17 August 2009.
9. D. McWilliams, 'The Two Tigers', *Business & Finance*, 1996.
10. See <http://www.enterprise-ireland.com>, accessed 17 August 2009.
11. R. Miller and M.J. O'Sullivan, 'The Luck of the Israelis', *The Wall Street Journal*, 5 December 2006.
12. ibid.
13. A.T. Kearney/Foreign Policy Globalization Index 2002, 2003, 2004, 2005, 2006, 2007.

14. See <http://www.investinisrael.gov.il>, accessed 17 August 2009.
15. ibid.
16. <http://www.moodys.com/cust/default.asp>
17. <http://www.standardandpoors.com/home/en/us>
18. <http://www.venturesource.com>
19. <http://www.fast500europe.com>
20. <http://www.investinisrael.gov.il>
21. R. DeVol and A. Bedroussian, 'Mind to Market: A Global Analysis of University Biotechnology Transfer and Commercialization', Milken Institute, September 2006.
22. Miller and O'Sullivan, 'The Luck of the Israelis'.
23. D. Breznitz, *Innovation and the State: Political Choice and Strategies for Growth in Israel, Taiwan and Ireland*, New Haven, Connectictut, Yale University Press, 2007.
24. Miller and O'Sullivan, 'The Luck of the Israelis'.
25. T.L. Friedman, *The World Is Flat: A Brief History of the Twenty-first Century*, New York, Picador, 2007.
26. T.L. Friedman, 'People vs. Dinosaurs', *New York Times*, 8 June 2008.
27. <http://www.investinisrael.gov.il>
28. Miller and O'Sullivan, 'The Luck of the Israelis'.
29. E. Neuman, 'Begorra, it's the hora', *Ha'aretz*, 6 September 2005.
30. H. Sher, 'Trail of the Tiger'.
31. M. Coleman, *The Best is Yet to Come*, Dublin, Blackhall Publishing, 2007.
32. D. McWilliams, *The Generation Game*, Dublin, Gill & Macmillan, 2008.
33. <http://www.gemconsortium.org>
34. <http://www.imf.org>
35. <http://www.worldbank.org>
36. <http://www.worldcat.org>
37. Greg Myre, 'Amid Political Upheaval, Israeli Economy Stays Healthy', *New York Times*, 31 December 2006.
38. M. Martin, 'The Flourishing Irish Entrepreneurs', *Irish Times*, 26 May 2006.
39. <http://www.doingbusiness.org>
40. *Irish Independent*, 3 March 2008.
41. <http://www.heritage.org>
42. <http://www.oecd.org>
43. <http://www.icsep.org>
44. E. Neuman, 'Begorra, it's the hora'.
45. <http://www.investinisrael.gov.il>
46. <http://www.oecd.org>
47. <http://www.gcr.weforum.org>
48. ibid.
49. E. Neuman, 'Begorra, it's the hora'.
50. *Irish Independent*, 30 April 2008.

51. <http://www.investinisrael.gov.il>
52. Miller and O'Sullivan, 'The Luck of the Israelis'.
53. D. McWilliams, 'Big Ideas for Small Countries', *Sunday Business Post*, 16 July 2003.
54. J. Kennedy, 'Innovation is Key for Irish SMEs', SiliconRepublic.com, 1 September 2005.
55. J. Lee, *Ireland, 1912–1985: Politics and Society*, Cambridge, Cambridge University Press, 1990.
56. <http://www.rte.ie/business/news/2006/0517/aerlingus.html>, accessed 20 September 2009.
57. D. Ahlstrom, 'Strategy for Success'.
58. T. Friedman, 'People vs. Dinosaurs'.
59. Y. Fachler, *Chutzpah – Unlocking the Maverick Mindset for Success*, Cork, Oak Tree Press, 2006.
60. D. McWilliams, 'Big Ideas for Small Countries'.
61. O. Zegen and Y. Mann, 'It's Not Only Ireland', *NRG*, 17 February 2008, available at: <http://reut-institute.org/en/Publication.aspx?PublicationId=3019>, accessed 16 January 2010.
62. Miller and O'Sullivan, 'The Luck of the Israelis'.
63. <http://www.idaireland.com>
64. <http://www.investinisrael.gov.il>

Chapter 10

1. A common approach of scholarship in both East and West appears to involve a focus on the contrasts between China and elsewhere, with many high quality examples found across numerous disciplines. Without diminishing the excellence and worthiness of such scholarship, the case must also be made for appreciating similarity where it can be found, and to recognise its significance.
2. Alexander Mundell, Nobel Laureate, described China and Ireland in these terms in 2007 at UCD's Confucius Institute Inaugural Conference during his presentation entitled 'Globalisation and the Rise of China's Economy – Causes and Consequences'.
3. For example, A. Graham, 'If China Spends its Trillions, Recession Could Be Averted', *The Guardian*, 15 October 2008. Graham, an economist and master of Balliol College, Oxford, questions what he calls 'the Anglo-Saxon model of unfettered capitalism' and contrasts it with what he terms 'Chinese capitalism', suggesting that more state control of the market may avert future economic meltdowns. See <http://www.guardian.co.uk/commentisfree/ 2008/oct/15/ economics-china>, accessed 17 September 2009.
4. The Irish Free State formally became the Republic of Ireland on 17 April 1949; the People's Republic of China (PRC) was proclaimed on 1 October 1949.

5. As just one example, Irish and Chinese workers built the transcontinental railroad in the United States in the 1860s, a major economic milestone in American history, which linked the eastern and western parts of the country for the first time. There are 'Chinatowns' in major cities throughout the world, and St Patrick's Day has attained a status akin to a quasi-global festival, celebrated far beyond the island of Ireland

6. EU-15 – Austria, Belgium, Denmark, Finland, France, Germany, Greece, Ireland, Italy, Luxembourg, the Netherlands, Portugal, Spain, Sweden and the UK.

7. For a detailed discussion, please consult L. Wang, 'Red Hot Dragon', *Business & Finance, Asia Supplements*, vol. 43, no. 18, pp. 8–11.

8. Vernon's product cycle states that there are four distinct phases or cycles in the life of a product – introduction, growth, maturity and decline. This framework is used to explain the diffusion of trade and manufacturing capacity, and relate this to foreign investment flows.

9. See, for example, E. Borensztein, J. DeGregorio and J. Lee, 'How Does Foreign Direct Investment Affect Economic Growth?', *Journal of International Economics*, vol. 45, no. 1 (1998), pp. 115–135.

10. D. Dollar, 'Outward-Oriented Developing Economies really Grow more Rapidly: Evidence from 95 LDCs, 1976–85', *Economic Development and Cultural Change*, vol. 40, 1992, pp. 523–44.

11. In many cases, a complete exemption from the tax can be received for a two-year period with a further reduction by half for the next three years (i.e. two years at 0 per cent and then a further three years at 7.5 per cent).

12. FDI in January was US$11.2 billion, 109.78 per cent more than in the corresponding month of last year: 'FDI Doubles Despite Tax Concerns', *China Daily*, 19 February 2008.

13. Hong Kong, politically part of China since 1997, was under British colonial rule from the Opium War period in the mid-nineteenth century. Hong Kong has a population of about 6.6 million with the majority being ethnic Chinese.

14. The official language of Taiwan is also Mandarin, though the written form of Mandarin used is the traditional version.

15. N. Hardiman, 'Politics and Markets in the Celtic Tiger Experience: Choice, Chance or Coincidence', Dublin, UCD Geary Institute, 2003.

16. Of these ETDZs, 37 were set up before 2000, primarily in the south-eastern coastal belt and 17 were set up after 2000, mainly distributed across the central and western regions of China. Overall, 32 are located in the south-eastern coastal belt, and 22 are located in central and western China. See *Report of Development Zones, 2006*, the Central Government of the People's Republic of China, January 2007.

17. The name 863 comes from the fact that the programme was created in the third month of the year 1986.

18. <http://www.worldmapper.org/display.php?selected=100>, accessed 17 September 2009.

19. According to the International Monetary Fund *Manual on Statistics of International Trade in Services*, 2002, available at: <http://www.oecd.org/dataoecd/32/45/2404428.pdf>, accessed 17 September 2008, these 'comprise international payments and receipts of franchising fees and the royalties paid for the use of registered trademarks. Other royalties and licence fees include international payments and receipts for the authorised use of intangible, non-produced, non-financial assets and proprietary rights (such as patents, copyrights and industrial processes and designs) and with the use, through licensing agreements, of produced originals or prototypes (such as manuscripts, computer programmes, and cinematographic works and sound recordings).'

20. See OECD, *Education at a Glance: OECD Indicators*, 2005.

21. P. Gunnigle and D. Maguire, 'Why Ireland? A Qualitative Review of Factors Influencing the Location of US Multinationals in Ireland with Particular Reference to the Impact of Labour Issues', *Economic & Social Review*, vol. 32, no. 1, 2001, pp. 43–67.

22. The figures of 21 and 1 within 211 are from an abbreviation of the twenty-first century and approximately 100 universities respectively.

23. 985 refers to May 1998, when former Chinese President Jiang Zemin announced extra funding for an elite group of Chinese universities in a speech on education policy in Peking University.

24. D.E. Bloom and D. Canning, 'Contraception and the Celtic Tiger', in *Economic and Social Review*, vol. 34, no. 3, Winter 2003, pp. 229–247.

25. ibid.

26. See United Nations Department of Economic and Social Affairs (DESA), *The World Economic and Social Survey*, Population Division, DESA, available at: <http://www.un.org/esa/desa>, accessed 17 September 2009.

27. T. Hesketh, L. Lu, and Z. Wei Xing, 'The Effect of China's One-Child Family Policy after 25 Years', *New England Journal of Medicine* 353, 2005, pp. 1171–1176.

28. These effects include a high sex imbalance – with males outnumbering females – sex selective abortion, infanticide, and other social effects possibly related to single child families.

29. M. Hennigan, 'Irish Economy: Ireland Is Faced with New Challenges as US Financial Sector Faces Retrenchment and Transformation', Finfacts Ireland, *Business & Finance* Portal, 20 September 2008, available at: <http://www.finfacts.ie/irishfinancenews/article_1014770.shtml>, accessed 17 September 2009.

30. Central Statistics Office, Ireland, 2009, available at: <http://www.cso.ie/statistics>, 17 September 2009.

31. UN Deptartment of Public Information, 2009, Summit on Climate Change, Meetings Coverage ENV/DEV/1069, available at: <http://www.un.org/News/Press/docs/2009/envdev1069.doc.htm>, accessed 17 September 2009.

32. *Financial Times*, 20 September 2009.
33. D. McWilliams, *The Generation Game*, Dublin, Gill & Macmillan, 2008, p. 201.

Chapter 11

1. Per capital gross domestic product (GDP) was purchasing power parity (PPP) $13,713 (at the 2005 price level) and the population was 3.541 million for Ireland in 1986, while these respective figures were PPP $203 and 60 million for Vietnam.
2. Both countries have a large Diaspora population living mainly in North America and Europe, which is about three million for Vietnam and seventy million for Ireland. See A. Nguyen Dang, 'Enhancing the Development Impact of Migrant Remittances and Disapora: The Case of Vietnam', *Asia-Pacific Population Journal*, vol. 20, no. 3, 2003; see also <http://www.irelandroots.com/roots4.htm>, accessed 13 September 2009.
3. D.F. McCarthy, 'Social Policy and Macroeconomics: The Irish Experience', Policy Research Working Paper no. 2736, World Bank, Washington DC, 2001, p.6.
4. ibid., Table 1, p. 5.
5. See B. Beary, 'Why Ireland's Economic Boom Is No Miracle', *The Globalist*, 30 May 2007, available at: <http://www.theglobalist.com>, accessed 13 September 2009.
6. See statistical information on annual per capita food output, Vietnam, General Statistics Office Vietnam (GSO), available at: <http://www.gso.gov.vn/default_en.aspx?tabid=491>, 1996, accessed 13 September 2009.
7. International Monetary Fund database, available at: <http://www.imf.org/external/data.htm>, accessed 13 September 2009.
8. For example, see P. Honohan and B. Walsh, 'Catching Up with the Leaders: The Irish Hare', in Brookings Panel on Economic Activity, Washington, DC, 2002; O. Blanchard and B. Bosworth, 'Comments and Discussion', *Brookings Papers on Economic Activity*, vol 1, 2002, pp. 58–77; R. McSharry and P. White, *The Making of the Celtic Tiger: The Inside Story of Ireland's Boom Economy*, Dublin, Mercier Press, 2000; and M.J. O'Sullivan, *Ireland and the Global Question*, Syracuse, New York, Syracuse University Press, 2006.
9. This ranking is compiled annually by the Heritage Economic Freedom Foundation, <http://www.heritage.org/Index/>. The earliest year with data available is 1995.
10. Global Entrepreneurship Monitor (GEM) Report 2007 for Ireland (Table 2.1, p. 26), available at <http://www.enterprise-ireland.com>, accessed 13 September 2009.
11. OECD Statistics Database, available at: <http://www.oecd.org>, accessed 13 September 2009.

12. OECD, *Ireland: Towards an Integrated Public Service*, OECD Public Management Reviews, 2008, Table 1.1, p. 15.

13. D.C. North, *Institutions, Institutional Change and Economic Performance*, Cambridge, Cambridge University Press, 1990.

14. See Lucas, 1993, p. 270.

15. MacSharry and White, *The Making of the Celtic Tiger*, p. 209.

16. ibid., p. 217.

17. NESC, *Strategy into the 21st Century*, Dublin, NESC, 1996, p. 60.

18. From the mission statement of IDA Ireland, available at <http://www.idaireland.com/home/index.aspx?id=8>, accessed 13 September 2009.

19. NESC, *Strategy 2006: People, Productivity, and Purpose*, Dublin, NESC, 2005.

20. K. Jacobsen, *Chasing Progress in the Irish Republic: Ideology, Democracy and Dependant Development*, Cambridge, Cambridge University Press, 1994, p. 177–78.

21. F. Sautet, 'Why Have Kiwis Not Become Tigers? Reform, Entrepreneurship, and Economic Performance in New Zealand', in B. Powell (ed.) *Making Poor Nations Rich: Entrepreneurship and the Process of Economic Development*, Stanford Economics and Finance, 2008, p. 388.

22. From the NESC's website, <http://www.nesc.ie/>.

23. L. Baccaro and M. Simoni, 'The Irish Social Partnership and the "Celtic Tiger" Phenomenon', IILS Discussion Paper, DP 154, 2004.

24. See R. O'Donnell and D. Thomas, 'Partnership and Policy-making' in Healy, Reynolds *et al.* (eds), *Social Policy in Ireland: Principles, Practice and Problems*, Dublin, Liffey Press, 1998, pp. 117–146.

25. Honohan and Walsh, 'Catching Up with the Leaders: the Irish Hare', p. 31–32.

26. A typical ABP includes representatives from government (divisions concerned with training or economic development), 'social partners' (trade unions, farmers and business associations) and the 'community sector' (groups active in matters ranging from welfare to crime-fighting). See OECD, *The Economic Survey of Ireland 2006*, OECD, 1996.

27. See 'National Spatial Strategy for Ireland 2002–2020', Department of Environment and Local Government, Dublin, 2002, available at: <http://www.irishspatialstrategy.ie/pdfs/Completea.pdf>, accessed 13 September 2009.

28. MacSharry and White, *The Making of the Celtic Tiger*, p. 26.

29. ibid.

30. M. Martin, Minister of Education and Science, 1999, from the website for enterprise education in Irish primary schools, <http://www.cdu.mic.ul.ie/bi_gnothach/page20.html>, accessed 13 September 2009.

31. NESC, *Strategy into the 21st Century*, Dublin, NESC, 1986, p. 263–4.

32. From the IDA's website, available at: <http://www.idaireland.com/home/sitetool.aspx?id=3&content_id=1>, accessed 20 October 2008.

33. Author's calculations with data from EUKLEMS database, available at: <http://www.euklems.net/>, accessed 20 September 2008.

34. D.F. McCarthy, 'Social Policy and Macroeconomics: The Irish Experience', Policy Research Working Paper no. 2736, World Bank, Washington DC, Table 1, p. 4

35. OECD, *Regulatory Reform in Ireland*, Paris, OECD, 2001.

36. The World Bank, *Doing Business*, 2008, available at: <http://www.doing business.org/>, accessed 20 September 2008.

37. From Department of Finance, *Ireland – Stability Programme*, Dublin, Department of Finance, December 2003, available at <http://www.finance.gov.ie>, accessed 13 September 2009.

38. From 'Transport 21' website, <http://www.transport21.ie/Home/Home_Page/index.html>, accessed 13 September 2009.

39. Deloitte, *Closing the Infrastructure Gap: The Role of Public–Private Partnerships*, Deloitte, 2006, available at: <http://www.deloitte.com>, accessed 13 September 2009.

40. *A Time for Change: Industrial Policy for the 1990s* ('The Culliton Report'), 1992, available at: <http://www.esri.ie/publications/>, accessed 20 October 2008.

41. 'The Work of IDA Ireland', speech by John Dunne, Chairman, IDA Ireland at the Transitions Ireland Lunch, 27 January 2004, available at: <http://www.idaireland.com>, accessed 20 October 2008.

42. From the IDA's website, <http://www.idaireland.com/home/index.aspx?id=64>, accessed 20 October 2008.

43. World Bank, Data & Research, 1993, available at: <http://www.worldbank.org>, accessed 20 October 2008.

44. D. Perkins, 'Industrial and Financial policy in China and Vietnam', in J.E. Stiglitz and S. Yusuf (eds), *Rethinking the East Asian Miracle*, World Bank and Oxford University Press, 2001, p. 272.

45. Transparency International, available at: <http://www.transparency.org/>, accessed 13 September 2009.

46. The number of labour strikes rose from 387 in 2006 to 541 in 2007, and by about 300 over the first three months of 2008, with increasing scale.

47. Congressman Lê Văn Cuông stated that the problem of 'bribing for promotion or power [in government agencies] occurs in every place and at every level', Dai Doan Ket, October 21, 2008, available at: <http://baodaidoanket.net>, accessed 13 September 2009.

48. The Congress X documents, Vietnam's Communist Party, 2006.

49. World Bank, Data & Research 1999, available at: <http://www.worldbank.org>, accessed 20 October 2008.

50. T. Crampton, 'Politburo Is Hesitating on Pact', *Herald Tribune*, 11 September 1999, available at: <http://www.iht.com/articles/1999/09/11/viet.2.t_0.php>, accessed 20 October 2008.

51. D. Perkins, 'Industrial and Financial Policy in China and Vietnam', p. 267.

52. The country's supreme ruling body, which consists of about thirteen to seventeen top leaders of the communist party.

53. The enlargement of Hanoi was pushed forward, regardless of the arguments by deputies of the National Assembly that 'the government had not spelled out a clear financial and technical plan for the expansion, failed to address the social and cultural impacts of the change, did not set out the zoning and development plans for the new Hanoi, and did not consider the limitations of managerial and administrative capacity that Hanoi faces even now', Economist Intelligence Unit, 'Vietnam: Moving into Fashion', London, EIU, 2008, p. 9, available at: <http://www.eiu.com/index.asp?rf=0>, accessed 20 August 2009.

54. E. Malesky, 'Gerrymandering – Vietnamese Style: The Political Motivations behind the Creation of New Provinces in Vietnam', paper presented at the Annual Meeting of the American Political Science Association, Philadelphia, PA, September, 2006.

55. A. Fforde and S. de Vylder, *From Plan to Market: The Economic Transition in Vietnam*, Boulder, Westview Press, 1996, p. 11.

56. See *Tuoitre*, 21 July 2008, available at: <http://www.tuoitre.com.vn/Tianyon/Index.aspx?ArticleID=269773&ChannelID=13>, accessed 13 September 2009.

57. For example, in a survey conducted by the *Saigon Times* in 2007, 56 per cent of parents were of the view that 'the school fees are heavy' and 31 per cent were of the view they did not have sufficient money to pay the school fees for their children, see 'The burden of education expenses', *Saigon Times*, 2 May 2008, available at: <http://www.thesaigontimes.vn/Home/thoisu/doisong/5335/>, accessed 20 October 2008.

58. The market freedom index published by the Heritage Freedom Foundation consists of ten components which include the business freedom and trade freedom sub-indices. These index and sub-indices range from ten to a hundred where higher numbers are better.

59. See 'Foreign Direct Investment in Vietnam Triples in 2008', *China Post*, 27 December 2008, available at: <http://www.chinapost.com>, accessed 16 January 2010.

60. L. Anh Nguyen, 'Intel's Vow in Vietnam', *Forbes*, 26 November 2007, available at: <http://www.forbes.com/business/global/2007/1126/085.html>, accessed 20 October 2008.

Chapter 12

1. The Home Rule movement began in 1873 when the Home Rule League campaigned for the creation of an Irish Parliament within the ambit of overall British rule. The movement gathered strength under the leadership of Charles Stuart Parnell.

2. The India freedom movement aimed to end British colonial authority in India, and what are now its surrounding countries. The movement's chief political vehicle was the Indian National Congress party.

3. Eamon de Valera was the dominant political figure of twentieth century Ireland, having played a key role in the 1916 Rising, the War of Independence and the subsequent founding of the state. He served over sixteen years as taoiseach and fourteen years as president.
4. Jawaharlal Nehru was one of the leading Indian statesmen of the twentieth century, having served as prime minister from 1947 to 1964. He was the first prime minister of independent India in 1952.

Conclusion

1. M. J. O'Sullivan, 'Was John Law Irish?', forthcoming in *Economie en Irlande*, Groupe de Recherches en Etudes Irlandaises, Caen, Universite de Caen, 2010.
2. C. Cleary, 'Take Israel as an Economic Model', *The Examiner*, 8 January 2010, available at: <http://www.examiner.ie/opinion/letters/take-israel-as-an-economic-model-109191.html#ixzzocJgEEOUN>, accessed 11 January 2010.

Further Reading

Official Reports and Policy Papers

Baccaro, L. and Simoni, M., 'The Irish Social Partnership and the "Celtic Tiger" Phenomenon', IILS Discussion Paper, DP 154, 2004.

Cassidy, M., 'Productivity in Ireland: Trends and Issues', *CBFSAI Bulletin*, Spring 2004, pp. 83–105.

Credit Suisse Research Institute, *Report on Intangible Infrastructure*, London, Credit Suisse Research Institute, November 2008.

DeVol, R. and Bedroussian, A., 'Mind to Market: A Global Analysis of University Biotechnology Transfer and Commercialization', Santa Monica CA, Milken Institute, September 2006.

Dornbusch, R., 'Credibility, Debt and Unemployment: Ireland's Failed Stabilization', NBER Working Paper no. 2785, Cambridge MA, NBER, 1988.

ESRI, *A Time for Change: Industrial Policy for the 1990s* ('The Culliton Report'), Dublin, ESRI, 1992.

Flinter, D., 'The Transformation of the Irish Economy: the Role of the Public Policy', CIT Working Paper 052112, Clemson University Centre for International Trade, 21 December 2005, pp. 5–7.

Förster, M. and Mira d'Ercole, M., 'Income Distribution and Poverty in OECD Countries in the Second Half of the 1990s', OECD Social, Employment and Migration Working Paper, 22, OECD, 2005, p. 11.

Government of Scotland, *Taking Forward the Government Economic Strategy – A Discussion Paper on Tackling Poverty, Inequality and Deprivation in Scotland*, Edinburgh, Government of Scotland, 2008.

Hodge, S.A., 'US States Lead the World in High Corporate Taxes', Fiscal Fact 119, Washington DC, The Tax Foundation, 18 March 2008.

Honohan, P. and Walsh, B., 'Catching Up with the Leaders: the Irish Hare', *Brookings Papers in Economic Activity*, vol. 1, 2000, pp. 1–77.

McCarthy, D.F., 'Social Policy and Macroeconomics: the Irish Experience', Policy Research Working Paper no. 2736, Washington DC, World Bank, 2001, p. 6.

McMahon, E.J., 'Enough Is Enough: Why and How to Cap New York State's School Property Taxes', Albany, New York, Empire Center for New York State Policy, March 2008.

NESC, *Strategy into the 21st Century*, Dublin, NESC, 1996.

NESC, *Strategy 2006: People, Productivity, and Purpose*, Dublin: NESC, 2005.

OECD, *Growing Unequal? Income Distribution and Poverty in OECD Countries*, OECD, 2008.

OECD, *Ireland: Towards an Integrated Public Service*, OECD Public Management Reviews, 2008.

OECD, *Regulatory Reform in Ireland*, OECD, 2001.

Pendall,R., Drennan, M.P. and Christopherson, S., 'Transition and Renewal: The Emergence of a Diverse Upstate Economy', Washington DC, Brookings Institution, Centre on Urban and Metropolitan Policy, January 2004.

Pendall, R. and Christopherson, S., 'Losing Ground: Income and Poverty in Upstate New York', Washington DC, Brookings Institution, Metropolitan Policy Programme, September 2004.

Sapir, A., 'Globalisation and the Reform of European Social Models', *Bruegel Policy Brief*, vol. 1, November 2005.

UNCTAD, Assessing the Impact of the Current Financial and Economic Crisis', Geneva, UNCTAD, January 2009.

Books

Breznitz, D., *Innovation and the State: Political Choice and Strategies for Growth in Israel, Taiwan and Ireland*, New Haven, Connectictut, Yale University Press, 2007.

Coleman, M., *The Best is Yet to Come*, Dublin, Blackhall Publishing, 2007.

Considère-Charon, M., *Irlande: Une Singulière Intégration Européenne*, Paris: Economica, 2002.

Cornwall, J. (ed.), *The Capitalist Economies: Prospects for the 1990s*, Aldershot, Edward Elgar, 1991.

Crouch, C. and Wolfgang S. (eds), *Les Capitalismes en Europe*, Paris, La Découverte, 1996.

Dooge, J. (ed.), *Ireland in the Contemporary World*, Dublin, Gill & Macmillan, 1986.

Fachler, Y., *Chutzpah – Unlocking the Maverick Mindset for Success*, Cork, Oak Tree Press, 2006.

FitzGerald, G., *Reflections on the Irish State*, Dublin, Irish Academic Press, 2003.

Fforde, A. and de Vylder, S., *From Plan to Market: The Economic Transition in Vietnam*, Boulder, Westview Press, 1996.

Friedman, T.L., *The World Is Flat: A Brief History of the Twenty-first Century*, New York, Picador, 2007.

Hamel, G., *The Future of Management*, Cambridge, Mass., Harvard Business School Press, 2008.

Heikkinen, S. and van Zanden, J.L. (eds.), *Explorations in Economic Growth*, Amsterdam, Aksant, 2004.

Jacobsen, K., *Chasing Progress in the Irish Republic: Ideology, Democracy and Dependent Development*, Cambridge, Cambridge University Press, 1994.

Joannon, P. (ed.), *De Gaulle and Ireland*, Dublin: Institute of Public Administration, 1991.

Keogh, D., *Ireland and Europe, 1919–1948: A Diplomatic and Political History*, Dublin, Gill & Macmillan, 1988.

Kirby, P., *The Celtic Tiger in Distress: Growth with Inequality in Ireland*, Basingstoke, Palgrave, 2002.

Leach, D., *Fugitive Ireland: European Minority Nationalists and Irish Political Asylum, 1937–2008*, Dublin, Four Courts Press, 2009.

Lee, J., *Ireland, 1912–1985: Politics and Society*, Cambridge, Cambridge University Press, 1990.

Maher, E. and Neville, G. (eds), *France–Ireland: Anatomy of a Relationship*, New York, Peter Lang, 2004.

Maignant, C. (ed.), *Le Tigre Celtique en Question*, Presses Universitaires de Caen, 2007.

McSharry, R. and White, P., *The Making of the Celtic Tiger: The Inside Story of Ireland's Boom Economy*, Dublin, Mercier Press, 2000.

McWilliams, D., *The Generation Game*, Dublin, Gill & Macmillan, 2008.

Miller, R., *Ireland and the Middle East: Trade, Society and Peace, 1948–2006*, Dublin, Irish Academic Press, 2005.

Mishrif, A., *Investing in the Middle East: The Political Economy of European Direct Investment in Egypt*, London, I.B. Tauris & Co, 2010.

North, D.C., *Institutions, Institutional Change and Economic Performance*, Cambridge, Cambridge University Press, 1990.

O'Hearn, D., *Inside the Celtic Tiger: The Irish Economy and the Asian Model*, London, Pluto Press, 1998.

O'Mahony, M. and B. van Ark (eds.), *EU Productivity and Competitiveness: an Industry Perspective. Can Europe Resume the Catching-up Process?*, Luxembourg: Official Publications of the European Communities, 2003.

O'Sullivan, M.J., *Ireland and the Global Question*, New York, Syracuse University Press, 2006.

Powell, B. (ed.) *Making Poor Nations Rich: Entrepreneurship and the Process of Economic Development*, Stanford Economics and Finance, 2008.

Smith, N.J., *Showcasing Globalization? The Political Economy of the Irish Republic*, Manchester, Manchester University Press, 2005.

Stiglitz, J.E. and Y. Shahid (eds), *Rethinking the East Asian Miracle*, New York, World Bank and Oxford University Press, 2001.

Tonra, B., *Global Citizen and European Republic*, Manchester, Manchester University Press, 2006.

Journal Articles

Agostini, C.A., 'The Impact of State Corporate Taxes on FDI Location', *Public Finance Review*, vol. 35, no. 3, May 2007, pp. 335–360.

Baer, W. and Nogueira Leite, A., 'The Economy of Portugal within the European Union: 1990–2002', *The Quarterly Review of Economics and Finance*, vol. 43, 2003, pp. 738–754.

Barry, F., 'Economic Integration and Convergence Processes in the EU Cohesion Countries', *Journal of Common Market Studies*, vol. 41, no. 5, 2003, pp. 897–921.

Barry, F., 'Peripherality in Economic Geography and Modern Growth Theory: Evidence from Ireland's Adjustment to Free Trade', *The World Economy*, vol. 19, no. 3, 1996, pp. 345–65.

Bloom, D.E. and Canning, E., 'Contraception and The Celtic Tiger', in *Economic and Social Review*, vol. 34, no. 3, Winter 2003, pp.229–247.

Brennan, P., 'Croissance Économique et Exclusion Sociale: Eléments du Problème', *Études Irlandaises*, vol. 24, no. 2, 1999, pp. 155–162.

Dollar, D., 'Outward-oriented Developing Economies really Grow more Rapidly: Evidence from 95 LDCs, 1976–85', *Economic Development and Cultural Change*, vol. 40, 1992, pp. 523–44.

Färe, R., Grosskopf, S. and Margaritis, D., 'Productivity Growth and Convergence in the European Union', *Journal of Productivity Analysis*, 25, 2006, pp. 111–141.

Fortin, P., 'The Irish Economic Boom: What Can We Learn?', *International Productivity Monitor*, no. 3, Fall 2001, pp.19–32.

Gottheil, F., 'Ireland: What's Celtic about the Celtic Tiger?', *The Quarterly Review of Economics and Finance*, vol. 43, 2003, pp. 720–37.

Gunnigle, P. and Maguire, D., 'Why Ireland?: A Qualitative Review of Factors Influencing the Location of US Multinationals in Ireland with particular reference to the impact of labour Issues', *Economic & Social Review*, vol. 32, no. 1, 2001, pp.43–67.

House, J.D. and McGrath, K., 'Innovative Governance and Development in the New Ireland: Social Partnership and the Integrated Approach', *Governance: An International Journal of Policy, Administration, and Institutions*, vol. 17, no. 1, January 2004, pp. 29–58.

Krugman, P.R. and Venables, A.J., 'Integration, Specialization and Adjustment', *European Economic Review*, vol. 40, 1996, pp. 959–67.

Macedo, J. Braga, 'Converging European Transitions', *The World Economy*, vol. 23, no. 10, 2000, pp. 1335–1365.

Midelfart, K.H., Overman, H.G. and Venables, A.J., 'Monetary Union and the Economic Geography of Europe', *Journal of Common Market Studies*, vol. 41, no. 5, 2003, pp. 847–68.

Powell, B., 'Economic Freedom and Growth: The Case of the Celtic Tiger', *Cato Journal*, vol. 22, no. 3, Winter 2003.

Temple, J. and Voth, H.J., 'Human Capital, Equipment Investment, and Industrialization', *European Economic Review*, vol. 42, 1998, pp. 1343–62.

Index

Figures are indicated by **bold** page numbers, tables by *italic* numbers.